MW00604397

EXPLORING
--- *the* ---
ST. CROIX
RIVER VALLEY

EXPLORING
--- *the* ---
ST. CROIX
RIVER VALLEY

Adventures on and off the Water

ANGIE HONG

University of Minnesota Press

Minneapolis • London

The University of Minnesota Press gratefully acknowledges the generous assistance provided for the publication of this book by the Hamilton P. Traub University Press Fund.

Copyright 2024 by Angie Hong

All photographs taken by Angie Hong unless otherwise credited.

All rights reserved. No part of this publication may be reproduced, stored in a retrieval system, or transmitted, in any form or by any means, electronic, mechanical, photocopying, recording, or otherwise, without the prior written permission of the publisher.

Published by the University of Minnesota Press
111 Third Avenue South, Suite 290
Minneapolis, MN 55401-2520
http://www.upress.umn.edu

ISBN 978-1-5179-1640-4 (pb)

A Cataloging-in-Publication record for this book is available from the Library of Congress.

Printed in China on acid-free paper

The University of Minnesota is an equal-opportunity educator and employer.

30 29 28 27 26 25 24   10 9 8 7 6 5 4 3 2 1

To Charlie and Molly, my ever-ready nature companions,

and for Gary, who always packs us plenty of snacks

before we head into the woods

CONTENTS

PROLOGUE

A River, a Mussel, a Lullaby

July 30, 2017—St. Croix River

IT WAS A BEAUTIFUL SUMMER DAY, AND THE RIVER SEEMED TO stretch endlessly in all directions—river, forest, water, sand. My five-year-old son and I were balanced atop my brand-new stand-up paddleboard, fully immersed in an epic outdoor adventure. The sun shone brightly, the water was warm, and all was right in the world.

We began our St. Croix River journey that day in Marine on St. Croix, a tiny town located twelve miles north of Stillwater that is the site of Minnesota's first commercial lumber mill. Today, Marine is a great place to enjoy an ice-cream cone, watch the Mill Stream flow through the basement of the Brookside Bar and Grill, and revel in small-town charm.

Only minutes after leaving town, we already felt as though we had entered a wilderness. Great blue herons and bald eagles flew overhead, and we seemed to be the only people on the river. There were no boats, no houses, and no pesky intrusions from the modern world.

"I want to swim down the river," my son, Charlie, announced, as he launched himself overboard and began dog-paddling next to our paddleboard. Our pace slowed to a crawl—but was there anywhere else we needed to be?

Over the next five and a half hours, we explored every foot of that wide blue river. We lay on our bellies and held our breath as we

Charlie dips his toes in the St. Croix River north of the Arcola High Bridge.

Ferns and moss surround a tiny waterfall on the Lower St. Croix River south of Marine on St. Croix.

watched freshwater mussels trace lazy circles ever so slowly in the river's red sand. We floated through a vast, unending labyrinth of backwater channels where frogs leaped and turtles basked. On a wooded hill, we paused to inspect a miniature waterfall that cascaded over rock and emerald fern.

We snacked and swam, paddled and napped. Little by little, the sun slowly slid lower toward the horizon.

By the time we reached the Arcola High Bridge, still more than three miles from the Boom Site Wayside where we planned to get off the water, we had both grown a little weary. Nevertheless, Charlie was awestruck by this soaring bridge that arches gracefully over the water. The water there is deep and blue, and we paused to swim for a while.

Then it was time for lullabies and stories. Four hours had passed since we'd first set sail, and still there was river ahead. By now, the sun was setting, and the air was soft and pink. I sang as we paddled. Together, Charlie and I crafted an elaborate fairy-tale kingdom, where wiener dogs rode paddleboards and beavers built castles of wood.

Eventually, we arrived at the wayside beach, where my husband stood waiting with two towels and a bundle of snacks. The St. Croix River whispered goodbye, and we promised to return again soon.

● ● ●

I have spent nearly twenty years working as an environmental educator in the St. Croix River Watershed, and during this time I've fallen firmly and permanently in love.

The St. Croix River is a 169-mile ribbon of blue that cleaves the land between Minnesota and Wisconsin. In the surrounding watershed, you'll find small towns vibrant with local art, music, dining, and festivals. Board a kayak or canoe, however, and you could easily spend an entire day on the water without seeing another person. The St. Croix is close enough to Minneapolis–St. Paul to allow for a pleasant day trip, and yet it's vast enough that you could lose yourself there for a week if that is your goal. This unique combination of accessibility and wildness makes the St. Croix Watershed utterly intoxicating.

My husband, Gary, and I moved to Stillwater in 2011, when I was pregnant with Charlie. For the first several months, we joked that it felt like we were on vacation every day. I had always appreciated the natural beauty of the St. Croix Valley, but once we moved there I developed an intense desire to root in, explore, and really get to know this place we now called home. Now it feels as though we have woven ourselves into the fabric of the St. Croix, and my experiences on the river, in the woods, and on the prairies are inextricably entwined with that of raising a child and growing through life.

I hope that this book will inspire you to explore the St. Croix Watershed, either for the first time or with new appreciation. The book is divided into two main parts. In the first, I share recommendations for places to find beautiful prairies, towering trees, unique geologic formations, and your own river story. This is by no means an exhaustive list of places to visit, but rather a curated collection of destinations that highlight different parts of the watershed and different types of experiences.

In the second part, I offer practical advice on outdoor activities for spring, summer, fall, and winter, as well as tips for enjoying the

outdoors with children, seniors, or on your own. Woven throughout is a continuing story of restoration and renewal. A landscape
revival is underway, and you are invited to join.

Featured destinations within this book are coded as beginner,
intermediate, or advanced, based on the level of outdoor experience needed for an enjoyable visit.

Beginner = state parks, county parks, and nature centers
with clearly marked trails, bathrooms, drinking water,
and services. Most offer ADA accessibility.

Intermediate = easy to access locations that may have
trails or nearby outfitters but lack services such as visitor
centers, bathrooms, and water.

Advanced = wilderness experiences that require
pre-planning and your own equipment.

If you're nervous about venturing out to explore new places, I'd encourage you to read through the Outdoor Safety section in the Tips on Exploring chapter near the end of the book, where I offer advice for trip planning and classes that can build your outdoor skills.

In this guide, I draw from my professional experience and interviews with people who live, work, and recreate in the region. I also share stories and photographs from the many years I've explored the St. Croix River Watershed while hiking, biking, swimming, paddling, snowshoeing, and skiing with family and friends. Unless otherwise noted, I have taken the photographs, although I included photographs taken by people I interviewed to help you see the watershed through their eyes as well.

Go forth and explore the St. Croix Watershed! I hope you find some magic while you're here.

Upper St. Croix River near Riverside Landing, Wisconsin

The river bluff in Houlton, Wisconsin,
glows in the autumn sun.

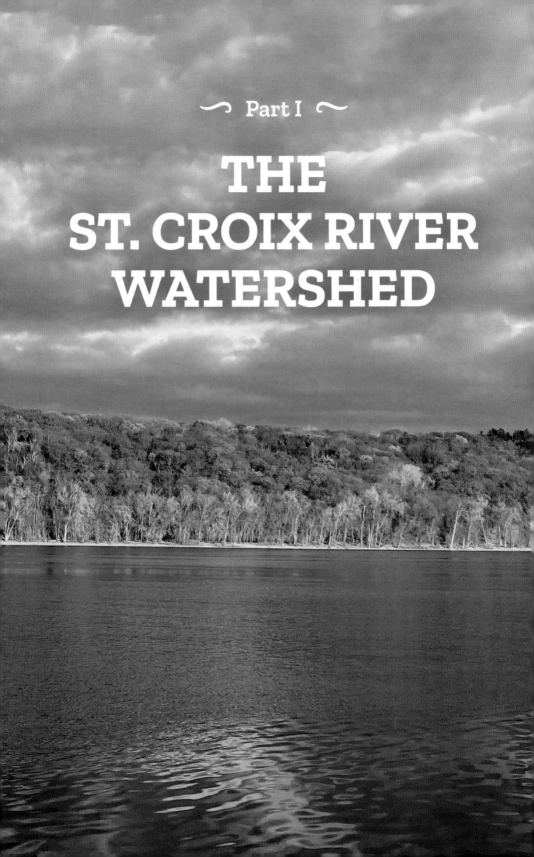

~ Part I ~

THE ST. CROIX RIVER WATERSHED

THE ST. CROIX RIVER BEGINS ITS JOURNEY IN SOLON SPRINGS, Wisconsin, just south of Lake Superior, before flowing 169 miles south to meet the Mississippi River in Prescott. Its largest tributary, the Namekagon, begins at Namekagon Lake in the heart of the Chequamegon–Nicolet National Forest in northern Wisconsin. Nearly eight thousand square miles of forest, farm, and prairie drain to the St. Croix River, forming a heart-shaped watershed that is wide in the river's upper reaches and gradually tapers as it flows south toward its confluence with the Mississippi River.

Together, the St. Croix and Namekagon Rivers form the St. Croix National Scenic Riverway, and both enjoy special protections through the National Wild and Scenic Rivers Act. Shoreline development is restricted, as are dams, impoundments, and new river crossings. As a result, visitors to the St. Croix and Namekagon can enjoy the beauty and solitude of nature, with minimal intrusions from the modern world.

The Story Begins . . .
or Perhaps It Continues

Sometimes it's hard to know when to begin the story of a place. We could begin the story of the St. Croix River in 1968, when Senators Gaylord Nelson and Walter Mondale led the U.S. Congress to pass the Wild and Scenic Rivers Act. Were it not for that legislation, the St. Croix and Namekagon Rivers today might be lined with mansions and vacation homes, choked with weeds and silt, or hidden behind now-shuttered factories.

Perhaps we should start earlier. When glaciers retreated fourteen thousand years ago from the land now known as Minnesota and Wisconsin, the meltwater formed massive rivers that carved into the soil and rock beneath, leaving behind towering bluffs along the riverways and dappled lakes throughout the forests and prairies. For thousands of years, people lived here along the shores of these rivers and lakes: they hunted deer, tapped maple trees, fell in love, raised children, buried parents.

Often the story begins in 1837, when Ojibwe and Dakota tribes ceded thirty-five million acres of land in what is now east-central Minnesota and western Wisconsin to the United States government. During the following century, white settlers forcibly re-

Sun dog at Afton State Park

moved Indigenous people from the land, decimated the forests, transformed prairies into farmland, and built cities with houses, roads, and factories.

"People need to know the true history, which no one has ever been taught in school," explains Sharon Day, executive director of the Indigenous Peoples Task Force. "Indigenous people inhabited North America for thousands of years, and we knew how to take care of the water. We had irrigation and waste disposal practices. When white folks came here, the rivers were in pristine condition. It didn't take more than 150 years for them to pollute almost every river in Minnesota."

"We've never lost our connection to this space," says Keeli Siyaka, a member of the Sisseton Wahpeton Dakota community who worked previously as an environmental justice educator for Wakan Tipi Awanyankapi, a Native-led organization in St. Paul. "It's important to bring Native people back here and involve them in decisions on how the land is managed."

The 1837 treaties between the U.S. government and Indigenous tribes designated land in the southern portion of the St. Croix River Watershed (Washington County in Minnesota and portions of Pierce and St. Croix Counties in Wisconsin) as Dakota land, and land farther north as Ojibwe land. The U.S. government and Ojibwe tribes signed additional treaties in 1842 and 1854. During this same period, Wisconsin and Minnesota

FEATURES OF THE ST. CROIX RIVER WATERSHED

- one national park
- one national forest
- one national wildlife refuge
- two national scenic trails
- three national historic landmarks
- twelve state parks
- eight state trails
- six state historic sites
- ten state forests
- sixty-five state natural areas
- more than 150 properties listed on the National Register of Historic Places
- the St. Croix Scenic Byway
- the reservation lands of four Ojibwe tribes

became states, in 1848 and 1858, respectively. This transition in human cultures and power was anything but peaceful.

The United States and the Dakota fought a bloody war in 1862 that ended with the hanging of thirty-eight Dakota men in Mankato, Minnesota, and the deaths of more than three hundred Dakota elders, women, and children who were sent to an internment camp on Pike Island, which is now part of Fort Snelling State Park. The Dakota Expulsion Act of 1863 made it illegal for Dakota people to reside within the borders of the newly formed State of Minnesota and, to this day, the law has yet to be repealed. Today, four Ojibwe tribes occupy reservation land within the St. Croix River Watershed—the St. Croix Chippewa Indians of Wisconsin, the Mille Lacs Band of Ojibwe, the Lac Courte Oreilles Band of Lake Superior Chippewa Indians, and the Fond Du Lac Band of Lake Superior Chippewa.

Wild and Scenic Designation

As difficult as it is to know when to begin the story of a place, it is even more challenging to know when the story will end.

By 1965, Minnesota and Wisconsin had both been states for more than one hundred years, the forests had regenerated within the St. Croix Watershed, and the river again ran clear and clean. A new threat emerged when Northern States Power Company (now Xcel Energy) announced its intention to build a coal-fired power plant on the river just south of Stillwater in Oak Park Heights, Minnesota.

Local residents worried that the St. Croix would suffer the same fate as the Mississippi, Cuyahoga, and other urban rivers across the country that had become choked with pollution and devoid of natural beauty. They called on Wisconsin Senator Gaylord Nelson and Minnesota Senator Walter Mondale, who advocated fiercely against construction of the new power plant but were ultimately unsuccessful.

Though the Allen S. King Generating Station was indeed constructed on the banks of the river, Nelson and Mondale ignited a national conversation that eventually inspired Congress to pass the Wild and Scenic Rivers Act of 1968, which established the National Wild and Scenic Rivers System. The act declared that the

The St. Croix River watershed

Upper St. Croix River (above Taylors Falls) and seven other U.S. rivers with "outstandingly remarkable scenic, recreational, geologic, fish and wildlife, historic, cultural, or other similar values" worthy of protection should be "preserved in free-flowing condition, and . . . protected for the benefit and enjoyment of present and future generations."

In 1972, the Lower St. Croix River was added to the National Wild and Scenic Rivers System as well. Today, the National System protects more than thirteen thousand miles of riverway in 226 rivers

across the United States. The St. Croix is the only federally protected Wild and Scenic River in Minnesota and one of only two in
Wisconsin.

For its part, in 1968, the Northern States Power Company donated twenty-five thousand acres of land to create the St. Croix
National Scenic Riverway. This included giving seven thousand
acres to the National Park Service, thirteen thousand acres to
Minnesota, and five thousand acres to Wisconsin. Without this do-
nation of land, Wild River State Park in Minnesota and Governor
Knowles State Forest in Wisconsin might not exist today. As for
the power plant in Oak Park Heights, it has been in operation since
1968 but is scheduled to be decommissioned in 2028.

What Is a Watershed?

A watershed is an area of land that all drains to the same lake, river,
stream, or ocean.

Minnesota is divided into ten major watersheds, with two-
thirds of the state draining to the Mississippi River, then onward
to the Gulf of Mexico. Northern and northwestern Minnesota
drain to the Rainy and Red Rivers, which flow to Hudson Bay in the
Arctic Ocean. The northeastern Arrowhead region drains to Lake
Superior, with water flowing through the Great Lakes and eventually to the Atlantic Ocean.

Wisconsin has twenty-four major watersheds. Two-thirds
of the state drains to the Mississippi River. Far northwestern
Wisconsin goes to Lake Superior, and the remaining watersheds
along the eastern edge of the state flow to Lake Michigan.

Like nested Russian dolls, major watersheds subdivide into
smaller lake and river watersheds, each of which can be divided
even further into subwatersheds.

The St. Croix River Watershed is 7,760 square miles and covers portions of ten counties in Minnesota and nine counties in
Wisconsin. After gathering water from rivers, lakes, streams, and
wetlands across this vast and varied landscape, the St. Croix carries it onward to the Mississippi River.

We are connected with the land, water, and people who live
above and below us in a watershed. Runoff pollution from farming and development in Minnesota and Wisconsin contributes to

East Boot Lake in northern Washington County, Minnesota

catastrophic water pollution downriver in the Mississippi, as well as a dead zone in the Gulf of Mexico that is as large as the state of New Jersey. By the same token, when we work to restore water and habitat in the St. Croix River Watershed, we can improve our own lives as well as those of people and wildlife who live more than one thousand miles away.

Ecoregions

The St. Croix River Watershed lies at an intersection between multiple different ecoregions in Minnesota and Wisconsin. In the southern portion of the watershed, the landscape was originally a mix of prairie and oak savanna, dotted with patches of hardwood forest around lakes, rivers, and valleys. Today, most of the native grasslands have been lost to farming and development, and trees have moved in to fill the spaces that were once kept clear by grazing bison and periodic fires.

Farther north within the watershed, the natural environment transitions to pine forests, pine barrens, and northern hardwood forests. Though these areas were logged extensively during European American settlement, many trees have regrown, and this northern region is now mostly forested.

Throughout the watershed there is water, water, everywhere. There are hundreds of lakes, thousands of miles of rivers and streams, and hundreds of thousands of acres of wetlands that provide critical habitat for rare plants, migrating waterfowl, reptiles, and amphibians.

The Story of the River Continues

Time is like an accordion, and, depending on your perspective, the story of the St. Croix River could be very long or very short.

During the past two hundred years, the St. Croix River Watershed has experienced tremendous destruction, transition, growth, and renewal. For people who live here today, the events of the 1800s might seem like ancient history, yet the past two centuries are just a blink in the eye of geologic time. Is it possible that our current time marks the beginning of a new era for the St. Croix River, when we come together to restore prairies, woods, and waters that were nearly lost to human ambitions?

As you read about places to explore and enjoy nature in the St. Croix River Watershed, pay attention to the stories of people who are working hard to plant trees, tend rain gardens, and sow native seeds into fallow fields. Listen for the voices of Ojibwe and Dakota people who live in the region today and share their wisdom and perspectives through art and activism.

The story of the river is still being written. Where do you fit in?

ST. CROIX NATIONAL SCENIC RIVERWAY

THE MOST OBVIOUS PLACE TO BEGIN EXPLORING THE ST. CROIX RIVER Watershed is on the river. The Namekagon and St. Croix Rivers combined offer more than 250 miles of scenic opportunities to paddle, fish, swim, and explore, all within a designated National Scenic Riverway.

The northernmost reaches of the St. Croix and Namekagon are best traveled by kayak or canoe and are wilderness at its finest. South of Stillwater, the St. Croix becomes wider and deeper, and you are more likely to find motorboats and millionaires.

The riverway is home to 41 species of mussels, five of which are on the federal endangered species list; 111 species of fish; and 240 species of birds, including 60 species identified as being of greatest conservation need.

Planning a Paddling Trip on the St. Croix or Namekagon River

Your first step in planning a day or overnight paddling trip on the St. Croix or Namekagon River should be the National Park Service website: www.nps.gov/sacn. There, you will find river maps, recommended routes, safety and gear lists, links to check river levels, and other important information. National Park Service visitor

Gary and Charlie join me for a day on the Upper St. Croix River.

A stand-up paddleboard rests on a sandbar north of the Arcola High Bridge.

centers are located at 401 North Hamilton Street in St. Croix Falls, Wisconsin, and at W5483 U.S. Highway 63, Trego, Wisconsin. Both are wheelchair accessible and have exhibits, a bookstore, and restrooms. It is particularly important to check river levels before you head out on the water. The St. Croix River can flood and be unsafe during the spring snowmelt, and there are stretches that become shallow and hard to navigate in the late summer and fall.

If you own your own canoe or kayak, it is technically possible to do a multiday trip along the riverway without spending money on anything but food and gas. North of US Highway 8, riverside campsites are available on a first come, first served basis, and do not require a permit or reservation. Between U.S. Highway 8 and the Arcola High Bridge (near Stillwater), a free annual camping permit from the National Park Service is required. The Namekagon and St. Croix River campsites are similar to those you find in the Boundary Waters Canoe Area Wilderness in northern Minnesota: they have latrines, campfire rings, and sometimes picnic tables, but no water or indoor bathrooms.

In Minnesota, canoes, kayaks, and paddleboards longer than ten feet must be licensed through the Minnesota Department of Natural Resources (DNR): www.dnr.state.mn.us/licenses/water craft. Wisconsin does not require licenses for nonmotorized watercraft.

Shuttle Services and Watercraft Rental

On the National Park Service website, you can find information about private companies offering shuttle services; canoe and kayak rental; and guides for fishing, hunting, and paddling trips within the St. Croix Riverway: www.nps.gov/sacn/planyourvisit/goodsandservices.htm. There are several places along both rivers where you can rent tubes to float downriver and then be picked up at the end of your trip. If you'd like to use your bike instead of a shuttle, be sure to bring a bike lock and helmet and pack a small bag with a change of clothes and a bottle of water that you can leave with your bike at the takeout each day.

What to Pack

You'll want to bring food, water, sunscreen, a hat, sunglasses, bug spray, and a first aid kit. Our family usually also brings a fishing pole, a slingshot, a couple of books, a hammock, and fold-up stadium seats to use during rest and play time. Be sure you have a life jacket for each person in the canoe or kayak. Children under thirteen years of age are required to wear life jackets at all times when on board.

If you'll be camping, invest in a waterproof dry bag to protect your camping gear. You'll have to pack relatively lightly to ensure there is enough space in your canoe. If you are self-shuttling with a bike, I recommend dropping off your bike at the takeout each morning and then riding back to pick up your vehicle and camping gear at the end of the day so that you can travel more lightly on the water.

As for clothing, dress in layers so you can easily adjust as the temperature rises and falls during the day. Wear breathable clothing made of wool or synthetic fabric that dries relatively quickly if it gets wet. You will need to step into the water multiple times during your trip, so wear shoes that can get wet. River sandals or water shoes work well during the summer; in the spring or fall, when the water is cold, you'll be more comfortable in rubber boots with wool socks underneath.

The truck is all packed and ready to roll.

Join a Guided Kayak Trip with Wild Rivers Conservancy of the St. Croix and Namekagon

New to kayaking or the St. Croix River Watershed? The Wild Rivers Conservancy of the St. Croix and Namekagon is the official nonprofit partner of the St. Croix National Scenic Riverway. It promotes land conservation, water quality protection, river corridor and watershed stewardship, and celebration of the river and its watershed.

Wild Rivers offers day trips and overnight kayaking excursions on the St. Croix and Namekagon Rivers with experienced staff who can help you navigate the riverway and learn about the wildlife, geology, and cultural history of the watershed. Overnight camping trips are fully supported, with Wild Rivers Conservancy providing a shuttle, campsite, kayak, paddle, life jacket, camp kitchen supplies, food, and professional guides.

For a truly comprehensive experience, try a three-day Namekagon paddle. It will take you down the Namekagon River from Cable to Springbrook, Wisconsin. To learn more, visit www.wildriversconservancy.org/learn-explore/paddle-adventures.

Explore Six Stretches of the St. Croix National Scenic Riverway

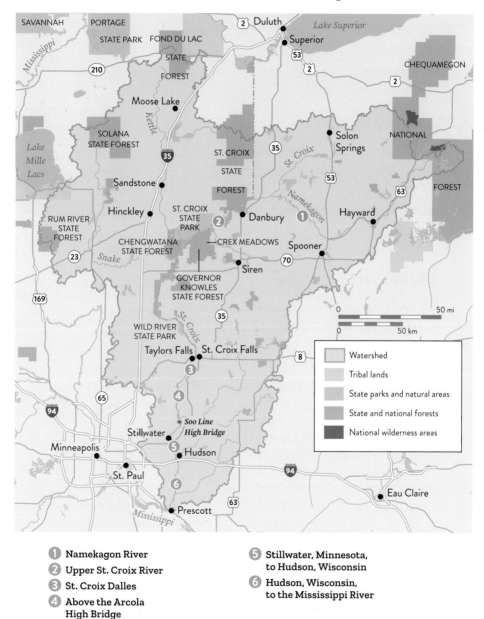

1. Namekagon River
2. Upper St. Croix River
3. St. Croix Dalles
4. Above the Arcola High Bridge
5. Stillwater, Minnesota, to Hudson, Wisconsin
6. Hudson, Wisconsin, to the Mississippi River

Namekagon River above the confluence with the St. Croix River

❶ Namekagon River

*Wisconsin north woods, crystal clear water,
and terrific trout fishing*

Intermediate

As it flows from the Chequamegon–Nicolet National Forest to its confluence with the St. Croix River, the Namekagon passes through small towns with Northwoods charm, long stretches of semi-wilderness, and prime cabin and camping country in north-western Wisconsin. The Namekagon is well known for its abundant brook and brown trout, and also offers opportunities to fish for sturgeon, bass, and muskellunge.

Most people explore the Namekagon by canoe or kayak, but there are stretches where the water is deep enough to use small motorboats with shallow drafts. However, personal motorized watercraft (jet skis) are prohibited on the entirety of the river.

The Namekagon is a dynamic river that changes from one mile to the next and from season to season. Through some stretches, the river is rocky and difficult to navigate. In others, it passes through wide, slow-moving flowages. When the snow melts in the spring, water levels surge and the river can become dangerous. By late summer, low water levels and beaver dams can make it difficult to paddle, especially in the uppermost reaches.

Numerous outfitters offer canoe, kayak, and tube rental along the upper and lower Namekagon River. See www.nps.gov/sacn/planyourvisit/namekagon-outfitters.htm to find locations and contact information.

PADDLE, BIKE, REPEAT:
FOUR DAYS ON THE NAMEKAGON AND ST. CROIX RIVERS

June 2020

During our first day on the Namekagon River, we watched brook trout scatter in threes and fours as our canoe parted the water. Their greenish-gold bodies contrasted against the river's sandy bottom, and we could clearly see the red on their fins as they darted

An ebony jewelwing damselfly perches near the water.

A doe munches on aquatic plants as she watches our canoe pass.

Marsh milkweed in bloom along the Namekagon

Charlie poses with an ebony jewelwing.

away. Ebony jewelwings fluttered along the water's edge. These brightly colored damselflies have shiny turquoise bodies with dark black wings. Like dragonflies, they lay their eggs in the water and live as aquatic insects during their nymph stage. After metamorphosis, they emerge as brilliantly colored flying insects that feast on gnats, mosquitoes, and other smaller insects. Other treasured sightings of the day included a deer munching river grass, blueflag iris and swamp milkweed in bloom, and a three-ridge mussel.

It's hard to say which of us was most excited for the trip. I was eager to see the Namekagon for the first time; my eight-year-old son had just read *My Side of the Mountain* and was ready to play the protagonist in a real life, outdoor adventure; my husband yearned to escape work for a few days; and the dog was just relieved that she didn't get left behind.

We started our trip at the County Road K landing on the Namekagon River near Trego, Wisconsin, and ended four days later at the Lower Tamarack landing on the St. Croix River, forty-seven miles downriver. To avoid a shuttle or bringing two cars, I

Three-ridge mussel, among the forty-one freshwater mussel species in the St. Croix and Namekagon Rivers

brought my mountain bike and rode back to our put-in at the end of each day to bring our truck and camping gear to the next location. The strategy worked really well on the first day but became progressively harder each day after that because of the sandy conditions on most of the smaller roads.

Riding through the Namekagon Barrens Wildlife Area on day three, I was treated to a stunning view of pine-oak barrens, a globally rare habitat that features scattered pines and oaks amid a prairie landscape. The rolling hills and wide-open views are unlike anything else in the surrounding Northwoods forest, but the soft sand road was a callous snare that left me feeling as though I was riding my bike across a never-ending series of sand dunes.

We were surprised to see how much the river changed from day to day. In some places, it was rocky and filled with rapids. In other locations, it was a long flat ribbon of crystal clear water flowing over miles and miles of golden sand. Around us, the landscape changed as well, from pine forest to silver maple floodplain, interspersed with wetlands, cold-water tributaries, and islands large and small.

Though we saw other people in canoes, kayaks, fishing boats, and inner tubes along the way, there were many occasions when we traveled for several hours without seeing anyone else. It was at these times that we encountered the most wildlife: a deer swimming across the river from north to south, a bald eagle resting on a fallen log at the river's edge, a beaver gliding silently beneath the canoe, and dozens of softshell turtles slipping stealthily into the water as we passed. Each day stretched out long and lazy beneath the summer sun in an endless sequence of simple actions—paddle, swim, hunt for frogs, paddle, bask, repeat. We ended our trip feeling dirty, exhausted, and entirely content.

Namekagon River between County Road K and Whispering Pines

Skiers glide through the woods in the American Birkebeiner. Courtesy of Sinthang Has.

OFF THE WATER

Skiing the Birkie in Hayward and Cable, Wisconsin

EACH YEAR IN FEBRUARY, approximately thirty thousand winter enthusiasts arrive in northwestern Wisconsin to participate in and watch the American Birkebeiner, an annual cross-country ski race known by most people as "The Birkie." The 51K and 55K Birkie marathons and the 24K Kortelopet race attract ten thousand skiers each year, including Olympians, international and national team members, and local amateurs from Minnesota, Wisconsin, Michigan, and Canada. It is one of twenty ski marathon events held around the world as part of the Worldloppet.

"I feel like skiing is the closest to flying you can get without a machine," says Josh Leonard, an environmental educator at Belwin Conservancy, who has skied the Birkie twice. "It's a really ergonomic way to use your big muscle groups because you use everything at once—legs, arms, and even abs."

The Birkie trail system has more than sixty-two miles of hilly, forested trails winding from Cable to Hayward and back. Within the forest are numerous steep ridges and glacial potholes filled with wetlands and small lakes. Aspen, red oak, white pine, red pine, basswood, and maple trees line the trail. The trail system overlaps with the Chequamegon Area Mountain Bike Association (CAMBA) trails. Together, these two trail systems offer year-round opportunities for skiing, mountain biking, hiking, and trail running, with numerous special events, races, and youth programs.

"It is such a hard course," laughs Sinthang Has, a teacher at Harding High School in St. Paul, who now has ten Birkies under his belt. "There are so many hills, and I wonder, 'Why do we go up all those hills?' My heart is racing the whole time."

Both Leonard and Has agree that cross-country skiing is as much a lifestyle as a sport. "You have to have dedication to go outside in the dark and the cold to train for this thing that no one watches," says Leonard. Has jokes about catching Birkie fever.

"I'm not going to stop now that I have a ten-year streak going. A Birch-legger is some-one who has finished twenty Birkies and now that's my goal."

The American Birkebeiner was modeled after the Birkebeiner Rennet in Norway, which honors and re-creates a historic Norwegian event from 1206. According to the American Birkebeiner Ski Foundation, "Two warrior soldiers, called 'Birkebeiners' because of the birch-bark leggings they wore, skied infant Prince Haakon to safety during the Norwegian civil war. Prince Haakon subsequently became King of Norway, and the Birkebeiner soldiers became a Norwegian symbol of cour-age, perseverance, and character in the face of adversity."

Sinthang Has hopes to complete twenty Birkies.
Courtesy of Sinthang Has.

Though cross-country skiing has its roots in Scandinavian culture, the sport here in Minnesota and Wiscon-sin is becoming more culturally diverse as new people move to the region and embrace the joy of winter snow and ice. When he taught at Como High School in St. Paul, Leonard worked with students from Burma, Laos, and other tropical countries. Many saw snow for the first time when they moved to Minnesota, but they were eager to strap on skis and learn to glide. "Eh Tah Lerc was one of those students, and he actually made the varsity ski team during his first year of skiing," says Leonard. "Another student was named Wa Wa. She loved to ski and would scoot around the field with a huge smile on her face." Has guesses he might be the first Cambodian to ski the Birkie, but he feels it's important to represent his culture. "Sometimes you have to be the one who is the forerunner," he says.

In addition to hosting the annual Birkie, the American Birkebeiner Ski Founda-tion has worked with Landmark Conservancy, a nonprofit conservation organization serving twenty counties in western and northwestern Wisconsin, to establish perma-nent land conservation easements for more than five hundred acres of land near Cable. The Telemark Forest Preserve and Mt. Telemark Conservancy are open to the public for low-impact uses including backcountry hiking, cross-country skiing, snowshoe-ing, bird-watching, and wildlife viewing; they are permanently protected from devel-opment. The adjacent Mt. Telemark Village will soon include a community center; a paved trail for roller skiing, walking, and hiking; a mountain bike park and trails; an observation tower; a sledding hill; and skating ponds.

Learn more about the Birkebeiner and access trail maps at www.birkie.com. ◇

Sunrise over the St. Croix River at Riverside Landing

② Upper St. Croix River

A wilderness experience, surrounded by forest and public lands

Advanced

The St. Croix River begins its journey at Upper St. Croix Lake in Solon Springs, Wisconsin, thirty miles south of Lake Superior. When glaciers retreated from Minnesota and Wisconsin fourteen thousand years ago, Lake Superior drained southwestward through what are now the Bois Brule and St. Croix River Valleys. Today, the Bois Brule flows north from Solon Springs to Lake Superior, while the St. Croix River flows south to the Mississippi River and eventually the Gulf of Mexico. Both rivers are fed by groundwater springs that are the modern remnants of glacial meltwater that seeped into the ground and filled sandstone aquifers beneath the forests, wetlands, and grasslands of today's landscape.

The first eight miles of the St Croix River meanders through marsh and bog before entering the St. Croix Flowage near Gordon. Gordon Dam, at the southwest end of the flowage, marks the beginning of the St. Croix National Scenic Riverway. From there, the next twenty miles of the river are shallow and filled with small rapids. This is a very isolated stretch of water with no towns nearby. In fact, if you make it this far north, it is entirely possible that you will have the river to yourself.

After its confluence with the Namekagon, the St. Croix River travels another seventy-seven miles until it reaches a dam at St. Croix Falls, Wisconsin. The untamed upper river has numerous class I and II rapids and flows through vast stretches of undeveloped public lands, including St. Croix State Forest and St. Croix State Park in Minnesota, Governor Knowles State Forest in Wisconsin, Chengwatana State Forest in Minnesota, and Wild River State Park in Minnesota. As with the Namekagon, most people explore the Upper St. Croix River by canoe or kayak, but it is possible to use small motorboats in some areas. Personal motorized watercraft are prohibited.

Because the upper river is so isolated, it is important to study river maps, check river levels, and plan your trip carefully ahead of time. During the spring snowmelt, that area can be dangerous, and when water levels get low, it is virtually impossible to paddle

Gary and Charlie wade in the St. Croix River downriver of its confluence with the Namekagon.

FANCY LADIES
ON THE ST. CROIX RIVER

September 2010

It was approaching midnight on a summer Thursday as I finished strapping my very large canoe to my very small car and glanced at my weekend packing list one last time. Canoe, paddles, and life jackets? Check. Sleeping bag, propane, and fixin's for s'mores? Check. Flowing scarves, bangles, and ruffled skirt? Got 'em. A fancy lady always travels in style, especially when she's camping.

By one o'clock the next day, my friends and I were gathered in a Maplewood front yard, all of us dressed in skirts and faux jewels, surveying the expanse of camping paraphernalia strewn across the lawn and trying to figure out how to stuff it all into four dry bags to carry in two canoes. A passing car slowed to a crawl, then returned from the opposite direction only minutes later. Neighborhood children hovered, looking perplexed.

"Where are you going?" asked a little girl watching from the sidewalk.

"Camping on the river," we replied. "Want to know why we're dressed like this?"

In my circle of friends, girls' weekend camping is an annual tradition. Each year, we choose a new destination and a new theme for our trip. One year, we stormed the pine forests of northern Minnesota dressed as Lumberjills with axes and saws. Another year, we brandished pirate flags as we paddled across Lake Winnibigoshish. In 2010, we floated down the St. Croix River as a pack of giggling ladies garbed in dresses.

We set up camp at Sandrock Cliffs, a rustic National Park Service campsite near Grantsburg, Wisconsin. On Friday night, the beauty and solitude of the location was somewhat marred by ravenous mosquitoes and the drunken louts who were camping nearby. By late Saturday morning, the loud boys were gone, leaving only us women and the mosquitoes to fight for the remaining territory. With a twinkle in our eyes, we donned our dresses and headed up the road to Norway Point Landing.

By early August, the Upper St. Croix River is usually too shallow for canoeing. That year, however, consistent rains had kept the water flowing throughout the summer. It took us a little more than five hours to paddle from Norway Point back to our campsite—and that included a long and leisurely lunch break at the Nelson's Landing picnic area.

We did have to navigate several stretches of rapids along the way, which caused a bit of mild panic within our group. Rapids are marked on National Park Service river maps, but we had been so busy planning our outfits that year, we hadn't really reviewed the maps as thoroughly as we should have. Luckily, we negotiated the whitewater successfully, without losing a single bangle or charm.

During our St. Croix River canoe trip, we observed softshell and painted turtles sunning on rocks, an eastern hognose snake swimming across the river, and a merganser that ran on top of the water like a cartoon character. We basked in the sun of a cloudless sky and watched bald eagles soaring in the wind. We saw only two other boats on the river, with not a single building, house, or road in sight. ◇

sections of the upper river, even with a kayak. Be sure to bring a first aid kit and change of clothes—especially warm clothes—and be prepared to shelter on the river's edge for several hours or even overnight if the weather changes. Even in the middle of summer, cold rain can come up unexpectedly. There are very few roads, and landings can be as far as ten miles apart. Cell phone reception is limited along most of the upper river.

With proper planning, the upper river offers an unparalleled wilderness experience. Between Riverside Landing (Wisconsin State Highway 35) and Thayer's Landing (Minnesota State Highway 48 and Wisconsin State Highway 77), the river is slow and

OFF THE WATER

Northwest Passage Gallery in Webster, Wisconsin

Located in Webster, Wisconsin, Northwest Passage is a residential treatment center for children that combines nature, experiential programming, community engagement, and arts to create a therapy program for youth who are struggling with depression, addiction, and other mental health challenges. The center is perhaps best known for its In a New Light program, which was developed in 2010.

In a New Light trains youth in nature photography and empowers them to find beauty in the world around them and themselves. Participants hike, explore the Namekagon and St. Croix Rivers by canoe, learn how to use special equipment such as underwater cameras, and even have opportunities to participate in trips to more distant locations such as Costa Rica, Yellowstone, and the Everglades. The program is supported by the National Park Service, Sea Grant, National Park Foundation, St. Croix Valley Foundation, Wisconsin Arts Board, National Endowment for the Arts, and Arts Midwest.

The Northwest Passage Gallery, operated in partnership with Burnett Area Arts Group, showcases the work of regional artists and In a New Light participants and also rents out studio and classroom space. It is open Thursday through Sunday and is worth a visit if you are in the area. The gallery is located at 7417 North Bass Lake Road in Webster.

Photography from In a New Light can be viewed online and purchased at purchase.inanewlight.org. The following photographs and stories are reprinted with permission and shared as examples of the beautiful art created by youth in the program. ◊

meandering, with hundreds of sand bar islands that are perfect for a picnic or lazy afternoon nap. As it flows past St. Croix State Park, the river comes to life with numerous rapids. You are more likely to see deer and eagles on the upper river than people, and visitors have the opportunity to disconnect from technology and reconnect with nature.

To me, Derek's photograph "Streaming Life" shows that the river is full of energy, full of life in a constant flow. And I feel like my life is just like the river—I have all this energy, and my life is now just beginning for the first time.

About Derek: "My name is Derek. I am seventeen years old, and I am from Superior, Wisconsin. I have been through a lot in life with my family and friends. I have had a lot of problems with substance abuse, but I am turning things around thanks to Northwest Passage. My dream is to be an underwater welder when I get older. For me, nature photography is a way to get away from all my problems. It was something I didn't really know about or care about when I came here, but the more I worked at it, the more I turned out to love it. Now it's my passion."

"Streaming Life," by Derek, 17

For me, De'Vante's "Green Dragonfly" symbolizes hope and also brings a smile to my face. It is so fragile and delicate, but so beautiful at the same time, and when it flies it is so fast and powerful. We all have many sides.

About De'Vante: "I'm De'Vante, I'm sixteen and from Madison, Wisconsin. I've made mistakes in the past, but now I'm working on getting trust back from my loved ones. Photography has helped me express the artistic and creative side in me, and there's no better way to do that than taking pictures out in nature."

"Green Dragonfly," by De'Vante, 16

About Chris: "Hey, my name is Chris and I'm from Madison, Wisconsin. The way I see it is, life is a roller coaster. It starts pulling out of the station and going up and up and up . . . until it drops, and my life so far has been that huge scary drop. But, between you and I, my coming to Passage is right after that first dip. Now I'm going up, and all I see in my future is going up and up. The way I see photography is almost as a therapeutic retreat. Taking a breathtaking picture is something that puts hope into my life and makes me feel very excited, and also like I'm possessing a secret skill. I feel like there is no better way to express such a great artistic passion in my life but doing just this."

"Freezing Namekagon," by Chris, 15

About Clayton: "My name is Clayton. I am a young Native American from Lac Courte Oreilles, Wisconsin. I used to be a menace to my society. But now that I'm taking pictures, my chance for success is much greater because I can help my community and show the world anyone can change. I hope that when others see my work it can inspire them to change and let them know that there is a better life out there for them than hanging in the streets. My plan for the future is to successfully finish Northwest Passage and Challenge Academy and then teach others the right path in life."

"Searching for a Meal," by Clayton, 17

I had no idea that sponges even existed in freshwater. But they're everywhere. When I saw this one, I thought it was unique and beautiful. In life, sometimes the best things are the ones you never knew were even there.

About Anthony: "My hometown is the Superior–Duluth area, it is amazing and beautiful. My favorite thing to do is motocross. My other hobby would be anything in the outdoors. I have been struggling with meth addiction since I was fourteen. I have been in too many run-ins with the law since then. I have had this bad struggle with drugs, and I'm just starting to change my life around. I'm planning on going into the military when I am eighteen."

"Sponge," by Anthony, 16

Overlooking the St. Croix River at the western terminus of the Ice Age National Scenic Trail in Wisconsin's Interstate State Park. The hiking trail from here to Potawatomi State Park in Door County, Wisconsin, is one thousand miles long.

③ St. Croix Dalles

Towering basalt cliffs, hiking trails, and paddlewheel riverboats

Beginner

The St. Croix River near Taylors Falls, Minnesota, and St. Croix Falls, Wisconsin, is one of the most popular and action-packed sections of the entire riverway. Known as the St. Croix Dalles, this area is characterized by tall, basalt rocks that form a dramatic gorge with towering cliffs on either side of the river.

On the north end of St. Croix Falls, a sixty-foot hydroelectric dam stands where once there was a waterfall. Built in 1907, this dam marks the official divide between the Upper and Lower St. Croix River. Just south of Taylors Falls, there is an Interstate State Park on each state's side of the river. Both parks offer great hiking trails and amazing geology. Minnesota's park was established in 1895 and Wisconsin's in 1900. Together, they formed the first interstate park in the nation.

The towering basalt at Minnesota's Interstate State Park is great for exploring or for a game of hide and seek.

In Minnesota's Interstate State Park, you can find numerous cylindrical potholes in the basalt, which were formed by the grinding action of sand and small stones swirling in strong currents when meltwater from Glacial Lake Duluth carved the modern St. Croix River Valley. Some of the largest potholes are six feet wide and twelve feet deep.

Wisconsin's Interstate State Park, the larger of the two parks, has nine miles of trails and includes the Centennial Bedrock Glade and Interstate Lowland Forest State Natural Areas. The hot, dry conditions and thin soil atop the boulders here create a microhabitat that supports lichens and rare prairie plants,

Enjoy a leisurely ride through the St. Croix Dalles aboard a historic paddlewheel boat in Taylors Falls, Minnesota.

including the prairie fameflower, a succulent that grows only in the upper Midwest.

One of the most popular ways to explore this stretch of the river is by paddlewheel riverboat. Taylors Falls Scenic Boat Tours (www.taylorsfallsboat.com) offers numerous day and evening trips with food, drinks, and entertainment. The trips are a great way to learn about the history and geology of the area and are suitable for large groups and people of all ages and abilities. The boats are semi-accessible for standard-size manual wheelchairs.

The 6.6 miles between the St. Croix Dalles and Osceola is also one of the most popular stretches for canoeing and kayaking. It's an easy paddle with beautiful scenery. Three companies in the area offer boat rental and shuttle services:

Eric's Canoe Rental www.ericscanoerental.com

Taylors Falls Canoe and Kayak Rental
www.taylorsfallscanoeandkayakrental.com

Riverwood Canoe Rental www.riverwoodcanoe.com

The twin towns of St. Croix Falls and Taylors Falls have restaurants, gas stations, and stores, as well as numerous tourist attractions. Head to https://thestcroixvalley.com/ to find information about popular activities, including the Osceola and St. Croix Valley Railway, Wild Mountain and Trollhaugen ski areas, St. Croix Festival Theatre, and Fawn-Doe-Rosa petting zoo.

Canoes and kayaks on the St. Croix River between Taylors Falls and Osceola

"Playstation" by Bridget Beck was constructed in 2009 and includes swings, slides, and lookout posts.

OFF THE WATER

Franconia Sculpture Park, Shafer, Minnesota

One day a few years back, I had a day off work and wanted to do something fun with my son, spend time outside, and maybe see some art. And the dog needed a walk. With luck, a solution presented itself in the form of the Franconia Sculpture Park, located along Minnesota Highway 95, just south of Taylors Falls, Minnesota.

As we drove north to Franconia from our home in Stillwater, I worried. Gray clouds hung overhead, and sprinkles kept landing on the windshield. But shortly after we arrived, a warm sun emerged from the clouds and we were able to enjoy a playground fit for Dr. Seuss: mirrors reflecting a prairie in bloom, a shed with black spots and a face that looked exactly like my dog, and an art installation by 2019 Open Studio Fellow Molly Valentine Dierks that reminded me an awful lot of my mind.

In her installation, Dierks captures key phrases from "I Worried," one of Mary Oliver's most beloved poems, on a series of brightly colored road signs that seem out of place amid the natural beauty of the surroundings. That day, the questions leapt out and confronted me as we wandered past towering creatures of steel and through a waving sea of bluestem and coneflower.

"Will the garden grow?"

I paused and gazed at a buzzing bee atop the purple petals of a coneflower in bloom.

"Was I right, was I wrong?"

Which of the many possible incidents could she be asking me to recall?

"Can I do better?"

If you are a perfectionist like I am, the answer is always yes.

I have always been a fan of Oliver's poetry, and it was a grounding experience to read her words of wisdom while standing in a field of flowers with a warm breeze on my back. Oliver had a special way of writing about nature that reminds us that simple and everyday experiences can also be spiritual and enlightening. Dierks's installation is a beautiful tribute to the poet, who died in 2019 at the age of eighty-three, the same year the signs took root in the prairie.

Franconia Sculpture Park sits on fifty acres of land near the intersection of U.S. Highway 8 and Minnesota Highway 95 in Franconia Township. The gargantuan sculptures and art installations are immediately visible from the road. There are easy mowed and gravel walking trails leading from the parking area to the ever-growing art collection, which now includes more than one hundred works. From April through October, golf carts are available for people with mobility challenges to rent. Franconia Sculpture Park also offers artist residencies, live music, film showings and other public programs, a small indoor gallery, and youth summer camps.

In 2022, Franconia initiated a new project, *4Ground: Midwest Land Art Biennial,* in collaboration with more than twenty arts, environmental, and tribal organizations. The goal of the project is to raise awareness about environmental issues affecting communities in the St. Croix River Watershed; boost tourism; and celebrate the art, land, and history of the rural Midwest. During the summer, partnering organizations host site-specific land art and public programs at locations across the watershed, including Franconia Sculpture Park.

Franconia Sculpture Park is located at 29836 St. Croix Trail in Shafer, Minnesota. The grounds are open 365 days a year from 8 a.m. until 8 p.m. The visitor center is open daily from April 15 until November 15 and on weekends during the winter. Dogs are allowed on leashes. Learn more at www.franconia.org. ◊

A bumblebee on
purple coneflower

The Arcola High Bridge soars above the St. Croix River approximately halfway between Marine on St. Croix and Stillwater.

4 Above the Arcola High Bridge

Braided channels, islands, and backwaters within an hour of the Twin Cities

Intermediate

The Arcola High Bridge, also known as the Soo Line High Bridge, is a steel railroad bridge that crosses the St. Croix River five miles north of Stillwater. The bridge was built in 1910, and as the name implies, it soars high above the river, creating a dramatic subject for photographs. It is listed on the National Register of Historic Places and also marks an important transition along the river.

From Osceola to the St. Croix Boom Site, the river divides and rejoins itself in a series of braided channels, islands, and labyrinthine backwaters as it passes by William O'Brien State Park and the quaint, historic town of Marine on St. Croix in Minnesota and the St. Croix Islands State Wildlife Area in Wisconsin. You'll see more pontoon and fishing boats here than on the Upper River, but personal watercraft are prohibited, and there are wake and speed rules for motorboats.

Numerous freshwater mussel beds lie within this portion of the river, and you may be surprised to discover that cell service is

An emerald kingdom awaits in the backwaters of the St. Croix River near Log Cabin Landing in Scandia, Minnesota.

relatively nonexistent, even though you are less than an hour from Minneapolis and St. Paul. To prevent the spread of invasive zebra mussels, boats are not allowed to travel upriver from below the Arcola High Bridge. As a result, the riverway between the St. Croix Dalles and here remains quiet and natural.

TRACING LAZY CIRCLES IN THE SAND

Beneath the clear brown water, the mussel paused, resting softly on the sand. Behind it, a long arcing trail unfurled. Puff. The mussel exhaled, sending a small burst of water out of its body, and in doing so, it traveled one centimeter farther across the river bottom. Rest, exhale, repeat.

Mussels trace lazy circles in the soft sand on the river's bottom.

Pimpleback mussel

Plain pocketbook mussel

A freshwater mussel gaps open, showing its soft flesh inside.

The water lapped gently against the sandbar, and a heron glided across the water to perch on a fallen tree. Rest, exhale, repeat. Overhead, the sun slid slowly down the sky and into the horizon. Hour by hour, the ribbon grew longer as the mussel in the river slowly, ever so slowly, traced its circles in the sand.

The St. Croix River Watershed is considered one of the premier environments for freshwater mussels in the world and it is home to five species listed under the Federal Endangered Species Act: Higgins' eye, sheepnose, snuffbox, spectaclecase, and winged mapleleaf. "The St. Croix River is a rare example of a complete and intact river ecosystem," explains Marian Shaffer, an aquatic biologist with the National Park Service. "In fact, all of the freshwater mussel species that existed in the St. Croix Riverway before European settlement are still here today." This diversity and abundance of mussels in the St. Croix is an indication of good water quality and a healthy ecosystem.

Elsewhere in the United States, almost two-thirds of all native mussel species are threatened, endangered, or already extinct. In the Mississippi River, twelve mussel species have disappeared, leaving twenty-eight species remaining. These mussels help tell the story of a river, nearly destroyed by pollution, that is slowly returning to good health.

When the U.S. Army Corps of Engineers and National Academy of Science surveyed the Mississippi River in the Twin Cities during the 1970s, they found only nine species of mussels, and only in a small section of the river. Mussels are filter feeders, which makes them particularly vulnerable to water pollution, and the Mississippi River was one of the most polluted during the early twentieth century. Minneapolis and St. Paul dumped untreated sewage into the river until 1938, and factories spewed chemicals into the water until the Clean Water Act was passed in 1972. Today, native mussels are making a comeback in the Mississippi, and researchers have even reintroduced Higgins' eye and winged mapleleaf mussels in some locations. Many of these reintroductions have been with mussels that originated in the St. Croix.

A mussel breathes and eats by drawing water in through a body part known as an incurrent siphon. The mussel absorbs oxygen from the water as it passes over its gills and it also filters out tiny plankton and nutrients, which it absorbs into its body and shell. Once this process is complete, the mussel shoots the water out through its excurrent siphon, propelling itself forward ever so slightly. Rest, exhale, repeat.

In addition to making slow forward progress, a female mussel also performs elaborate dances and uses mimicry to lure fish to her side when she is carrying mussel babies, known as glochidia. Intrigued by a flash of movement or what appears to be a minnow, a fish swims closer to investigate, and the mussel releases her young with a burst. The glochidia attach to the fish's gills and hitch a ride for a few weeks until they are large enough to drop off onto the river bottom and begin lives of their own.

In 2021, researchers with the National Park Service, Wisconsin DNR, and University of Minnesota made a startling discovery when they found a population of elderly spectaclecase mussels living in the St. Croix River above the St. Croix Falls Dam. Since it was constructed in 1905, the dam has blocked mooneye, goldeye, and other fish from swimming upriver, thereby dashing the parental hopes of spectaclecase mussels living above the dam that use

Charlie takes a break from paddling through the backwaters near Marine on St. Croix, Minnesota.

mooneye and goldeneye as their larval host. So, the adult mussels in that location are now well over one hundred years old.

The newest threat for North American freshwater mussels are invasive zebra mussels, which originally came from the Caspian Sea. The zebra mussels attach themselves to any surface they can find, including boat docks, submerged rocks, and native mussels, and disrupt the natural food web. The National Park Service prohibits boats from traveling upstream on the St. Croix River past the Arcola High Bridge north of Stillwater to protect the upper reaches of the river where zebra mussels haven't yet invaded.

The mussel's journey is both slow and long. As the curving path in the sand grows steadily longer, years turn into decades and sometimes even a century. Answering machines give way to cell phones, and typewriters to computers. Past the river bluff, a prairie becomes a farm becomes a subdivision. Still the mussel carries on, carving circles in the sand. Rest, exhale, repeat.

OFF THE WATER

Osceola & St. Croix Railway, Osceola, Wisconsin

All aboard the Pumpkin Express! It was a gorgeous fall weekend and a scenic train ride on the Osceola & St. Croix Railway seemed like the perfect way to spend the day with my in-laws, who were visiting from Milwaukee. At the time, my son was just shy of three years old and still firmly in the Thomas the Tank Engine stage of childhood.

We boarded a vintage train in Osceola, Wisconsin, and enjoyed a short forty-five-minute round-trip ride upriver to Dresser and back. We disembarked at the train depot, which had been transformed into a fall harvest festival with food, music, games, hayrides, and, of course, pumpkins. We stayed and played a while, picked out the perfect pumpkin, and spent a while exploring the station and train cars in Osceola before heading home.

Minnesota's first railroad was built between St. Paul and St. Anthony in 1862. By 1871, two additional railway connections had been added to serve the sawmills of Stillwater, which processed vast amounts of milled lumber from forests in the St. Croix River Watershed. The Minneapolis, St. Paul and Sault Ste. Marie Railway, commonly known as the Soo Line, opened in 1884 and carried passengers between Chicago; Minneapolis–St. Paul; Duluth–Superior; Winnipeg, Ontario; and Sault Ste. Marie, Michigan. It was originally built by a group of flour mill owners in Minneapolis who wanted to send shipments to Sault Ste. Marie without passing through Chicago.

Today, the Soo Line tracks are owned by the Canadian National Railway and are part of a larger network that connects most of Canada with a north–south rail corridor that leads to the Gulf of Mexico. The Arcola High Bridge is still actively used by freight cars that transport a wide variety of goods, including petroleum, chemicals, grain, and fertilizers. Meanwhile, the vintage passenger trains in Osceola are owned and operated by the Minnesota Transportation Museum.

The Osceola & St. Croix Railway offers trips lasting forty-five minutes to an hour and a half from Osceola to Marine on St. Croix and Dresser, with special themed rides such as the Pumpkin Express, pizza train, fall color tours, and wine tasting at local Wisconsin wineries. Trains to Marine on St. Croix cross the St. Croix River on the 1887 Cedar Bend Drawbridge and turn around at William O'Brien State Park. The trains run on Saturdays and Sundays, May through October.

There are accessible bathrooms in the depot and two of the train cars, as well as a lift to help people in wheelchairs enter the train. Wheelchairs may not be able to move between rail cars, however. You can find more information at transportationmuseum.org. ◇

Waiting for the Pumpkin Express to arrive in Osceola, Wisconsin

Passing through the Hudson Swing Bridge aboard St. Croix River Cruises'
Grand Duchess.

⑤ Stillwater, Minnesota, to Hudson, Wisconsin

Paddlewheel riverboats, motorboats, party boats,
restaurants, and walking trails

Beginner

Below the Arcola High Bridge, the Lower St. Croix River changes dramatically. At the St. Croix Boom Site, the river widens, and
dramatic limestone and sandstone bluffs rise up along either side.
The short stretch between here and downtown Stillwater is a party
zone during the summer, when pontoons and motorboats line the
islands, and large groups of people gather at the Boom Site to enjoy
picnics and makeshift bonfires.

From Stillwater on, the river is wide and deep and is technically classified as a lake. Here you'll find motorboats, pontoons,
speedboats, and yachts. I would not recommend paddling a canoe
or kayak through this stretch unless you go in the early morning
and stay close to the shore.

Sailboats at sunset in Hudson, Wisconsin

If you want to rent a boat, there are several places to do so:

Stillwater Boat Rentals—pontoons (www.stillwaterboatrentals.com)

Ole Sawmill Marina (Stillwater)—pontoons (www.facebook.com/OleSawmillMarina)

Your Boat Club (Stillwater)—daily and multiday boat rentals (https://yourboatclub.com/locations/boat-rentals-st-croix-river-mn)

Rent St. Croix (Stillwater)—jet skis (https://rentsaintcroix.com/)

Beach House Marina and Boat Rental (Bayport)—pontoons (https://boatrentalmn.com/)

St. Croix Donut Boat Rentals (Hudson) (telephone, 612-470-4134)

Beanie's Marina (Lakeland)—pontoons (http://beaniesmarina.com/)

Summer Tuesdays on the St. Croix in Stillwater,
one of many local community festivals

The easiest way to get on the river between Stillwater and Hudson is aboard a paddlewheel riverboat. Stillwater River Boats (https:// stillwaterriverboats.com) operates cruises out of Stillwater, and Afton–Hudson Cruise Lines (https://stcroixrivercruises.com) has boats out of Hudson and Afton. Both companies also charter boats for large group events.

If you want a truly unique experience, you can book a trip on a gondola through Gondola Romantica (www.gondolaromantica. com). The rides are geared toward couples and travel around Still-water and under the historic Lift Bridge.

Even if you don't get on the water, there are many other ways to enjoy this stretch of the St. Croix River. You'll find restaurants, parks, and walking trails near the river in Stillwater and Hudson and public swimming beaches in Bayport, Minnesota, and Hudson, Wisconsin. The 4.7-mile paved St. Croix River Crossing Loop Trail connects the historic Lift Bridge in Stillwater with the new St. Croix Crossing south of town (State Highway 36) and is popular for walking and biking.

A WORKSHOP ON THE WATER FOR LOCAL ELECTED OFFICIALS

October 17, 2016

In my professional life, I help to coordinate an annual Workshop on the Water that brings city council members, county commissioners, and other local officials out on the river to learn about policies and ordinances that help to protect habitat and water quality. The event is cosponsored by Wild Rivers Conservancy of the St. Croix and Namekagon, National Park Service, Minnesota DNR, Wisconsin DNR, Minnesota Extension, and the East Metro Water Resource Education Program.

In 2016, eighty local leaders from Minnesota and Wisconsin gathered aboard the *Grand Duchess*, departing out of Hudson, to learn about riverway regulations, how to prevent runoff pollution, and how to protect wildlife habitat. For some, learning about stormwater policies and erosion control ordinances was new territory. Others had been at every workshop since the series began in 2009 and could now talk about phosphorus, infiltration, and visual screening like old pros.

For a special touch that year, I decorated the tables with stories collected by Susan Armington, a local artist with a talent for mixing images and words to create two- and three-dimensional images. My hope was that these quotations from community residents would help to ground our workshop in a shared sense of purpose and love for the river.

Sitting on an island all day long, it was just a blast. It was... you couldn't have had more entertainment or joy or connections or whatever. We cooked on it, we played on it, we rode our bicycles, destroyed toys.

We called ourselves basically river rats 'cause we were out there till you couldn't see. It'd get buggy, so much water...

We actually ate raw arrowheads and you know it was such a blast, it was so much entertainment, that it's like, "where are our parents?" We didn't need to know. They were down at the other end of the island or they were up on shore or we'd swim across, go clamming, hiking, or exploring... it was just unbelievable you know. Huck Finn didn't even come close.

— *Quotation from a St. Croix River resident,*
collected by Susan Armington

Susan first connected with the St. Croix River as an artist in residence for the St. Croix Watershed Research Station in 2013. During this time, she organized several events in local river communities to gather stories from people who live, work, and play here. When I told her about the workshop I was planning, she passed me an overflowing folder full of handwritten notes to share with the attendees, saying, "I want these stories to be used for good, to protect the St. Croix River."

> The St. Croix River is sacred.
>
> I have been coming to the St. Croix since I was a kid. Those day trips were full of camping, boating, and burgers. I live here now. I have found great healing in the valley.
>
> My most treasured times have been at the unknown places where few people hike and fewer boats and snowmobiles invade. I have walked there with dear friends and alone but always with my dear companion (my dog). He has lived all but four months here with me. We live at the end of a dirt road in the solitude of the woods. When we hike the river, as we descend to the lowest part of the valley, I can feel the solidifying action—what grounds me. The water... the massive movement... the continuous power of the water. It stuns me. I stare at it, taking in as much as I can.
>
> I have experienced many changes since I have lived here. To others, it might look like or be called loss. I know that the gifts of life have been illuminated through these losses and I am so grateful. Everyday grateful. I may not always live here, but that is not something to consider right now. I deeply connect with the river... now.
>
> — *Quotation from a St. Croix River resident,*
> *collected by Susan Armington*

For the local decision-makers attending that year's St. Croix River Workshop on the Water, the stories that Armington had collected were a reminder of the values that we share in common, even when we disagree about politics and candidates. We love the river. We want clean water. We want vibrant communities.

The river is our story, and the actions that we take today determine the outcomes that we'll see in twenty, forty, or one hundred years. Working together, we can write a story that we'll want to tell our grandchildren and that they'll want to share with theirs. ◊

The historic Lift Bridge in Stillwater, Minnesota, is now part of a multiuse trail for cyclists and pedestrians.

OFF THE WATER

St. Croix Crossing Loop Trail—Stillwater, Minnesota, and Houlton, Wisconsin

The historic Lift Bridge in downtown Stillwater is an iconic sight along this stretch of the river. When friends come to visit us in Stillwater, we often buy ice cream at Leo's Grill & Malt Shop or Minnesota Nice Cream on Chestnut Street and then stroll across the bridge and back to enjoy views of the river down below. Another simple but thoroughly enjoyable pastime in Stillwater is to sit on a bench in Lowell Park and watch the Lift Bridge rise and lower every half hour as paddleboats, yachts, and other watercraft pass beneath.

A 4.7-mile paved loop connects the Lift Bridge with the newer St. Croix Crossing, approximately one and a half miles farther south, which is popular for walking, running, and biking. The story of how this new bridge and the current loop trail came to be is quite the adventure.

The historic Lift Bridge was constructed in 1931 to replace an earlier timber bridge, which had caught fire and partially collapsed in 1909. As early as the 1980s, the communities of Stillwater and Houlton had determined that the Lift Bridge was past its prime. With only two narrow lanes of traffic, there were massive backups during rush hour and when vehicles were stopped to lift and lower the bridge. The line of idling cars and trucks would extend along several blocks of city streets in downtown Stillwater.

By 1995, the Minnesota Department of Transportation (DOT), Wisconsin DOT, and the Federal Highway Administration had determined that the best course of action was to build a new, larger bridge to span the St. Croix River. Due to the protections of the Wild and Scenic Rivers Act, however, new river crossings are not permitted.

Over the next two decades, a battle ensued between the state and federal transportation agencies, local communities, the National Park Service, St. Croix River Association (now called Wild Rivers Conservancy), environmental and historic preservation groups, and other stakeholders. Eventually, in 2011, U.S. Senator Amy Klobuchar proposed special legislation that exempted the new St. Croix Crossing from riverway protections and allowed it to be built.

Along with this decision, the many governmental and nonprofit entities involved agreed to a mitigation package to offset the historic, aesthetic, and environmental impacts of building a new bridge. During construction, the project managers relocated threatened and endangered mussels in the St. Croix River, restored the river bluff, replaced lost wetlands, and implemented strict erosion control and stormwater management practices. Funds were also provided to an intergovernmental group called the St. Croix Basin Team to conduct a basin-wide water quality study and assist local

communities in planning for future growth. Last, but certainly not least, the group agreed to preserve the historic Lift Bridge and maintain it for pedestrian use as part of a larger loop trail.

In 2017, the new St. Croix Crossing opened, and by 2020 the St. Croix Crossing Loop Trail was complete. Rising 110 to 150 feet above the river, the St. Croix Crossing offers dramatic views of the St. Croix River and Stillwater below. There are three viewing platforms on the bridge with space to stop and rest or take photographs. The loop

Charlie and I pause for a photograph from the top of the newly built St. Croix Crossing.

trail is smooth, well-marked, and relatively easy, unlike the long, steep climb from the Lift Bridge to the top of the river bluff on the Wisconsin side.

Parking is available in downtown Stillwater and near the Sunnyside Marina on the Minnesota side, and in Wisconsin near the top of the hill and at the St. Croix Crossing main trailhead near County Road E and Wisconsin Highway 64. The trail has bathrooms in several locations and self-serve bike repair and tire-filling stations at the main trailhead (Wisconsin) and the Browns Creek Trailhead (Minnesota), which is just north of the historic Lift Bridge. From there, trail users can continue all the way into St. Paul via the Brown's Creek and Gateway Trails.

DIRO Outdoors, Herman Electric Bikes, and Pedego Electric Bikes all offer rentals in downtown Stillwater if you wish to explore and need a bike. Learn more and download maps of the local trails at www.discoverstillwater.com/things-to-do/biking -hiking-trails. ◊

Lake St. Croix Beach

6 Hudson, Wisconsin, to the Mississippi River

A wide channel through bluffs and floodplain forest,
past motorboats and millionaires

Beginner

South of Hudson, the St. Croix River continues its wide, slow journey south to the Mississippi River. For the first five miles, you'll see homes and mansions along the Minnesota side of the river as it flows past a series of small towns—Lakeland, Lakeland Shores, Lake St. Croix Beach, St. Mary's Point, and Afton. After that, the last ten miles of the river become much quieter, as it passes by Afton State Park (Minnesota), Kinnickinnic State Park (Wisconsin), St. Croix Bluffs Regional Park (Minnesota), and Carpenter Nature Center (Minnesota). You are still more likely to see motorboats than canoes in this stretch, but the river does regain some of its wildness.

Finally, the St. Croix seems to almost hit a dead end as it reaches a wide levee at Point Douglas Park and then merges with the Mississippi River at Prescott, Wisconsin. You will instantly notice the change in color as the relatively clear St. Croix River flows into the muddy Mississippi. In aerial photographs, the rivers appear midnight blue and chocolate brown. Here, you'll see multiple vehicle and railway bridges and barges on the Mississippi River, carrying gravel and other freight south to other cities and states.

The parks listed above all offer public access to the St. Croix River for swimming, fishing, and boating, and there are public swimming beaches in Lake St. Croix Beach and the town of Troy, Wisconsin.

Wide blue water near Afton, Minnesota

ST. CROIX—RIVER OR LAKE?

Fans of Aerosmith, sing it with me: "Nah na, nah na, dude looks like a lady!" Did you know that state and federal agencies classify the St. Croix from Stillwater to Prescott as a lake, not as a river? I don't know about you, but that dude sure looks like a river to me. If I drive across the bridge to Wisconsin, I say I'm crossing the river. Tourists arriving at the Stillwater River Boats climb aboard a riverboat, not a lake boat. And let's not forget that it's called a Wild and Scenic River. As it turns out, the St. Croix's got more than a few secrets concealed beneath its rippled surface.

Sue Magdalene, a former scientist with the St. Croix Watershed Research Station, developed the first ever Lake St. Croix, State of the Lake Report and talks about many of the river/lake's idiosyncrasies. For example, you might be surprised to learn that the St. Croix "River" from Stillwater to Prescott is not only classified as a lake, but is actually considered to be four lakes! Equally surprising, water quality and clarity in the St. Croix improves from north to south. By the time it reaches the Mississippi River, it is usually cleaner than it is up in Stillwater.

Experts at the Watershed Research Station have been studying the St. Croix for years. Through studying sediment cores collected from the river (ahem ... lake) bottom, they know that the St. Croix changed significantly in the 1950s during the rise of conventional agriculture. The cores are collected by inserting long tubes into the river bottom to extract layers of silt, sand, and sediment. The cores look somewhat like tall, thin layer cakes. Because the sediment layers accumulate in chronological order, these cores offer a glimpse into the past and help researchers understand how the river and its surrounding landscape interacted in previous decades.

After 1950, the amount of phosphorus flowing downriver into Lake St. Croix increased significantly, creating a ripple effect that affected diatoms (algae), macroinvertebrates (bugs), and other parts of the ecological web as well. As the St. Croix Basin continued to develop during the 1980s and 1990s and more natural areas were converted to agriculture and residential land, phosphorus levels continued to climb. Algae blooms became more common, and people swimming and boating in the St. Croix started to notice. A comprehensive assessment of the St. Croix and its tributaries

Paddlers approach the St. Croix River's confluence with the Mississippi River near Prescott, Wisconsin, during the St. Croix River Association's centennial anniversary event.

was conducted in the late 1990s and the data formed the basis for both Minnesota and Wisconsin to declare Lake St. Croix officially impaired due to too much phosphorus. More than twenty years later, the landscape in the St. Croix Watershed has continued to change and there has been much work to improve water quality as well.

Part of what makes the St. Croix so difficult to study is the fact that it has characteristics of both a river and a lake. There are actually four distinct pools—Stillwater to Hudson (Willow River), Hudson to Afton (Valley Creek), Afton to the Kinnickinnic River, and the Kinni to Prescott. Naturally formed ridges on the lake bottom prevent deep water in each of these pools from moving downstream. Within each pool, the water stratifies during the summer, with colder water sinking to the bottom and warmer water remaining at the top. As a result, from June until September, the St. Croix could best be described as a warm shallow river flowing over the top of four deep, cold lakes. During the spring and fall, changing temperatures cause the water to "turn over" and mix together, typical behavior for a deep lake. During the winter, the four pools become isolated again.

Between the first and fourth pool, interesting changes happen in the St. Croix. Water from the shallow channel upriver comes pouring into the first deeper pool near Stillwater, creating turbid conditions that churn up sediment and nutrients. By the time the water reaches Hudson, some of the sediment has had time to settle out. This pattern continues for each subsequent pool. Though tributary streams like the Willow and Kinnickinnic bring in additional sediment and nutrients, there is still an overall improvement in water quality and clarity by the time water flows out of Lake St. Croix into the Mississippi.

Magdalene's State of the Lake Report examined other interesting patterns. For example, through analyzing climate records and water data collected by the Metropolitan Council and volunteers, she found that wetter, high-flow years produced turbid conditions, with poorer water clarity and higher levels of phosphorus in the water. Because the water is moving faster those years, there is less time for algae to grow. In contrast, drier, low-flow years tend to have better water clarity and lower phosphorus levels but also result in more algae growth. These wet and dry cycles last about ten years each, making it hard to determine if the St. Croix is getting better or worse unless you know where you are in the decadal weather pattern and look at long-term trends.

As local communities continue working to restore the St. Croix River, scientists at the Watershed Research Station continue studying long-term water quality trends. Where are our efforts succeeding? Where do we still need more work? The long-term goal is to nurse the St. Croix—both the river and the lake—back to good health for people, wildlife, and even the lowly diatoms.

Moms and kids prepare for a hike in the prairie at Carpenter Nature Center.

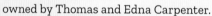

OFF THE WATER

Carpenter St. Croix Valley Nature Center, Denmark Township, Minnesota

Spectacular views of the St. Croix River and delicious apples in the fall

Since opening in 1981, Carpenter Nature Center has worked to protect native habitat and introduce children and adults to the wonders of nature. Carpenter's Minnesota campus contains 425 acres of oak savanna, restored prairie, and wooded ravines along the St. Croix River, just north of its confluence with the Mississippi; land that was once owned by Thomas and Edna Carpenter.

A bee collects nectar from a late-blooming fall aster.

Inside the visitor center, you'll find live raptors and reptiles and interpretive displays. Outside, a large pond and rain garden filled with native plants collect and treat runoff from the parking lot and building. There is a small orchard by the entrance road that sells apples, pumpkins, honey, and maple syrup in the fall. An observation deck in the middle of the savanna overlooks the St. Croix River and a 1.4-mile trail through restored prairie on the west side of County Road 21.

"The Carpenters loved gardens," explains former program director Mayme Johnson. "By building a rain garden and water garden, the nature center found a way to honor the family's legacy while also protecting the St. Croix River."

My favorite time to visit Carpenter is during the fall, when you can enjoy the beautiful gold and pur-

Sand, sedges, and fall colors along the St. Croix River

ple colors of the prairie, hike down to the river and build stick forts in the woods, and buy apples to bring home. The nature center also holds an annual Apple Festival in early October with pick-your-own apples, cider-making demonstrations, live music, live animal programs, children's activities, and more.

Carpenter uses integrated pest management (IPM) to reduce the need for insecticides and fungicides in its apple orchard. IPM is a comprehensive strategy that includes the use of nonchemical insect traps; careful attention to weather patterns, disease emergence, and insect life cycles; and lots of manual labor.

If you'd like to spend more time at Carpenter, there are numerous nature programs for adults, families, youth, and school groups throughout the year, including summer camps for children ages 5–15.

Carpenter's Minnesota campus is located at 12805 St. Croix Trail South, Hastings, Minnesota 55033. Plan ahead before you go, as the building and trails are only open from 8 a.m. until 4:30 p.m. Newer paved trails around the administrative building, near the orchard, and near the wetlands are flat and easily wheelchair accessible.

Carpenter Nature Center also owns three hundred acres of prairie and woods along the St. Croix River at 300 East Cove Road, Hudson, Wisconsin 54016. The trails on the Wisconsin campus are open year-round from sunrise to sunset, and the site is home to the Al and Laurie Hein Visitor Center, which opened in summer 2022.

There is no parking permit or entrance fee at either location. Dogs are allowed but must be kept on-leash at all times. Learn more at https://carpenternaturecenter.org. ◊

STEWARDSHIP STORY

Renewal and Restoration
Lessons from a Garden

Sometimes you think you have a really good idea, like planting vegetable gardens at your office. Full of enthusiasm, you put your family to work and spend an entire day tearing out sod, piecing together scrap lumber, and hauling in dirt. It is hard work, but you feel proud.

Then it is the next year, and you think it will be easier, but it's not. This time it's only you, your kid, and the dog. Last year's dirt is rock hard and full of weeds. You dig, you hammer, you sweat. There is a truck full of new soil to unload and only a six-year-old to help. But he does. He rakes the rich, black dirt smooth while you shovel and haul one wheelbarrow after another. Shovel, haul, shovel.

Finally, it is time to plant. That part—the long-awaited planting—is finished so surprisingly quickly. By then the sun has set, you're covered in dirt, and the dog has ticks. But at last, the garden is planted.

You can learn many lessons from a garden. One is that few things worth doing in life happen easily or quickly. Whether you're training for a race, raising a child, or trying to restore the St. Croix River, it can take months, years, or even a lifetime of hard work and relentless forward motion to succeed.

In the example of a race, there is at least an end point at which your work is done and the long-sought goal accomplished. Like most other things in life, however, the garden is never finished. The garden is an endless cycle of hoeing and planting, weeding and tending, preserving before the winter

A red-and-black-striped bee hovers above purple prairie clover in a restored shoreline planting. Courtesy of Blue Thumb—Planting for Clean Water.

and then starting over in the spring. Planting seeds and harvesting tomatoes are the shortest, sweetest tasks in a never-ending, though worthwhile and satisfying, job.

Gardening also shows us how hard it is to transform the earth from one thing into another. In the still of the night, while the freshly raked soil lies smooth and brown, the weeds have already begun to creep in and take over. Maple seed helicopters spiral to the ground, ready to reclaim the garden as a forest. As the summer progresses, the edging cracks and the hand-painted markers fade. To preserve the garden requires constant tending, tending, tending.

Even when we aim to turn the process in reverse—changing farm field back to prairie or restoring a degraded lake—nature seems to fight the transformation. Natural resource managers will tell you that it is always easier to protect a lake, river, forest, or prairie than to restore it to good health once it is damaged. Converting an old field into prairie is like trying to plant a ten-acre garden. Though the work gets easier as the plants fill in, it requires constant tending, tending, tending to survive those first few years.

The larger the garden, the harder the job becomes. The St. Croix River basin is 7,760 square miles. That's nearly five million acres of land to tend.

In 2004, the St. Croix Basin Team set a goal of reducing phosphorus flowing into the river by 20 percent in order to reduce algae blooms and restore the river to good health. Minnesota and Wisconsin signed an official agreement to work toward this goal in 2006, and a study and plan (TMDL—total maximum daily load) was approved by the U.S. Environmental Protection Agency in 2012.

Today, the gardeners work, hoeing and weeding, planting and tending. They plant rain gardens in cities and buffers on stream banks in farm fields. Here they patch a crumbling ravine to keep sediment and nutrients out of the river; there they convert perennial crops to pastureland so that the soil will hold when it rains. As in gardening, the work is never-ending, though worthwhile and rewarding.

The garden teaches us two final lessons. The first is that many hands make the workload lighter. One person can plant a garden, though it is hard and bitter work, but one person can't restore a river and neither can one agency or one organization. When everyone works together, the impossible becomes realistic. When all levels of government work together and in partnership with Indigenous tribes, nonprofits, community groups, private landowners, and local residents, the garden begins to flourish.

Finally, the garden urges us to teach and involve our youth. Those kids will amaze you with what they can already do—planting trees, weeding rain gardens, stenciling storm drains, and planning events. They burst in with new ideas and enthusiasm, ready to help us tend the garden—not just in the future, but also today. If you show them, they will learn how to sow the seeds and nurture the plants. Equally important, the garden will teach you how to trust children and hand them a rake and a shovel. ◊

PRAIRIES AND GRASSLANDS

One man, one family driven from the land; this rusty car creaking along the highway to the west. I lost my land, a single tractor took my land. I am alone and bewildered.

— John Steinbeck, *The Grapes of Wrath*

ABUNDANCE CAN BE SURPRISINGLY FRAGILE. NATIVE GRASSLANDS once covered 40 percent of the United States, including one-third of Minnesota and 6 percent of Wisconsin. When the first European settlers hauled their wagons across the Mississippi River and into the western United States, they gazed out at a vast, unending prairie, mind-numbingly unbroken by hill or tree. Surely in this land where grass grew taller than man, wheat and rye would prosper as well. When first turned under, the prairie soil was indeed fertile, and so they plowed and planted more. Soon farm fields, instead of prairie, stretched as far as the eye could see. Then one day, the rain stopped, the soil became parched, the shallow roots of the farm crops withered, and the land blew away in the wind.

During the 1930s, the United States endured both an economic depression and a severe drought. The deep-rooted prairie grasses that grew naturally in the Great Plains were able to find moisture during the driest of summers, but the farm crops that replaced them died quickly, leaving nothing behind but bare soil. During the ensuing Dust Bowl, clouds of dirt darkened the sun, burying

Aster in the oak savanna at Standing Cedars Community Land Conservancy

Restored prairie at Lake Elmo Park Reserve. Courtesy of Brett Stolpestad, Washington Conservation District.

homes and hopes in their wake. John Steinback's novel *The Grapes of Wrath* perfectly captures the desperation and darkness of the era, as the Joad family joins thousands of others fleeing Oklahoma for greener pastures in California.

Today, less than 2 percent of the native grasslands in the United States still remains. However, for the intrepid explorer, it is still possible to find pockets of remnant and restored prairie, oak savanna, and pine barrens within the St. Croix River Watershed. In these places, you can expect to see big and little bluestem, Indiangrass, bergamot (bee balm), pale purple coneflower, black-eyed Susans, compass plant, blazing star, pussytoes, and prairie phlox. Other "indicator species," including leadplant, kittentails, pasque flower, and bird's-foot violet, are usually found only in remnant prairies that were never plowed.

Putting Down Roots

The real magic of a prairie happens belowground, beneath the waving heads of the bluestem, coneflower, compass plant, and blazing star. With sprawling root systems that grow five, ten, or even fifteen feet deep, prairie flowers and grasses can withstand the ravages of nature, finding water in the midst of drought, retaining life during the most frigid winters, and even surviving fire. Tiny nodules along the lengths of their sinewy roots produce nitrogen compounds that help the plants to grow. When some of these roots eventually slough off, the fixed nitrogen is released, making it available to other plants and helping to fertilize the soil.

Oak savanna is a transitional habitat between prairie and forest that is common in the southernmost portion of the St. Croix Watershed. Tall grasses and flowers grow in this habitat, but there are also scattered oak trees. As with prairie, oak savanna is a fire-dependent ecosystem that historically existed in locations where natural and human-caused fires were common. The deep roots of the prairie plants and the thick bark of the oaks enable both to survive fires that kill off most species of trees and shrubs.

A lesser-known type of grassland that can also be found in the St. Croix Watershed is called pine barrens. This globally endangered ecosystem is found in dry, acidic soils and features scattered jack pines growing among prairie grasses and low-growing shrubs such as hazelnut, sand cherry, prairie willow, and blueberry. Pine barrens are located in the north-central portion of the watershed near the Wisconsin towns of Grantsburg and Danbury.

A milkweed pod bursts open, exposing the silken seeds within.

Oak savanna at Belwin Conservancy in Afton, Minnesota

While exploring the prairies and oak savannas in the St. Croix Watershed, you may be lucky enough to find wildlife such as thirteen-lined ground squirrels, meadowlarks, bobolinks, red fox, monarch butterflies, and rusty-patched bumblebees. In pine barrens, you can find common nighthawks, eastern whip-poor-wills, sharp-tailed grouse, gopher snakes, prairie skinks, and many other animals.

Human Influence

Habitat restoration efforts in the St. Croix Watershed today are guided by land surveys that were conducted between 1832 and 1907 when European Americans first began settling in the region. Though these maps accurately record the land cover as it was at the time, the ecosystems here had already coevolved with human influence over the past ten to twelve thousand years. Archaeological records show that people have lived on Grey Cloud Island (Mississippi River, southern Washington County) for more than two thousand years, and a recent excavation led by the University of Minnesota found remains of a seven-hundred-year-old village located near the St. Croix River south of Marine on St. Croix. Likewise, pictographs on a basalt outcropping along the St. Croix River north of Stillwater are estimated to be five hundred to one thousand years old. Though older archaeological discoveries are less abundant, it is widely accepted that humans have lived in the land now known as Minnesota for twelve thousand years and in modern Wisconsin for ten thousand years.

Oak savanna and pine barrens are two examples of human-influenced ecosystems in the St. Croix River Watershed. In these transitional zones between forest and prairie, people used fire to maintain open areas as a way to attract large game animals like bison and elk. They also cultivated edible and medicinal plants such as blueberry and purple coneflower (Echinacea).

Today, land managers use prescribed fire to restore and maintain prairie, oak savanna, and pine barrens on public and private lands in the region and to fight the continual encroachment of trees, shrubs, and invasive species.

Prairie bales in winter at Pine Point Regional Park in Washington County, Minnesota

Ten Places to Visit Prairies and Grasslands in the St. Croix River Watershed

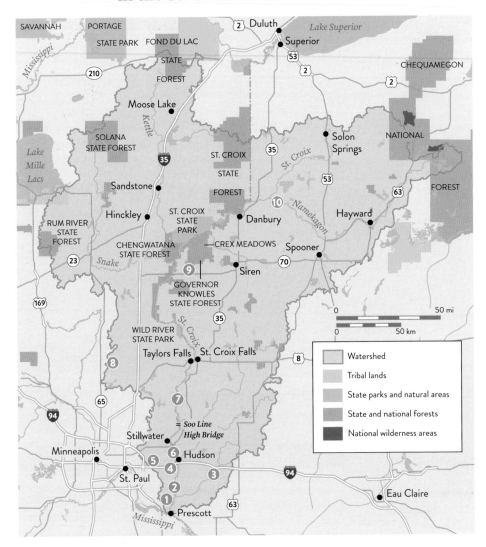

1. Lost Valley Prairie Scientific and Natural Area, Denmark Township, Minnesota
2. Afton State Park, Afton, Minnesota
3. Kelly Creek Preserve, Kinnickinnic, Wisconsin
4. Belwin Conservancy, Afton, Minnesota
5. Lake Elmo Park Reserve, Lake Elmo, Minnesota
6. St. Croix Savanna Scientific and Natural Area, Bayport, Minnesota
7. Standing Cedars Community Land Conservancy, Osceola, Wisconsin
8. Fish Lake Nature Trails at Cedar Creek Ecosystem Science Reserve, East Bethel, Minnesota
9. Crex Meadows State Wildlife Area, Grantsburg, Wisconsin
10. Namekagon Barrens State Wildlife Area, Danbury, Wisconsin

Wide open landscape at Lost Valley Prairie Scientific and Natural Area

1 Lost Valley Prairie Scientific and Natural Area, Denmark Township, Minnesota

A hidden prairie amid rolling farmland

Intermediate

"Mom! You are not seriously going to wear that, are you?" We had just climbed out of the car at the end of a dusty farm road, and Charlie was staring at me, aghast, as I placed a giant cowboy hat firmly on my head and sauntered over to the faded wooden sign that marks the entrance to Lost Valley Prairie Scientific and Natural Area. Ignoring him, I began unloading supplies for an impromptu picnic, humming "Home, Home on the Range" as I worked.

I will spoil the suspense now by telling you that we saw neither deer nor antelope on the prairie that day. We did find black swallowtail butterflies, gopher holes, and too many birds to count.

Lost Valley Prairie contains 320 acres of prairie in southern Washington County and is located three miles north of Carpenter Nature Center. It is classified as an Audubon Important Bird Area (IBA) and is home to a wide array of native prairie plants, including little bluestem, prairie dropseed, side-oats grama, hairy grama, Indiangrass, big bluestem, puccoon, stiff gentian, and prairie smoke.

Minnesota's Scientific and Natural Areas program was created in 1969 to protect "exceptional places where native plants and ani-

Monarda, also known as bee balm and wild bergamot

Yellow coneflower

mals flourish; where rare species are protected; and where we can know, and study, Minnesota's fascinating natural features." To date, there are 168 Scientific and Natural Areas (SNAs) in the state protecting more than 192,000 acres of public land. The program protects an additional 12,800 acres of private land through Native Prairie Bank easements.

The primary goal of the Scientific and Natural Areas program is to protect Minnesota's natural heritage and ensure that examples of intact, pristine habitat are not lost from any ecological region of the state. SNAs also provide opportunities for nature-based recreation, education, and scientific research. Unlike state parks, most SNAs do not have designated trail systems and do not allow camping or organized social events. They are wonderful destinations to visit if you really love nature and want to see high quality habitat, but they are not very well suited for novice explorers, families with little kids, or people with mobility issues.

When my son and I visited on that steamy August afternoon, we made a critical error that I hope you'll avoid if you go. We wore shorts. By the time we left, our legs were tattered, itching, and covered in seeds after wading through the tall and tangled plants of a summer prairie without the benefit of a clearly marked and well-maintained trail.

To access Lost Valley Prairie SNA, travel 2.4 miles east on 110th Street from Manning Avenue South, then turn left on Nyberg Avenue South and follow it to the road's end. There is no parking permit or entrance fee. No dogs allowed. Lost Valley Prairie is a suitable destination for quiet adventures, including hiking, snowshoeing, bird-watching, and photography.

The prairie loop trail at Afton State Park

② Afton State Park, Afton, Minnesota

Challenging trails and hike-in camping

Beginner

Just up the road from Lost Valley Prairie, Afton State Park offers a prairie experience with modern amenities, including paved and unpaved trails, a visitor center with indoor bathrooms, camping, picnic tables, and a beach.

Afton State Park is well known as one of the best places for serious hiking and trail running within thirty minutes of the Twin Cities. The park's 1,600 acres contain prairie and woods and are crisscrossed by steep ravines that plunge three hundred feet from the bluff-top to the St. Croix River below. You'll find oak, aspen, birch, and cherry growing in the wooded ravines, and floodplain forest with silver maple and cottonwood trees along the river.

In upland areas of the park, the Minnesota DNR is working with volunteers to restore oak savanna and expand and improve patches of remnant prairie on the property. As recently as the 1980s, ecologists had documented numerous areas with high-quality remnant bluff prairie at the park. Without the benefit of fire and grazing, those patches have since been taken over by red cedar. Today when you visit, you might see herds of goats munching their way across the hillsides as they clear out bushes and shrubs so that prairie plants can grow again.

Though the prairie at Afton State Park is lower quality than that at Lost Valley Prairie SNA, you can still expect to find prairie pasque flowers and woodland ephemerals in the spring; butterfly weed and puccoons on the summer prairie; and sunflowers and blazing star in the fall.

If you really want to push your body to the limit, try signing up for the annual Afton Trail Run, which is held each year over Fourth of July weekend. The event offers 25- and 50-kilometer races, run entirely on trails, with seven long climbs per loop. It has been held annually since 1994 and attracts runners from around the United States and other countries. John Storkamp, founder of Rocksteady Running and the Afton Trail Run, believes strongly in caring for the land in places where his races are held. The Afton Trail Run donates about $60,000 per year to Afton State Park and encourages volunteers to help maintain trails and remove invasive species in the park. Learn more at www.aftontrailrun.com.

Afton State Park is located at 6959 Peller Avenue South, Hastings, Minnesota 55033. The park has twenty-eight hike-in campsites, two group campsites, and a small collection of camper cabins and yurts near the group sites. The Bluebird and White Pine cabins are accessible, as is the Coyote Yurt. A Minnesota State Park vehicle permit is required, which costs $35 per year or $7 for a day

A charred field after a prescribed burn. Controlled fires are one strategy commonly used during prairie restoration efforts.

Goats nibble on invasive buckthorn. In recent years, the Minnesota DNR has used goats as an additional tool for habitat restoration at Afton State Park.

permit. Dogs are allowed but must be kept on-leash at all times. Learn more about the park at www.dnr.state.mn.us/state_parks/afton.

③ Kelly Creek Preserve, Kinnickinnic, Wisconsin

Restored prairie and oak savanna with a cold-water spring and brook trout

Intermediate

As you step into the prairie at Kelly Creek Preserve, you'll be greeted by towering compass plants and cup plants, literally buzzing with bees. A short walk through the waving flowers and grasses will take you to the headwaters of Kelly Creek. Here, cold, clear water pulses out of a limestone outcropping and gives birth to a stream full of caddisflies, freshwater shrimp, brook trout, and wetland flowers. A towering oak grows straight up out of the rock and stands guard over the water and wildlife below.

Kelly Creek Preserve is one of four noncontiguous parcels of land owned by the Kinnickinnic River Land Trust, a nonprofit organization based in River Falls, Wisconsin, that works to protect the Kinnickinnic River and its surrounding watershed. The land

Kelly Creek Preserve is located northeast of River Falls, Wisconsin.

trust owns three thousand acres of land in the watershed, including ten miles of shoreline along the "Kinni."

The 170 acres of land draining to the Kinni are home to more than forty threatened, endangered, and special concern plants and animals. Protecting upland prairie and oak savanna areas, like at Kelly Creek Preserve, provides habitat for a wide variety of insects, birds, reptiles, amphibians, and mammals, and also helps to protect water quality within the springs and streams. Kelly Creek pumps out 700,000 gallons of cold, clear water per day and is one of six tributary streams to the Kinnickinnic River.

From the parking lot at Kelly Creek Preserve, it is a short (less than a quarter mile) hike down to the spring where Kelly Creek begins. Bring rubber boots or river sandals if you want to wade in the water, but be forewarned that it is freezing! There are also a few easy walking loops through the prairie on mowed trails. The prairie here was planted in 2000–2003 and features a mix of tall grasses such as big bluestem and Indiangrass, as well as forbs, including cream gentian, cup plant, compass plant, goldenrod, and asters.

The preserve is located on County Road J in the Town of Kinnickinnic, in St. Croix County, a few miles south of U.S. Highway 94. Access is from a shared private gravel road off County Road J, approximately a quarter mile east of the bridge over the Kinnickinnic River. A sign marks the entrance but can be hard to see from the main road. Find more information at https://kinniriver.org.

An oak tree stands watch over the rock where the springs originate.

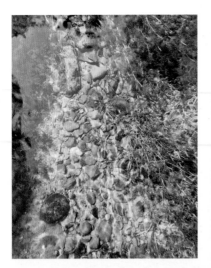

(Top left) *Pebbles in the water* (Top right) *Cream gentian* (Bottom) *Monarch on a cup plant*

On the north side of County Road J, the Wisconsin DNR owns about one hundred acres of land along the Kinnickinnic River that is also open to the public for hiking and fishing. There is a spot to put in and take out canoes and kayaks where the river crosses the road.

④ Belwin Conservancy, Afton, Minnesota

Bison, special events, and environmental education for St. Paul Schools

Beginner

Belwin Conservancy protects 1,500 acres of prairie, savanna, and woodlands in Afton, Minnesota, including two hundred acres along Valley Creek that were set aside by Charlie and Lucy Bell in 1970. The Conservancy provides environmental education programming for St. Paul students through a partnership with St. Paul Public Schools and has spent decades working to restore tallgrass prairie and oak savanna on the parcels of land that it owns. Most enticingly, Belwin has bison.

People gather around a winter solstice bonfire at Belwin Conservancy in Afton, Minnesota.

Watching bison run off the truck and into the prairie at Belwin's annual Bison Festival in May.

These giant mammals once roamed North America in massive herds that could be found from Alaska to the Gulf of Mexico and as far east as New York and Georgia. They play an important role in the prairie ecosystem by working the soil with their hooves as they graze, cycling nutrients, and helping native wildflowers and birds to thrive. The Belwin bison spend their winters at NorthStar Bison in Rice Lake, Wisconsin, and are released into the prairie each spring.

A dragonfly perches in the prairie.

FINDING LIGHT IN THE DARKNESS

December 22, 2016

We drove quietly through the winter night, down a dark and winding road. I could tell my son was tired by the nature of his questions—deep and searching, the way he often speaks in the gentle minutes just before sleep. "How would the world be different," he asked, "if I had never been born?" No one ever warned me that five-year-olds could be so philosophical.

Not too long afterward, we pulled into the almost hidden entrance of Belwin Conservancy and rolled slowly down a narrow driveway, tires groaning in the snow. Finally, we rounded one last curve and saw a gargantuan bonfire ablaze in a clearing near the edge of a pond. It was like something out of a dream, this golden light hidden away deep in the woods on the longest and darkest night of the year.

Dozens of people were already gathered round the fire, bundled beneath hats and scarves. Their faces glowed warm in the light. Soon, Charlie found other children in the circle, and they laughed as they rolled in the snow, darting in and out of the shadows. Eventually, Susan Haugh, Belwin's program manager, grabbed everyone's attention to introduce Crow Bellecourt and Robin Day-Bedeau, two Ojibwe musicians who drummed and sang a few songs for the group.

After the music, storyteller Erika Rae shared a touching tale of a little girl named Estrella (the Spanish word for star), who loved sunshine and the prairie. As the story ended, Bellecourt and Day-Bedeau urged us to hold hands and dance slowly around the circle as they played one last song in the clear, cold night.

Belwin's Stagecoach Prairie in winter

THE FALL AND RISE OF THE BISON

Prior to European American settlers, the lives of bison and Indigenous people were inexorably linked. American Indians used every part of the bison for food, clothing, shelter, tools, jewelry, and religious ceremonies, and actively managed prairies and oak savannas with fire to maintain open areas for bison and other game.

As white settlers moved westward during the 1800s, they quickly decimated the bison herds, hunting from the open windows of trains, and even killing bison intentionally as a way to deprive Dakota and Lakota people of sustenance during the Sioux Wars. There were an estimated sixty million bison in North America in the late 1700s. By 1889, only 541 remained.

During the 1860s, a handful of private citizens began to capture and shelter bison to save them from extinction. The majority of bison living today are descended from the animals those people protected. Yellowstone National Park is the only place in the United States where wild bison have lived continuously since prehistoric times.

Eventually, Congress passed laws to protect bison from poaching and established several public bison herds outside Yellowstone at wildlife refuges in the western United States. Today, about 360,000 domestic bison are owned as livestock and 31,000 wild bison are living on public lands in the United States and Canada.

Sixty-three Native tribes, including the Prairie Island Dakota Community in Minnesota, have come together during the past twenty years to form the InterTribal Buffalo Council, which is restoring bison herds in order to solve food shortages and financial shortfalls, restore ecosystems, and honor cultural traditions. Tribes collectively manage more than twenty thousand buffalo on approximately one million acres of Tribal land in nineteen states.

RESTORING CONNECTIONS
TO THE LAND AND ITS PEOPLE

In 2008, Belwin introduced a seasonal herd of bison to a portion of its property that contains 130 acres of restored prairie. In the following years, staff at Belwin began to think critically about how their organization could help to restore connections between people and the land as well.

When program director Susan Haugh was hired in 2015, she set a goal of expanding Belwin's programming to reach new people who might not normally visit a nature center. "During my very first year, I met with more than fifty people from different communities," says Haugh. "I focused on meeting people and building relationships."

"Through Rory Wakemup, we got to know American Indian artists at the All My Relations gallery in Minneapolis. This also led to a new relationship with the Anishinaabe Academy," Haugh explains. "It started with field trips where we provided the space, and Native elders and teachers from the school provided instruction."

Eventually, the American Indian Family Center asked Belwin if they could build a sweat lodge on the land to use for spiritual ceremonies. "We don't charge them for the sweat lodge because we recognize that we have land here that was stolen from their ancestors," says Belwin's executive director Katie Bloome. "In fact, this new relationship helps us to connect more people to the land, which is part of our mission."

In addition to building connections with Indigenous-led organizations, Belwin has worked with Family Means to develop programs for people with dementia and is expanding a network of paved trails to improve accessibility for people with disabilities. "Some organizations look only at racial equity," Bloome says, "but Belwin believes it's important to address all barriers to accessibility."

For the staff and board at Belwin, one of the most important actions they have taken in recent years is to develop a land acknowledgment statement, in partnership with members of the Dakota Nation. "To do it right, you can't just hire someone to write a land acknowledgment or copy it from another organization's website," says Haugh. "We formed a committee to research and develop the statement and hired a Dakota woman to help us review and revise it as well."

The land on which Belwin Conservancy exists is the ancestral home of the Wahpekute Dakota people, original stewards of this region. We recognize that despite efforts to exterminate and diminish the Dakota, their connection to this land, water, history, and lifeways perseveres today. We pay our respects to their Elders past, present and emerging.

"Fifty years ago, the founders of Belwin recognized that children living in St. Paul didn't have the same access to nature as kids living here in the St. Croix Valley," Bloome says. "The history of our organization informs who we are today and where we go in the future."

Today, Belwin actively continues its land protection and habitat restoration work, in addition to offering a unique array of programming to connect people of all cultures with the land. A visit to Belwin is both a step back in time, to the days when bison roamed the prairies, as well as a glimpse at what the future could be.

VISIT BELWIN

The Stagecoach Prairie contains 280 acres of restored tallgrass prairie with five miles of family-friendly hiking trails of easy to moderate difficulty. During the winter, the trails are suitable for snowshoeing and are open dawn until dusk. Dogs are allowed on leashes. There is no parking permit or entrance fee. The address is 825 Stagecoach Trail South, Afton, Minnesota 55001.

The Bison Observation Platform is located at 15551 Division Street. Climb the platform to see bison roaming on 130 acres of prairie during the summer and early fall. This property is not open for hiking, but there are two and a half miles of trails on the north side of Division Street. Belwin holds a Bison Festival in late May when each year's new herd is released.

The Education Center at 1553 Stagecoach Trail South operates outdoor, environmental education programming for students at St. Paul Public Schools. The four-mile trail system winds through three hundred acres of rolling woodlands, prairie, and wetlands and is open to the public only during special events. No dogs allowed.

In addition to their school programming and habitat restoration work, Belwin hosts community events throughout the year, including a Bison Festival in the spring, Music in the Trees in August, and a Winter Solstice Bonfire in December.

Learn more about Belwin at www.belwin.org.

A lookout tower near the Hilltop Classroom at Belwin's Education Center. This portion of the property is open only for school groups and special programs.

Riding the multiuse trails at Lake Elmo Park Reserve on a warm December day.

⑤ Lake Elmo Park Reserve, Lake Elmo, Minnesota

Extensive outdoor recreation opportunities and large-scale habitat restoration underway

Beginner

As we lie on our backs in the grass, the warm September sun overhead makes me drowsy. The prairie rises up on either side of the trail, hiding us almost completely from anyone more than a few feet away. Little bluestem, turkey foot, bee balm, coneflower—the tall grasses and flower stems wave in the breeze. My son leans over to tickle my nose with a seed head and I jump up laughing. Farther down the trail, we find a dried milkweed pod and pull it open. The silken seeds float on the breeze like tiny fairies. Today, we are the only giants on the prairie.

Lake Elmo Park Reserve is an outdoor destination that beckons in all seasons. The 2,165-acre park contains more than fourteen miles of hiking trails and eight miles of multiuse hiking, horseback riding, and mountain biking trails. Many of these are groomed for cross-country skiing in the winter. There is a swimming pond and beach, a campground, several playgrounds and picnic areas, and a public boat launch with access to Lake Elmo.

During the winter, Lake Elmo Park Reserve grooms fourteen miles of trails for skate and classic style skiing.

Though the park is located only one mile north of U.S. Highway 94 and fifteen minutes from St. Paul, it offers a true nature experience. Eighty percent of the land has been set aside for preservation and protection and is actively managed to improve natural habitat pollinators, birds, and wildlife.

Recently, Washington County secured new funding through the Lessard-Sams Outdoor Heritage Fund, as appropriated by the Minnesota State Legislature. The county is using these funds to restore and improve 166 acres of prairie and oak savanna at Lake Elmo Park Reserve around Eagle Point Lake and in the north end of the park. One species of concern they hope to support is the endangered rusty-patched bumblebee, which was designated as the Minnesota state bee in 2019.

Historically, oak savanna existed in locations where the Dakota people lived. They set intentional fires to improve habitat for game and foraging grounds for bison, which grazed the prairie grasses. Oak trees were able to survive the fires due to their thick bark, but other, less sturdy trees were kept at bay. Today, most of Minnesota's historical oak savanna has been lost due to intensive or suppressed grazing, fire suppression, and introduction of non-native plant species.

Because prairie and oak savanna ecosystems are largely dependent on landscape disturbances such as fire and grazing, Washington County has incorporated grazing, haying, and fire into its long-term maintenance plan for Lake Elmo Park Reserve.

A black-eyed Susan on the prairie

If you hike at Lake Elmo during the spring, summer, or fall, you may stumble on a herd of grazing goats.

Lake Elmo Park Reserve has two entrances. The main entrance at 1515 Keats Avenue North leads to the Nordic Center, campgrounds, swimming pond, and boat launch. The western entrance at 2579 Inwood Avenue North offers access to multiuse trails. A Washington County Parks vehicle permit is required at both locations; this costs $30 per year or $7 for a day permit. There are approximately five miles of paved trails within the park. Dogs are allowed, but not in the campground, playgrounds, or swimming area, and must be on-leash at all times.

The prairie at St. Croix Savanna Scientific and Natural Area in Bayport, Minnesota, protects one of the best remaining examples of hill prairie in the St. Croix Riverway.

6 St. Croix Savanna Scientific and Natural Area, Bayport, Minnesota

A dazzling array of native prairie and oak savanna plants

Intermediate

A grasshopper perches on a tattered black-eyed Susan. Two red-and-black-striped beetles dance a tango atop a lilac spray of vervain. Gentle summer breezes carry the sound of laughter as an impish four-year-old boy balances carefully on a time-weathered rock. Around him, the swaying grasses, muted prairie colors, and tumbled down, lichen-covered boulders are exactly the same as they have been for more than a century. Not much changes at the St. Croix Savanna Scientific and Natural Area; in fact, that's kind of the point.

A bioblitz conducted in June 2020 documented 170 species of plants, animals, and fungus within the 154-acre St. Croix Savanna

(Above) *Beetles on hoary vervain. Photograph by Charlie Hong.* (Below) *Blue-eyed grass*

SNA. It is one of the best remaining examples of hill prairie in the Lower St. Croix National Scenic Riverway. While hiking there in the late spring, I've found a startling array of native wildflowers on the top of the ridge, including blue-eyed grass, yellow star flower, violet wood sorrel, and prairie violet. I was also beguiled once by an amazing star-shaped formation that I found growing halfway down a steep and sandy hill. After consultation with iNaturalist, I determined that it was a hygroscopic earthstar, which is a type of fungus I never even knew existed!

Bluff prairies occur on steep, rocky, south-facing slopes along stream valleys. Though most prairies in Minnesota were plowed to create farmland, there are several areas in Washington County that still contain patches of remnant native bluff prairie in locations where it was too steep and rocky to plow.

Bluff prairies in the region also offer ideal breeding habitat for eastern kingbirds, eastern meadowlarks, field sparrows, and American goldfinches. If you're lucky, you might even find a prairie skink or garter snake basking on one of the many large, exposed rocks.

Grasshopper on a black-eyed Susan

Though it looks like a flower, this hygroscopic earthstar is actually a type of fungus. The ball in the center splits open to release a cloud of spores, much like a puffball mushroom.

There are two ways to access St. Croix Savanna SNA. The first is to enter from the Inspiration neighborhood, on the northwest side of the property. Turn east onto Inspiration Parkway South from County Road 21, turn right onto Prairie Way South, and then right to the parking area. A more dangerous but visually dramatic way to enter is by parking along Minnesota Highway 95 south of Bayport, just before the railroad tracks. Skirt the edge of the road behind the guardrail and then climb up a steep hill into the SNA to find a stunning view of the St. Croix River down below. There is no parking permit or entrance fee. No dogs allowed.

7 Standing Cedars Community Land Conservancy, Osceola, Wisconsin

The land that time forgot

Intermediate

I'm standing in the middle of a prairie making a conference call on my cell phone because that's what working moms do. Every few minutes, I catch a glimpse of my son as he lopes into view, diving

Kids and a dog frolic in the prairie at Standing Cedars Community Land Conservancy in Osceola, Wisconsin.

into the bee balm and through the black-eyed Susans. Then suddenly he appears directly in front of me and, with a flourish, opens his hands to release a kaleidoscope of grasshoppers on me. The insects spring out in all directions, whizzing by in bursts of color—bright green, dull brown, yellow striped, and winged. I scream, half from terror but equally from delight.

The funny thing, we both agreed, is that the two of us had spent more than an hour attempting to collect insects at a county park closer to home earlier that month, but to no avail. In contrast, here at Standing Cedars, the air is practically humming with song from birds and bugs all around.

Standing Cedars is a community land conservancy in western Wisconsin that protects 1,500 acres along the St. Croix River in four separate, noncontiguous parcels. The largest of the four, Engelwood, was a ski area during the 1950s and 1960s. At 1,100 acres, it was the single largest undeveloped parcel of land on the Lower St. Croix River when it was purchased in 1995. Today, there is a hillside prairie with a wide variety of grasses and forbs, a lush maple-basswood forest flowing down the bluff to the St. Croix River, and scenic stands of birch along the prairie's edge.

Throughout the Engelwood property are notes from the past. Tall wooden poles that once carried skiers up the hill now blend

with trees in the woods. Two old trucks quietly rot among the raspberries and prickly ash. Deer trails wind lazily across the hillsides and over old stone walls that are slowly being swallowed by the earth.

At the Buffalo Skull tract, four miles farther north, there are twenty-two acres of high-quality prairie nestled within 245 acres of forest and old farm field. Follow deer trails from the prairie into the woods to find a coldwater spring running through a lush and verdant valley. Do not attempt to access Buffalo Skull in the winter without a four-wheel drive vehicle.

Charlie holds a grasshopper for review and consideration.

Wild lupine in bloom at the Buffalo Skull prairie

Dog friends Brandie, Molly, and Emma head out for a walk in the prairie at the Engelwood Tract. Standing Cedars allows dogs to run off-leash, except from April 15 to July 31, when ground birds are nesting.

Though small in comparison, the fifty-acre Tewksbury property offers beautiful views of the St. Croix River, a prairie, and remnants from an old quarry and farmstead.

The Englewood tract is located at 215 280th Street, Osceola, Wisconsin 54020.

Buffalo Skull is located at 2849 55th Avenue, Osceola, Wisconsin 54020.

Tewksbury is located at 645 Ridge Road, Osceola, Wisconsin 54020.

Parking and entrance is free at all locations within Standing Cedars. Dogs are allowed but must be kept on-leash from April 15 through July 31 during ground-bird nesting season. Learn more at www.standingcedars.org.

A birch tree frames the view at Fish Lake. The nature trails are open to the public and are part of the larger Cedar Creek Ecosystem Science Reserve.

8 Fish Lake Nature Trails at Cedar Creek Ecosystem Science Reserve, East Bethel, Minnesota

Sand prairie, oak savanna, research plots, and bison

Intermediate

"There's a skink in the outhouse!"

"A what?"

"It's a skink!" I scream, with an exclamation point.

It's entirely possible that you've never seen a lizard in Minnesota or Wisconsin. Of the roughly 150 native and nonnative lizard species found in North America, only four live in Wisconsin and three in Minnesota. One, and only one, lizard lives in the St. Croix River Watershed—the northern prairie skink.

Prairie skinks live in sand prairies, pine barrens, oak savannas, and sandy stream banks, where they can burrow to escape predators, hibernate, or remain cool during the midday heat of the summer. They eat crickets, grasshoppers, beetles, spiders, caterpillars, and other small invertebrates and possess an amazing ability to regrow their tails if they lose them when escaping predators.

On the day that my son and I visited Fish Lake Nature Trails, the little skink I found racing around my feet in the outhouse must

The prairie skink is one of only three lizard species that live in Minnesota.

have recently escaped becoming lunch because he or she was entirely without a tail.

The Cedar Creek Ecosystem Science Reserve is a University of Minnesota biological field station in East Bethel, Minnesota, on the western border of the St. Croix River Watershed. Fish Lake and the nature trail lie within the St. Croix Watershed, while Cedar Creek and the eastern portion of the Science Reserve are in the Mississippi River Watershed. Students and faculty use the site to research ecosystem responses to biodiversity loss, nitrogen deposition, elevated carbon dioxide, warming temperatures, changes in precipitation, and exotic species invasions. Cedar Creek hosts field trips for K–12 students, as well as public programs including Lunch with a Scientist and Ecology Book Club.

Within the Cedar Creek Ecosystem Science Reserve, the Fish Lake Nature Trails wrap around the south side of the lake and include a one-mile (one way) trail extension that leads south from Fish Lake to a bison viewing gazebo, which is staffed by trained interpretive naturalists on the weekends. Between the parking lot and the lake, the trail passes through a sand prairie that is filled with big bluestem, Indiangrass, rough blazing star, anise hyssop, and other common prairie plants.

This prairie transitions to a bur oak savanna south of the lake. While walking there, Charlie and I found toads leaping here, there, and everywhere. There were deer tracks in the sandy trail, and we could hear the sounds of sandhill cranes, wood ducks, and red-headed woodpeckers.

Rough blazing star in bloom in the oak savanna at Fish Lake Nature Trails

We came in hopes of seeing bison, which must have been roaming elsewhere in their two-hundred-acre enclosure, but were delighted to see red-headed woodpeckers instead. These birds are classified as a species of greatest conservation need in Minnesota and are most often found in oak savannas, where they nest in standing dead trees. Their populations are declining as oak savannas disappear, and they have also suffered from the well-meaning intentions of private landowners who often cut down dead trees, thinking they are unsightly and unnecessary.

The Fish Lake Nature Trails are open to the public daily during the summer from 8 a.m. until 4:30 p.m. No dogs, horses, bicycles, or motorized vehicles are allowed, and internal roads south and west of the trail are off-limits. A two-mile Savanna Loop Ski Trail is open only during the winter. Parking is located off Durant Street Northeast, one mile north of 229th Avenue Northeast (County Road 36). Learn more at www.cedarcreek.umn.edu.

The Helen Allison Savanna Scientific and Natural Area (SNA) borders Cedar Creek Ecosystem Science Reserve to the south and has eighty acres of remnant oak savanna growing amid vegetated sand dunes, with rare prairie, savanna, and sedge meadow species. There are no trails at the SNA but there is a parking lot on Durant Street Northeast (County Road 15), just south of 229th Avenue Northeast (County Road 36) to access the property.

If you're lucky, from a gazebo at the end of the trail you can see bison roaming the two hundred acres of oak savanna. On weekends, naturalist volunteers set up displays with bison fur and bones and answer questions.

Sandhill cranes gather by the thousands at Crex Meadows during the spring and fall migrations. Photograph by Gordon Dietzman.

9 Crex Meadows State Wildlife Area, Grantsburg, Wisconsin

Largest remaining pine barrens in Wisconsin with sandhill cranes in the spring and fall

Beginner

"When the sandhill cranes arrive in the fall they are absolutely spectacular," says Gordon Dietzman, a naturalist, nature photographer, and retired park ranger for National Park Service who considers Crex Meadows one of his favorite places to see and photograph wildlife. "The cranes are out in the fields during the day and then come into the wetlands to roost at night along Main Dike Road. You've got the sun setting, the moon rising, the belt of Venus across the horizon with cranes flying across the sky. It's my favorite time of year to visit."

The thirty thousand acres of land at Crex Meadows State Wildlife Area protect the largest remaining swath of pine barrens in Wisconsin, as well as a vast network of interconnected wetlands. The property also encompasses Crex Sand Prairie and Reed Lake

Meadow State Natural Areas. The landscape is intensively managed by the Wisconsin DNR and Bureau of Wildlife Management to protect this unique prairie-wetland ecosystem, which is home to 280 species of birds, 720 species of plants, more than 96 species of butterflies, and a wide variety of reptiles, amphibians, and insects.

Currently, Wild Rivers Conservancy is collaborating with the U.S. Fish and Wildlife Service to restore and manage oak savanna and grasslands within Crex Meadows and the nearby Fish Lake Wildlife Area in order to improve habitat for the endangered Karner Blue Butterfly. This tiny butterfly uses wild blue lupine as a host plant for its larva and can be found only in a handful of locations in the Midwest, including Crex Meadows.

In the early 1900s, most of the land within Crex Meadows was owned by the Crex Carpet Company, which harvested sedges and native prairie grasses to weave into carpets and furniture. In fact, the name "Crex" is derived from the true sedge wiregrass species of the genus *Carex* that were used to make the carpets. When the company went bankrupt during the Great Depression, the Wisconsin Conservation Department began envisioning a new long-term plan for the site.

Sunset over a marsh at Crex Meadows, near Grantsburg, Wisconsin. Photograph by Gordon Dietzman.

Sandhill cranes fly across the sky against the backdrop of a full moon. Photograph by Gordon Dietzman.

The Blanding's turtle is a special concern species in Wisconsin. Photograph by Gordon Dietzman.

Dietzman recommends visiting in the spring or fall when weather conditions are most favorable and nearly twenty thousand sandhill cranes descend on Crex Meadows to mate and nest. "There is an overlook on top of a hill near Rest Stop C, and it is a great place to watch the sun come down and see cranes and trumpeter swans," he says. "I've also seen black bear in that area. In fact, I once watched a bear run right through a flock of sandhill cranes."

"Winter can be pretty bleak up there," Dietzman cautions, "and by midsummer it can be hot and quiet. Chiggers come out in the summer as well, so it makes it hard to enjoy your visit."

Most people who visit Crex Meadows take the twenty-four-mile driving tour, which is easily accessible by car or fat-tire bike. There are also several short hiking trails at Crex Meadows that can also be used for snowshoeing or mountain biking. Another option is to bring a canoe or kayak to explore Phantom Lake and the Lower North Fork Flowage, where you can see Blanding's, snapping, and painted turtles; burnsi leopard frogs; and even otters. Early spring, when the ice is just beginning to melt, is a good time to look for otters swimming in open water near the roadway. Turtles are plentiful in June when females are traveling to and from their nesting locations.

Paddlers should stay off marshes where waterbirds nest during the spring breeding season and during waterfowl hunting seasons, which run from early September through mid-November.

Crex Meadows is located at 102 East Crex Avenue, Grantsburg, Wisconsin 54840. There is a visitor center with classrooms, an auditorium, exhibits, video room, and gift shop. Dogs are allowed but must be kept on-leash from April 15 through July 15 during ground-bird nesting season. Learn more at www.crexmeadows.org.

⑩ Namekagon Barrens State Wildlife Area, Danbury, Wisconsin

Remote pine barrens with sharp-tailed grouse viewing

Advanced

On the northeastern border of Burnett County and Washburn County, Wisconsin, the Namekagon Barrens Wildlife Area has 6,446 acres of land, divided into two different units. It is a premiere destination to see sharp-tailed grouse and is also home to turkeys, deer, bear, sandpipers, brown thrashers, and even the namesake Wisconsin badger.

I first stumbled on the Namekagon Barrens while canoeing from the McDowell Bridge Landing on the Namekagon River to the Riverside Landing on the St. Croix. After leaving my husband, son, and dog comfortably resting at a Riverside Landing campsite, I hopped on my mountain bike for a short ride back upriver to get our truck. How foolish I was!

Riding down Springbrook Trail through the Namekagon Barrens, the sand on the road grew deeper and deeper, until eventually I was forced to get off and drag my bike. Looking around, I felt a sense of utter bewilderment, as if I'd somehow been magically transported to the deserts of California.

The Northwest Sands Ecological Landscape of northwest Wisconsin is a globally rare ecological community that includes oak and pine barrens that grow on an irregular band of sand roughly 150 miles long and 10 miles wide. This meandering pile of sand is the remains of a glacier that began retreating from Wisconsin twenty-two thousand years ago. Throughout the region are spring ponds, cold-water streams, and a mosaic of different wetland types.

When European American settlers began logging the forests in this region during the mid-1800s, they drained numerous wetlands to create solid ground for farming and homes. As the settler population grew, they eventually pressed inward to the least desirable land, located in the barrens, during the early 1900s.

For hundreds of years, Ojibwe people had survived in this inhospitable region by burning the barrens to maintain an open landscape for wildlife and regular crops of blueberries. The sandy soils

The pine barrens at Namekagon Barrens State Wildlife Area are part of a globally rare ecosystem, comprised of prairie plants and scrub brush with scattered small trees.

are poor in nutrients, and the new homesteaders who arrived were unable to make a living from their small farms. The region was hit particularly hard during the droughts of the 1930s and the Great Depression, and, by the 1940s, nearly two-thirds of the land in the region was tax delinquent, including what is now Namekagon Barrens Wildlife Area.

In later decades, Wisconsin used federal financing to purchase some of the tax delinquent lands in the barrens and began working to restore wetlands and upland habitat as public wildlife areas. Other lands were given to counties and are now part of Wisconsin's county forest system.

When I called Gordon Dietzman to talk about Crex Meadows, he shared a memorable experience he had when photographing sharp-tailed grouse at Namekagon Barrens one spring. Male sharp-tailed grouse perform elaborate dances during the mating season in April and May, and people can reserve viewing blinds through Friends of the Namekagon Barrens Wildlife Area to watch the birds dancing in their leks (dancing grounds).

"The blinds are a quarter of a mile from the road, and you have to be out there well before daybreak," explains Dietzman. "So, I'm out there walking this path at 4:30 a.m. in the pitch dark because you aren't supposed to use a flashlight. It had rained the night before and it was a gorgeous morning. The stars were shining and there was only a little moon. I was following some tracks that sort

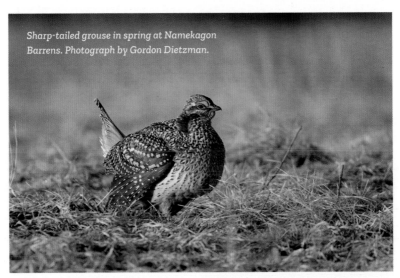

Sharp-tailed grouse in spring at Namekagon Barrens. Photograph by Gordon Dietzman.

of looked like deer tracks until I finally pulled out a light to get a better look. I saw that they were actually fresh wolf tracks, and I could see that there had been four wolves walking down that trail just before me."

Surveys conducted by the Wisconsin DNR estimate that there are fewer than five hundred sharp-tailed grouse left in Wisconsin. Of those, close to 75 percent live in Crex Meadows and Namekagon Barrens Wildlife Areas.

If you are interested in watching the sharp-tailed grouse dance, registration for the viewing blinds opens in mid- to late January. Visitors must agree to a pledge and follow several protocols when using the blinds, including arriving at least forty-five minutes before sunrise and remaining in the blind until the birds have left at the end of the display period. Often, there is still snow on the ground during the lekking season, so you'll need to dress warm and bring hot liquids to drink while you're there.

The Friends of the Namekagon Barrens Wildlife Area is a nonprofit organization that provides sharp-tailed grouse viewing opportunities, leads Natural Resource Foundation field trips for spring birding and hiking, raises funds for land expansion initiatives, supports Wisconsin DNR forest management to benefit sharp-tailed grouse, and conducts environmental education for children and the general public. www.namekagonbarrens.org. The Wisconsin Sharp-Tailed Grouse Society is a nonprofit organization working to protect grouse and increase their habitat: www.wisharptails.org.

The south unit of the Namekagon Barrens Wildlife Area is located two miles north of Wisconsin Highway 77 on Namekagon Trail. Turn left onto Springbrook Trail to access a parking lot with an overlook and view of the barrens. To get to the north unit, continue north on Namekagon Trail for two miles and go east on St. Croix Trail for one mile. According to the Wisconsin DNR website, "You'll know you are there when the sky opens wide and you can see for miles."

ATVs are common and popular on the town road trail system that runs through the barrens but are not allowed off-road or anywhere on the property. If you'd like a quieter experience, visit on a weekday when there is less motor traffic. There are no designated trails, but hiking, cross-country skiing, and snowshoeing is permitted anywhere within the Wildlife Area.

STEWARDSHIP STORY

Looking for Low Maintenance on a Large Scale

"Before I had grandchildren," says Nor Olson, "all of my pictures were of our prairie." We are standing in her kitchen, and Olson has just finished giving me a tour of her property, located in Stillwater Township just north of Silver Creek. When the Olsons bought their home a few years back, the land included an old farm field gone to weeds, as well as a rather large area of lawn surrounding the house. Having previous experience with prairies that she knew and loved, including fifty acres of land elsewhere in the township, Olson decided to bring the prairie to her new house as well. Now their home sits nestled between woods, a wetland, and a few acres of prairie—a microcosm of the habitats found in the St. Croix Valley.

When people move to the country, they are usually drawn by the rural character and the opportunity to be closer to nature. All too often, however, they find themselves tending to giant lawns, without the knowledge or resources to do something different with the land. Turf grass is an easy and relatively inexpensive landscaping option for developers converting farmland into three- to five-acre lots. Everyone knows how to maintain a lawn, and many people appreciate the aesthetic of a large lawn, as well as having the space for outdoor play and gatherings. At the same time, tending to any more than half an acre of grass can be a time-consuming venture. Even with a riding mower, one can easily spend several hours each weekend trimming grass, not to mention the weeding, watering, fertilizing, and pest management needed to keep a large lawn looking good. Turf grass is nonnative, provides no habitat for wildlife, and does little to prevent rainwater from running off into roadside ditches and nearby waterways.

Reducing weekly maintenance was a major motivation behind Nor Olson's decision to go native. "When I think of all the hours I have saved myself from mowing," she says, "I know it was all worth it."

That is not to say that the project happened without a considerable amount of effort. The Olsons spent about a year working with Minnesota Native Landscapes, a private company specializing in the installation and management of native plant communities, to prep the site by tilling it and applying herbicide to kill the weed bed before they planted. Next, they worked with the company to recontour the land so that water no longer runs off into the woods when it rains. Finally, the area was seeded with a mix of native wildflowers and grasses.

"Before, the water used to rush downhill through the old farm field and take out mature trees in the woods," Olson explains. Now, a berm along the edge of the prairie slows the water down and gives it a chance to soak into the ground before it reaches the trees. "It is kind of like a super-sized rain garden," she laughs.

Nor Olson stands in her restored prairie in Stillwater.

While maintenance was a motivation, the natural beauty of the prairie is Nor Olson's greatest reward. Though the prairie was relatively barren when I visited, the plants still charred from a prescribed burn the month before, the bare ground allowed us to spot several large animal burrows. We hypothesized they might belong to foxes or perhaps even a badger, which are known to prefer prairie as their habitat.

During the summer, the flowers and seed heads attract birds and butterflies in abundance. Then there is the amazing variety of the plants—purple coneflower, yellow black-eyed Susans, and feathery big bluestem. "I could just sit and look at it all day," Olson remarked as she grabbed another seed head in her hand and stopped to examine a plant coming up through the ashes. "Even though I know it will come back after the burn, I still love seeing it all return."

To learn more about creating your own prairie, visit www.dnr.state. mn.us/prairierestoration to download a prairie restoration handbook or www.BlueThumb.org to find local seed sources and businesses specializing in prairie restoration and management. In Minnesota, landowners can contact their county's Soil and Water Conservation District for advice and technical assistance. If the prairie planting will help fix a runoff or erosion problem affecting a lake or stream, the project may qualify for cost-share assistance. Other sources of information and advice include The Prairie Enthusiasts (www.theprairieenthusiasts.org) and Wild Ones–St. Croix Oak Savanna Chapter (stcroixoaksavanna.wildones.org). ◊

FOREST AND WOODS

They say that trees can speak to each other in a language we humans are too busy to hear and too self-absorbed to understand. Peter Wohlleben, a German forester who wrote the now famous book *The Hidden Life of Trees: What They Feel, How They Communicate* has learned that trees in a forest actually live as a community. They maintain interdependent relationships and share water and nutrients through underground fungal networks. They send distress signals about drought and disease through chemical, hormonal, and slow-pulsing electrical signals, and can also communicate through the air by releasing pheromones and other scents.

While traveling in New Zealand in 2016, my family and I visited the largest living kauri tree, a two-thousand-year-old giant known locally as Tane Mahuta—Lord of the Forest. Over the two thousand years that Tane Mahuta has grown ever so slowly from a tiny seed into a behemoth tree 169 feet tall, the world has experienced the rise of Christianity; the fall of the Roman Empire; western colonization of the Americas, Africa, and Australia; an industrial revolution; two world wars; and countless other changes. Does Tane Mahuta sense the enormity of change that has happened in its lifetime? Did it feel a mounting sense of loss as its community of kauri were slowly downed for timber? As every year, the chatter in the forest grew a little bit softer?

Charlie hikes along the trails at Pine Point Regional Park in Washington County, Minnesota.

I wonder, too, about the solitary trees planted in city yards and rolling farm fields. Do they feel the same loneliness of modern society that plagues so many of us? Do they long for a community of their own, with which to share signals and sustenance? Maybe the tree in your yard could use a couple of friends.

Though the St. Croix River Watershed contains large swaths of forest in its northern reaches today, the region was heavily logged in the 1800s and early 1900s. During the logging era, an estimated 150 logging camps sprang up along the St. Croix River and its tributaries, with some of the largest located near the modern towns of Hinckley, Minnesota; Trego, Wisconsin; Osceola, Wisconsin; and Stillwater, Minnesota. Trees felled in the northern reaches of the watershed were floated downriver to the St. Croix and then on to lumber mills in Taylors Falls, Marine on St. Croix, and Stillwater. So many trees filled the St. Croix that a person could walk from one bank to the other without ever touching water. It was called the River of Pines.

In a little more than fifty years, timber companies vanquished four million acres of pine forests with trees that were two hundred to three hundred years old. Today, the woods and forests of the St. Croix Watershed are but a shadow of the original forests that once covered the region.

According to the U.S. Forest Service, more than 50 percent of our nation's freshwater supply originates in forests. Forested watersheds stabilize streambanks, shade surface water, cycle nutrients, and filter pollutants. Trees also offer many other gifts to us humans. They provide oxygen for us to breathe and intercept carbon dioxide that would otherwise be released into the atmosphere. The canopy of a mature tree can intercept 1,600 gallons of water per year, helping to reduce stormwater runoff. Trees also afford food and shelter for migratory songbirds, pheasants, deer, pollinating insects, and a multitude of other animals.

As you go out in search of the St. Croix's famous forests, notice the changes in species composition across the watershed. In the south, you're most likely to find maple, oak, and basswood trees, while farther north, white pine, red pine, aspen, birch, and tamarack begin to dominate. In some southern forests, land managers are working to clear out second-growth trees and re-create the open oak forests that were once maintained by periodic fire and grazing. In the northern watershed, most of the forests are actively managed for timber harvest and wildlife habitat.

Sun-dappled forest in fall at Log Cabin Landing in Scandia, Minnesota

Nine Places to Wander in the Woods in the St. Croix River Watershed

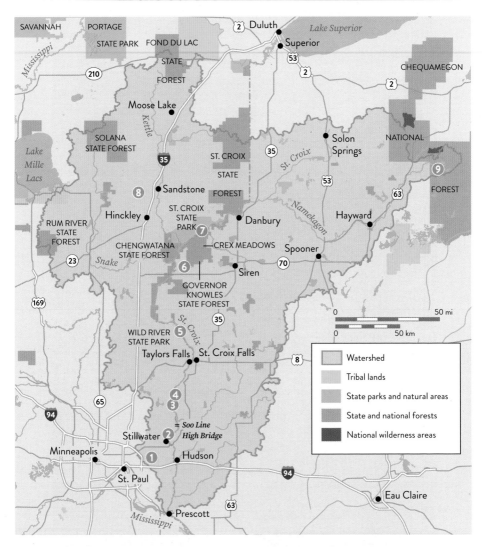

1. Sunfish Lake Park, Lake Elmo, Minnesota
2. Brown's Creek State Trail, Stillwater to Grant, Minnesota
3. William O'Brien State Park, Marine on St. Croix, Minnesota
4. Crystal Spring Scientific and Natural Area, Scandia, Minnesota
5. Wild River State Park, Center City, Minnesota
6. Governor Knowles State Forest, Danbury to Wolf Creek, Wisconsin
7. St. Croix State Park, Hinckley, Minnesota
8. Osprey Wilds Environmental Learning Center, Sandstone, Minnesota
9. Chequamegon-Nicolet National Forest, Wisconsin

① Sunfish Lake Park, Lake Elmo, Minnesota

*Maple, oak, and basswood forest with
woodland wildflowers in the spring*

Beginner

It would be easier to hike the trails at Sunfish Lake Park if it weren't for the woodland wildflowers that interrupt you at every turn. "Pause a moment," they say, "and notice that it is spring." If it weren't for the beaver that plopped into the water and is now carving a shimmering arc across a wooded pond, you could make it deeper into the park with less time spent dawdling by the water's edge. And when you finally crest the hill at the top of a glacial valley, you could quickly complete the rest of your journey if it weren't for the winding trail that branches and continues in both directions, leaving you to wonder which is the path less traveled and what would happen if you took it.

Sunfish Lake Park is a 284-acre park in Lake Elmo that features oak and maple forest in a rolling landscape with steep hills and numerous pocket wetlands. The park is recognized by the Minnesota DNR as a regionally significant ecological area and is home to a wide variety of wildlife, including red-shouldered hawks, bald eagles, the threatened Blanding's turtle, and at least

A birch-ringed pond in fall at Sunfish Lake Park in Lake Elmo, Minnesota

Rue anemone

Wild strawberry

six species of frogs. The park is also a likely location for the endangered rusty-patched bumblebee, which was recently named the Minnesota state bee.

During the spring, violets, Jack-in-the-pulpit, wild geranium, large-flowered bellwort, and strawberry dot the forest floor. Prior to the mid-1800s the landscape was shaped by periodic

fire, which maintained more open conditions than what is currently found on the site. Unfortunately, invasive buckthorn has crept into the park in recent years and threatens to crowd out native woodland wildflowers and shrubs, eradicating wildlife habitat in the process.

In 2020, Friends of Sunfish Lake Park secured a grant of $139,000 from the Minnesota

Yellow violet

Lessard-Sams Outdoor Heritage Council Conservation Partners Legacy Grant Program to remove buckthorn and restore native plants in forty acres of land in the park. A second grant in 2023 provided an additional $457,000 to continue this work on an additional 140 acres. The Friends of Sunfish Lake Park has mobilized dozens of community volunteers to complete this work, and it's likely you'll see signs of the buckthorn and brush clearing underway when you visit.

"Take a walk in this part of the park, and you will notice that the air is permeated with the unforgettable and invigorating aroma of freshly ground buckthorn," laughs Tony Manzara, the founder of the nature center. After it is cleared, park volunteers use the buckthorn mulch for trails and planting projects.

In *A History of Sunfish Lake Park,* compiled for the City of Lake Elmo in 2011, Judith Blackford writes, "Sunfish Lake Park is a critical haven for people. Nature affords us that escape to the wilderness—that tonic that Thoreau spoke of—as being essential to man's well-being. Communing with a wild deer brings one closer to our original place in nature, and it deeply resonates in our being that when we are in nature, we are home."

The entrance to Sunfish Lake Park is located at 10000 Stillwater Lane North, Lake Elmo, Minnesota, just north of Stillwater Blvd. There are separate trail systems for hiking, horseback riding, and mountain biking, and the trails are groomed for skiing in the winter as well. There is also a small nature center on-site that offers programming throughout the year. Learn more at https://sminc-lake-elmo.org/.

② Brown's Creek State Trail, Stillwater to Grant, Minnesota

Oak and maple forest in the Brown's Creek gorge and a popular multiuse trail

Beginner

Let it be known that I did not go out on the new Brown's Creek Trail before it was officially opened even though I really, really wanted to. As soon as the Minnesota DNR announced a "soft opening" at the end of October 2014, however, I was ready to roll.

A small set of rapids on Brown's Creek, beneath the stone arch bridge

I made an inaugural bike ride just before the weather turned cold, towing my son along in a Burley trailer, which meant that I spent half of the ride calling out interpretive features at the top of my lungs as we pedaled by. The 5.9-mile paved trail begins in downtown Stillwater and runs north along the St. Croix River, following a former railway corridor that was built in 1870 to connect Stillwater to downtown St. Paul. More recently, the Minnesota Zephyr operated a heritage railroad that used the tracks until 2008.

One mile north of town, the trail crosses over Minnesota Highway 95 and then travels two miles uphill through a steep, wooded gorge with views of Brown's Creek below. When the original rail line was constructed by the St. Paul and Pacific Railroad, this climb made it quite challenging to lay the track. According to the Minnesota Transportation Museum, "It climbed 299 feet on its way out of the St. Croix River Valley. The first four miles had an average 1 percent grade, with short stretches exceeding 2 percent. Half the six miles were on curves, some as sharp as 7.5 degrees."

An old rail car from the Zephyr, which used the rail line before it became a trail.

The forest in the gorge is comprised of sugar maple, red and white oaks, and basswood trees. During the spring, you can see many spring ephemeral wildflowers along the trail.

Just after passing under Stonebridge Trail, there is a small pull-off where you can get a view of the historic stone arch bridge that was part of the Military Road built to connect Point Douglas with Superior, Wisconsin, when Minnesota was still a territory.

Maidenhair fern along the Brown's Creek State Trail

Brown's Creek is a designated trout stream and the Brown's Creek Watershed District has been working for more than twenty years to protect trout and native fish and minimize flooding in the surrounding watershed. During conversion of the rail line into a paved multiuse trail, the watershed district worked with the Minnesota DNR and adjacent landowners to create a small floodplain area along the trail near the stone arch bridge and install underground treatment devices farther upstream to clean and cool stormwater runoff from roads and parking lots before it enters the creek.

After it leaves the gorge, the trail stays close to Brown's Creek, passing through the Oak Glen Golf Course and Brown's Creek Park. The watershed district has completed numerous stream restoration and protection projects at both locations. Within Brown's Creek Park, there are also walking trails south of the Brown's Creek Trail that wind through an enchanted forest of large and crooked trees. Look for the trails near the rest stop with four spinning color wheels.

After Brown's Creek Park, the trail and creek diverge, with the trail continuing west, roughly parallel to McKusick Road, and the stream's course

I pause by colorful graffiti beneath Stonebridge Trail.

Kids play with colorful spinning wheels along the Brown's Creek State Trail, near the Coldwater Stop.

leading northwest to its headwaters up in Withrow. A few miles past Manning Avenue, the Brown's Creek Trail meets up with the Gateway Trail. From there, you can continue all the way into downtown St. Paul.

Arriving at the intersection of the Brown's Creek and Gateway Trails for the first time back in 2014, I had the strange sensation of entering an alternate universe where people travel by bikes and skis instead of cars, surrounded by woods, like members of a nomadic forest tribe. Glancing back, I noticed that my son was fast asleep, lulled by the gentle rocking of his trailer, which was not unlike the gentle rocking of the trains that once rolled through these same woods. The early November air was still mild, and I decided to keep on riding, just a little bit farther.

The trailhead for the Brown's Creek State Trail is located at 401 Laurel Street East in Stillwater. Parking, bathrooms, and water are also available at the Coldwater Stop at Brown's Creek Park. Download maps of the trail at www.dnr.state.mn.us/state_trails/browns_creek.

Prairie and pines with sunset moon at William O'Brien State Park

③ William O'Brien State Park, Marine on St. Croix, Minnesota

Black ash swamp along the river, with skunk cabbage and marsh marigold in spring

Beginner

In search of spring on Mother's Day weekend, we headed north on Minnesota Highway 95 to William O'Brien State Park. I had hoped to canoe on the St. Croix River that May, but after seeing the river swollen, brown, and flowing fast, I decided I would have to wait until later in the summer. Instead, my mom and I settled for a leisurely stroll at William O'Brien, where we found delicate spring wildflowers scattered throughout the woods like charms from a broken bracelet.

The Riverside Trail at William O'Brien State Park is shaded by majestic white pines that create a natural cathedral over the banks of the St. Croix River. These trees are remnants of a four-million-acre pine forest that once blanketed the St. Croix River Watershed before European American settlers arrived and began logging in 1839. The Mill Stream, which originates in the park and flows through the village of Marine on St. Croix, was the site of Minnesota's first commercial sawmill. Today, you can enjoy a fish fry at the Brookside Bar and Grill as you watch the stream flow right through the basement of the restaurant, over a small waterfall on the opposite side of the street, and down to the St. Croix River.

When the park was first established in 1947, there were thirty state parks in Minnesota, but none located close to the Twin Cities area. That's when Alice O'Brien stepped up to donate 180 acres of land near Marine on St. Croix, which formed the seed for a new park to grow.

William O'Brien, Alice's father, was a lumber baron who purchased land owned by timber companies after they had finished logging the region. Today, when you visit the park, you can fish and swim in Alice Lake or enjoy hiking, camping, cross-country skiing, boating, and nature exploration amidst 1,653 acres of prairies, wetlands, and second-growth woods.

Marsh marigold

The first major land expansion for William O'Brien State Park happened in 1972–73, when a housing developer began to buy parcels of farmland in the surrounding area. The Minnesota Parks and Trails Council raced to line up purchase agreements for 750 acres of land, which now contain most of the upland trail system in the park. Later purchases in 1988, 1994, and 2007 added another 169 acres.

In 2010, Joan Grant and her children Hendrie and Ann sold ninety-seven acres of land, once known as 17 Springs Farm, to be added to William O'Brien State Park. It includes numerous springs and a trout stream that is a natural spawning area for native brook trout, as well as woods and a high-quality remnant prairie.

Most recently, the Minnesota Parks and Trails Council acquired sixty acres of land owned by Myron Lindgren in December 2021. Lindgren lived and farmed on the land for more than eighty years and says that his family used wood from the surrounding forest to heat their home prior to getting electricity in 1947.

Near the river, groundwater seeps keep the soil moist year-round. In the spring, you'll find marsh marigolds with cheery yellow flowers, as well as bodaciously large and stinky skunk cabbage.

Bloodroot, hepatica, and other spring wildflowers grow on slightly higher ground. These ephemeral flowers only appear in the early spring when trees and shrubs are still bare, and sunlight is able to reach the forest floor. Within a period of less than two months, they emerge, bloom, are pollinated by insects, set seed, and then return to a state of dormancy, hidden underground for the rest of the year. Bloodroot, named for its distinctive red sap, flowers for only a day or two before dying.

When the St. Croix runs high after the spring snowmelt and heavy rains, the river floods over its banks, scouring the surface of the floodplain and depositing silt and sediment when it subsides. Tall trees with shallow but far-reaching roots such as cottonwood, silver maple, box elder, and black willow are specially adapted for the frequent flooding. Upland, on the other side of Minnesota Highway 95, the landscape transitions to prairie, oak savanna,

Bloodroot

second-growth deciduous woods, and a vast network of wetlands and ponds.

William O'Brien has sixteen miles of hiking trails, most of which are groomed for cross-country skiing in the winter, as well as a campground with 185 individual sites and four group sites, a public boat launch onto the St. Croix River, and a swimming beach and fishing pier on Lake Alice, a backwater lake connected to the river.

New in 2023–24, the Minnesota DNR completed major changes in the riverside area of the park in order to improve accessibility for wheelchair users and people with limited mobility. It is one of three state parks where retrofits are planned and the DNR hopes that it will serve as a showcase for accessible outdoor recreation.

A Minnesota State Park vehicle permit is required, which costs $35 per year or $7 for a day permit. 16821 O'Brien Trail North, Marine on St. Croix, Minnesota 55047.

❹ Crystal Spring Scientific and Natural Area, Scandia, Minnesota

Red oak and basswood forest with a
groundwater-fed stream and tiny waterfall

Intermediate

There's a crack in the rock and water is pouring out. Liquid crystal tumbles down over moss and ferns, tossing tiny droplets that catch and glimmer on nearby spiderwebs. There is also a beach. The sand is soft and golden and if you run your hands through it, you can almost imagine an ocean lapping against your toes. Except, there isn't an ocean, because you are standing on a cliff (or more precisely, in a cliff) and the beach is actually a portion of the wall that used to exist before it crumbled and fell to the ground.

Crystal Spring Scientific and Natural Area (SNA) in Scandia was established in 2016 when former landowner Gregory Page worked with The Trust for Public Land and Minnesota DNR to permanently protect thirty-eight acres of land for scientific study and public understanding, as well as to maintain unique ecological and geological features on site. The SNA is located north of the former Tiller-Zavoral gravel mine, which is now a community solar

garden. In 2018, The Trust for Public Land protected an additional twenty acres that will expand the SNA and provide better public access. It contains a high-quality red oak–basswood forest on the top of the bluff, as well as sugar maple and white pine spreading down steep slopes and ravines. The real magic is the crystalline spring that pours out of the side of a rock wall, deep in an emerald chasm.

Five hundred million years ago during the Cambrian period, this part of Minnesota was covered by a shallow sea. Over time, the sand at the bottom of the sea compressed and became sandstone. Fast forward in geologic time to fourteen thousand years ago and you would find Minnesota covered by glaciers. When the ice retreated, the meltwater carved channels into the soft sandstone, creating the river valleys we see today.

Not all of the glacier water flowed away into the ocean. Some filled shallow depressions in the landscape, creating our modern-day lakes, and much of the water soaked into the ground where it still exists today in the form of freshwater aquifers. The Cambrian-Ordovician aquifer system covers portions of Minnesota, Iowa, Wisconsin, Illinois, and Missouri, and the most deeply buried portions actually contain saltwater.

Along the St. Croix Riverway, there are numerous locations where groundwater flows out of cliffs and rocks in the form of seeps and springs. At Crystal Spring SNA, a groundwater spring seeps out of the side of a cliff from between layers of Jordan sandstone. The flowing water continually undercuts the ledge, so that it carves deeper into the rock wall each year. In places, the sandstone sloughs away, leaving piles of golden soft sand. It's a beach from an ancient ocean, perched midway up a cliff in the middle of a Minnesota forest.

The spring-fed stream that flows through Crystal Spring SNA is one of the highest quality streams in the Carnelian–Marine–St. Croix Watershed District. A wide variety of aquatic insects and macroinvertebrates can be found in the upper reaches of the stream, while trout and other native fish inhabit the lower reaches of the stream where it flows into the St. Croix River.

A spring flows through a hardwood forest in the Crystal Spring Scientific and Natural Area.

If you head out to visit Crystal Spring SNA, be sure to plan ahead and take precautions to protect this fragile habitat. There is no bathroom on site, and no maintained trails. Bring insect repellent and wear good hiking boots or shoes. If you want bonus points, bring along a small trash bag as well to pick up bits of broken glass and litter you might find during your visit. The parking lot is located at 21777 Quarry Avenue North, Scandia, Minnesota 55073. You can find more info at www.dnr.state.mn.us/snas.

⑤ Wild River State Park, Chisago County, Minnesota

A transition zone between pine forest, hardwood forest, and oak savanna

Beginner

Located along the St. Croix River, just north of Taylors Falls, Wild River State Park has thirty-five miles of trails for hiking and cross-country skiing, as well as eighteen miles of river frontage. Nearly five thousand of the park's total 6,803 acres were donated by Northern States Power Company (now Xcel Energy) when the Wild and Scenic Rivers Act was established in 1968.

Like so many places in the St. Croix River Watershed, the story of Wild River State Park is integrally tied to the story of logging in the region. It was among the areas logged by settlers shortly after the 1837 treaty between the U.S. government and Ojibwe people and became the site of a fur trading post in 1847. As they denuded the forests, lumbermen sent the logs down the St. Croix River to sawmills in Marine on St. Croix and Stillwater, causing massive logjams downriver that could take days, weeks, or even months to clear.

In 1883, 150 million feet of lumber lodged in a narrow bend in the river near what is now Interstate State Park, forming a logjam that took fifty-seven days to clear. Seven years later, the St. Croix Dam and Boom Company built an enormous pile-driven dam across the river to control water levels and prevent future logjams. Nevers Dam remained in operation until 1954, when it was damaged by a flood and eventually removed.

Today, you can find Nevers Dam Landing on the Wisconsin side of the river, across from Wild River State Park. It is a quiet location to launch a canoe or kayak and appreciate the verdant second-growth forest that again lines the river's edge.

When visiting Wild River, look for silver maple and basswood in the floodplain along the river as well as restored oak savanna and prairie in upland areas. The Aspen Knob park boundary road is a beautiful location to find early fall maple, aspen, and birch colors.

Wild River State Park has more than 130 campsites, including backpacking, canoe-in, and horse camping sites. There are also six camper cabins. A Minnesota State Park vehicle permit is required, which costs $35 per year or $7 for a day permit. The park is located at 39797 Park Trail, Center City, Minnesota 55012.

A view of Wild River State Park from the visitor center overlook. Former Vice President Walter Mondale lived in the St. Croix River Watershed and was instrumental in establishing the U.S. Wild and Scenic Rivers Act during his time as a U.S. Senator.

Canoe on the river near Governor Knowles State Forest, Wisconsin

⑥ Governor Knowles State Forest, Wolf Creek to Danbury, Wisconsin

A fifty-five-mile forest on the wild upper reaches of the St. Croix River

Beginner–Intermediate

As you continue heading north along the St. Croix River beyond Taylors Falls and St. Croix Falls, you'll notice that the river and surrounding forest becomes wilder and dramatically less populated.

The fifty-five-mile stretch of river between the Wisconsin towns of Wolf Creek and Danbury, is buffered by the 32,500-acre Governor Knowles State Forest in Wisconsin and 62,000 acres of the Chengwatana State Forest and St. Croix State Park in Minnesota. Together, these protected forest lands create a wide, green swath of nature with almost no signs of human development other than occasional boat landings and one road crossing at State Highway 70.

Horsetail, big leaf aster, and woodbine   *Great white trillium*

Though it is a forest, one of the best ways to experience Governor Knowles State Forest is from the St. Croix River. There are nine public landings on the Wisconsin side of the river within this stretch, six of which offer motorized boat access, and nine public access points on the Minnesota side, all but one of which are limited to canoes and kayaks. From the water, you can enjoy ferns, aster, trillium, and woodland wildlife, amidst an endless ribbon of emerald green.

Off the river, Governor Knowles State Forest also has forty miles of hiking trails, forty miles of horse trails, and campgrounds along the river.

Three of the most popular hiking trails are the St. Croix Campground Trails (23409 West River Road, south of Wisconsin Highway 70), the Sandrock Cliffs Trail (begins north of the Wisconsin Highway 70 landing), and the Brant Pines Trail System (26001 Gile Road, near Danbury). During the winter, the Brant Pines trails are groomed for skiing as well.

From the Brant Pines Trail System, you can also access Brant Brook Pines State Natural Area, which has an old-growth stand of large red pines, as well as white and jack pines, Hill's oak, basswood, large-toothed aspen, and white birch. Beneath the trees are numerous native woodland plants, including bracken, spinulose wood fern, ostrich fern, wild geranium, and columbine The sandy-bottomed stream is fed by cold-water seeps and has native brook trout.

At the south end of Governor Knowles State Forest, horse riding trails begin at the Trade River Campground. The trail head is located six miles west of Wisconsin Highway 87 at 2988 Evergreen Avenue. There are forty campsites with horse tie posts, some with electrical hookups.

In addition to the equestrian campground, there are two other campgrounds and nine primitive backpack campsites within Governor Knowles State Forest. St. Croix Family Campground is on the south side of Wisconsin Highway 70, along the river, and has

thirty rustic campsites, some with electrical hookups. Sioux Portage Campground is a few miles southwest of Danbury and has sixty campsites.

A Wisconsin State Park vehicle permit is required at all campgrounds and picnic areas. This costs $28 per year or $8 per day for Wisconsin residents, and $38 per year or $11 per day for out-of-state visitors.

Ferns and wild yam

Overlooking Bear Creek from the fire tower at St. Croix State Park

⑦ St. Croix State Park, Minnesota

Largest state park in Minnesota and a fire tower with great views

Beginner

I took Charlie camping for the first time when he was eight months old. When the forest called, my mom and I loaded up baby and gear plus two giant white dogs and pointed the Prius north. We ended up at St. Croix State Park, where it is almost always possible to find a last-minute campsite, even when every other state park within four hours of the Twin Cities is full.

St. Croix State Park has thirty-four thousand acres and is bordered by both the St. Croix River and the Kettle River, which was Minnesota's first state-designated Wild and Scenic River. Like other forested areas in the St. Croix River Watershed, the land here was logged in the 1800s. Once the trees were cleared, settlers moved in to farm the land. Eventually, in 1934, eighteen thousand acres of farmland were purchased to establish the St. Croix Recreation Demonstration Area. The Civilian Conservation Corps

A fallen tree munched by a beaver is a sign that Beaver Creek isn't far away.

With baby Charlie at the top of the fire tower on his first ever camping trip in 2012

(CCC) and the Works Progress Administration (WPA) built campgrounds and roads, and nine years later, the land became St. Croix State Park.

Prior to the logging era, the land contained within St. Croix State Park was home to stands of virgin red and white pine. Today, the forests in the park are a mix of aspen and conifers. There is also a unique plant community called jackpine barrens. The thirty-four thousand acres of forested hills and rivers provide ample room for black bears, bobcats, coyotes, beavers, raccoons, gray and red fox, deer, and even wolves. Numerous species of birds, including warblers, flycatchers, eagles, owls, and osprey are all common within the park. As for wildflowers, keep your eyes out as you walk, and you may be lucky enough to find stemless lady's-slipper or moccasin flower.

Though the idea of taking a baby camping might seem intimidating, I think it's actually a pretty easy adventure, as long as you invest in a baby-carrying backpack and bring along a portable play yard to keep them contained while you're making meals and sleeping. To be honest, our camping trip proceeded much the same as any other. We hiked through the forest, climbed to the top of the fire tower to enjoy views of the winding Kettle River, and

Looking out over the St. Croix River

enjoyed quiet time, lounging around the campsite in the sunny afternoon.

With a constant stream of natural amusements in the form of rocks, birds, sticks, and pine cones, we never struggled to keep Charlie entertained, and when evening came, it was no harder to put him to sleep in the tent than it was at home.

If you're planning a first camping trip with a baby or young child, look for a park that is within easy driving distance of a town with services such as groceries, gas, and a doctor's office. Charlie had the bad luck to come down with croup while we were camping in St. Croix State Park, so we had to make an unplanned trip to Urgent Care in Sandstone, where we were able to get medicine and a quick checkup instead of driving home.

St. Croix State Park has more than two hundred campsites, including backpacking, canoe-in, and horse camping sites. There are also six cabins and two guesthouses at the park. Large groups can rent the Norway Point Center or Head of the Rapids Center, which accommodate 215 and 125 people, respectively, with showers, dining, and lodging. A Minnesota State Park vehicle permit is required ($35 per year or $7 for a day permit). The park is located at 30065 St. Croix Park Road, Hinckley, Minnesota 55037.

While you're in the area, consider visiting Hinckley Fire Museum on Old Highway 61 in downtown Hinckley. The museum is open Thursday through Sunday, May through mid-October and commemorates the Great Hinckley Fire, which burned a quarter-million acres of land in four hours on September 1, 1894. The fire leveled the town, killed more than four hundred people, and ended the logging era in the region. The museum is located at 106 Old Highway 61 South in Hinckley.

⑧ Osprey Wilds Environmental Learning Center, Sandstone, Minnesota

Experiential environmental education for people of all ages

Beginner

Osprey Wilds (formerly Audubon Center of the North Woods), is best known for its environmental education programming for K–12 youth, specializing in overnight and one-day experiences. The 780-acre property is also open to the public for hiking, snowshoeing, and cross-country skiing, in addition to offering adult and family programming and rental space for weddings, retreats, and

Colorful trees in fall at Osprey Wilds Environmental Learning Center near Sandstone, Minnesota

other large gatherings. For lifelong learners, Osprey Wilds also hosts Hamline University environmental education courses through the university's Graduate Professional Development Program.

When I first visited Osprey Wilds, I was most impressed by the silence. As I walked beneath a towering corridor of white pine, I heard nothing except the wind in the pines and the occasional calling of birds. There were no boats on the lake, no cars roaring past, and none of the endless chatter of lawn mowers, leaf-blowers, and hammers I hear when I'm outdoors at home.

Within Osprey Wilds, you can explore old-growth white and red pine groves,

Towering white pines along Grindstone Lake in Osprey Wilds

old-growth northern hardwood forest, birch and aspen forest, tall-grass prairie, oak savanna, and shrub-carr wetlands filled with dogwood and willow. The circle of life is evident in the standing dead trees, covered in woodpecker holes, as well as the carpet of baby maple trees that grows above Grindstone Lake. The forest here is an oasis where ecological connections remain intact, even as the surrounding landscape gives way to cornfields, churches, rural homes, and pine plantations.

The main building and seven miles of trails at Osprey Wilds are open to the public Monday through Friday, 8 a.m. to 4 p.m. Trails are groomed for skiing in the winter. Forty geocaches are hidden on the property. Osprey Wilds is located at 54165 Audubon Drive, Sandstone, Minnesota 55072. You can find more info at https://ospreywilds.org.

⑨ Chequamegon–Nicolet National Forest, Wisconsin

Beginner–Advanced

The Chequamegon–Nicolet National Forest covers more than 1.5 million acres of Wisconsin's north woods, including portions of the St. Croix River Watershed surrounding Namekagon Lake. Camping is available at Namekagon Lake Recreation Area on the north side of the lake, which is a family-friendly campground surrounded by hardwood and hemlock forest. Within the St. Croix

Mountain biking on the CAMBA trail system in Chequamegon–Nicolet National Forest, Wisconsin. Photograph by Connie Taillon.

Watershed portion of the Chequamegon–Nicolet National Forest are several notable locations worth visiting.

FOREST LODGE ON LAKE NAMEKAGON

A research site for Northland College

Nestled among old growth forest, this unique Northwoods retreat is situated on Lake Namekagon's pristine southern shoreline. The Forest Lodge was originally owned by the Northern Wisconsin Lumber Company but was later purchased by Crawford Livingston as a hunting and vacation property and passed down to his daughter Mary Livingston Griggs and then granddaughter Mary Griggs Burke. Mary Griggs Burke eventually donated the lodge and 872 acres of surrounding forest to the U.S. Forest Service.

Today, the Forest Lodge estate is owned by Northland College through a unique partnership with the U.S. Forest Service which preserves the estate as part of the National Historic Preservation Act. Northland uses the site for water science and forestry research and also offers occasional public education programs.

Overnight facility rentals are available for groups that are conducting or participating in official programs. The lodge is located at 22230 Garmisch Road in Cable, Wisconsin. Learn more at www. northland.edu/centers/soei/forest-lodge.

FAIRYLAND STATE NATURAL AREA, CABLE, WISCONSIN

Old growth hemlock forest with
undeveloped shoreline and wetlands

Covering 882 acres surrounding Forest Lodge is Fairyland State Natural Area (SNA), an outstanding example of a northern hardwoods forest that was designated as an SNA in 2007. Its 1.5-mile Forest Lodge Nature Trail includes a wooden pathway through a bog and passes through mature mesic and dry-mesic forest. Pick up an interpretive booklet at the parking lot to learn about the features along the trail that are marked by wooden posts.

Fairyland is home to bobcat, fisher, and coyote and is a mecca for migratory ducks in the spring and fall. Black ducks, mallards, ring-necked ducks, wood ducks, blue-winged teal, and hooded mergansers can all be seen along the lakeshore and in wetlands within the SNA. Fishing, hunting, hiking, and cross-country skiing are allowed.

To access Fairyland State Natural Area, head east from Cable on County Highway M. The parking area is nine miles outside town at the intersection of County Highway M and FR 203. Currently, public access is only allowed on the land located south of Garmisch Road.

ROCK LAKE NATIONAL RECREATION TRAIL

Mountain biking, hiking, and skiing

The Rock Lake National Recreation Trail is primarily managed as a narrow trail for classic cross-country skiing, with loops that are 1 to 9 miles long. The hilly trail is suitable for intermediate and advanced skiers. It travels through maple and oak forest, with occasional white pine, and past several small lakes. During the summer months, the trail is maintained for hiking.

From State Highway 63 in Cable, drive 7.5 miles east on County Highway M. The parking lot is on the right (south) side of the road. A trail pass is required, which costs $30 per year or $5 per day. www.fs.usda.gov/main/cnnf/passes-permits/recreation.

CHEQUAMEGON AREA MOUNTAIN BIKE ASSOCIATION (CAMBA) TRAIL SYSTEM

CAMBA manages more than 130 miles of mountain bike trails and 200 miles of mapped gravel routes in and around the Chequamegon–Nicolet National Forest and is a premiere destination for mountain biking in the Midwest. Trails are based out of Hayward, Seeley, Cable, Namekagon, and Bayfield. Access trail guides and maps at https://cambatrails.org.

The big event each year is the Chequamegon 40, a forty-mile mountain bike race that travels from downtown Hayward to the Great Hall in Cable, using the Birkebeiner Trail and other picturesque trails. The event has been held annually for more than forty years and attracts about 1,600 riders each year. During the weekend, there is a festival with live music, craft beer, and food trucks. Learn more about the race at www.cheqmtb.com.

CLAM LAKE ELK HERD

Elk in Wisconsin? Absent from the state for 130 years due to overhunting and loss of habitat, elk were reintroduced to the Chequamegon–Nicolet National Forest near Clam Lake in 1995. The town, now known as the Elk Capital of Wisconsin, is located ten miles east of Lake Namekagon, just outside the St. Croix Watershed boundary.

The best times to see elk are at dawn and dusk, especially during September and October. Look for them grazing in open areas along State Highway 77, County Road GG, and Forest Roads 204, 176, 173, and 339. Be aware that fall is also elk hunting season, so be sure to wear blaze orange or pink if you go hiking or walking along the roadways.

When the Wisconsin DNR first began to reintroduce elk to the Clam Lake area, it did so as a four-year experimental study, in partnership with the University of Wisconsin–Stevens Point. The first twenty-five elk were brought in from Michigan's Upper Peninsula. Since then, the herd has grown to roughly 330 animals. More recently, the DNR also brought in elk from Kentucky to increase genetic diversity. The long-term goal is to grow the herd to 1,400 elk.

To keep yourself and other people safe while viewing elk, slow down while driving, use your flashers to alert other drivers if you are stopping, stay in your vehicle, and do not feed, honk at, or call to the animals. Learn more about the Clam Lake Elk Herd at https://clamlakewi.com/elk-info.

SUPPORT FOR FOREST AND WOODLAND LANDOWNERS

The My St. Croix Woods program (www.mystcroixwoods.org) supports forest and woodland stewardship throughout the St. Croix River Watershed. The program was developed through a partnership of public and private organizations in Minnesota and Wisconsin to help woodland owners develop forest stewardship plans and connect with expert services, resources, and advice.

If you live in the watershed and have wooded or forested land, you can fill out a simple online form to receive a customized information packet in the mail. My St. Croix Woods also connects woodland landowners with workshops, consulting foresters, and cost-share and tax relief programs.

STEWARDSHIP STORY

Training the Next Generation to Be Keepers of the Trees
June 11, 2018

The sun shines on a May morning, and twenty-three tiny children gather round, faces upturned, smiling and eager to begin the day. Kim Lawler, a team leader with Tree Trust, and Joan Nichols, a Minnesota water steward in training, stand before the children with a young white oak that the students will soon plant in a grassy lawn behind their school.

"Who can tell me some things that trees do for us?" asks Lawler, as she cuts the tangled ball of roots, preparing the tree for planting. The first graders respond eagerly with hands waving in the air.

"They help the air."

"They make homes for animals like deer, squirrels, and robins."

"They soak up the water when it rains."

Lawler nods encouragingly to each new child who answers. "Yes," she says. "Trees do all these great things and when the rain comes down, they help to soak up the water so it doesn't go into the storm sewer that goes to lakes and rivers you want to swim in."

Protecting water resources is a big motivation behind the "Campus Greening" under way at Middleton Elementary and Lake Middle Schools in Woodbury, Minnesota. The project, a partnership effort of the South Washington Watershed District and South Washington County Schools, will convert fifteen acres of turf not in active use to prairie and native plantings, in addition to adding two hundred trees and two outdoor classrooms to the school property. The transformed campus will use less groundwater for irrigation, capture more rainwater on-site, create habi-

Joan Nichols and Kim Lawler prepare a group of kids to plant trees at Middleton Elementary in Woodbury.

Students at Middleton Elementary and Lake Middle School planted two hundred trees at their schools as part of a landscape restoration effort.

tat for birds and pollinators, and provide unique learning opportunities for the students.

South Washington's Campus Greening highlights the value of collaboration. In addition to providing a landscape design for the project, the watershed district recruited Tree Trust, a local nonprofit, to teach the students about trees and coordinate tree planting with sixty-seven classes. The U.S. Forest Service provided $5,000 in additional funding for the effort through its Urban Connections program. Joan Nichols and fellow steward in training Susan Goebel will help to design plantings and interpretive signs for the outdoor classrooms as part of their capstone project to become certified as Minnesota water stewards. The unique learning experiences and hands-on participation help students and teachers at the schools develop a sense of ownership as the project moves forward.

When they are done planting, Lawler gathers the first graders together one more time to share an important message. "You are what I call the keepers of the trees," she says. "You'll be here on this campus for another seven years as these trees are growing. It's your job to teach the younger kids who come to this school why you planted the trees and how to take care of them." She smiles, and the group gathers for a photograph with their tree. The next generation of tree keepers is trained and ready to serve. ◊

LAKES, RIVERS, STREAMS, AND WETLANDS

WHICH STATE HAS THE MOST LAKES? MINNESOTA or Wisconsin? Though Minnesota calls itself the Land of 10,000 Lakes, the Minnesota DNR notes that there are actually 11,842 lakes in the state. Minnesota Sea Grant puts the number closer to 14,380 if you count lakes that cross the United States–Canada border and divide up some of the larger lakes that function like connected but hydrologically independent basins. As for Wisconsin, anyone from the Cheesehead State will be quick to tell you that they actually have 15,074 lakes. Then again, Minnesota only counts lakes that are at least ten acres in size, whereas Wisconsin counts smaller bodies of water as well. Wherever you fall in this raging debate, you'll likely agree that there is a lot of water in the St. Croix River Watershed.

Between two million and fourteen thousand years ago, a series of glaciations swept through Minnesota and Wisconsin. When the glaciers melted and receded, they created most of the lakes, rivers, and groundwater aquifers that we see in our present landscape.

Sunset over Square Lake

143

Within the St. Croix River Watershed, water has carved through layers of soft sandstone to create steep bluffs like what we see along the St. Croix River. Glaciers also carved small dimples in the landscape that later filled with water to form lakes and wetlands. We call these prairie potholes.

The prairie pothole region of the upper Midwest is known as the "duck factory" and supports more than 50 percent of our nation's migratory waterfowl. In some parts of the watershed, lakes and wetlands are connected by small streams that are navigable by canoe or kayak. Historically, Dakota and Ojibwe people used these water trails to travel between places where they gathered wild rice, tapped maple trees for syrup, and hunted wild game.

Today, rivers and lakes in the St. Croix River Watershed bring hundreds of thousands of tourists to the region each year. Between lakes, streams, rivers, and wetlands, there are literally thousands of places to swim, fish, paddle a canoe, or relax and watch wildlife while you are here. The Northwoods lakes are calling, and when we answer the call, they'll ask that we stay awhile, put down some roots, and help to care for the land and the water.

Charlie wades across the secret waterfall near Standing Cedars Community Land Conservancy.

IN QUEST OF THE PERFECT SUPPER CLUB

August 19, 2022

A few years ago, my friend Tom and his husband Dean began a multiyear quest to find the perfect Wisconsin supper club. It must serve brandy old-fashioneds, surf and turf, and popovers. Kitschy decor and taxidermy are a bonus. Live music and a lakeside location? Essential.

Inspired by Tom and Dean's culinary adventures, my husband and I set out one Friday night in August on a mini road trip to Balsam Lake Lodge in Polk County, Wisconsin. Our son was away on vacation for the week and, finding ourselves surprisingly lonely and bored, we decided that the fifty-five-minute trip from Stillwater to Balsam Lake was just short enough to be classified as "going for a drive."

It had stormed all day, but the rain cleared around five o'clock, and the setting sun bathed the rolling countryside in a soft, warm glow, accented by occasional rainbows streaming from the clouds.

As we pointed our car north along Wisconsin Highway 65, the scenery gradually transitioned from bucolic pastures dotted with cows to winding hills that cut through maple and oak forests. Here the road grew increasingly steep and narrow, and the windows rattled as we drove over the bumps.

Nature was downright flamboyant that evening. As if a sunset and rainbows weren't enough, we were also treated to a mother doe with two spotted fawns, sandhill cranes, and a pair of white swans gliding gracefully across a lily-covered pond.

Balsam Lake Lodge serves up Northwoods Wisconsin with a capital W. We walked in the door to find live music, a bachelorette party dressed up as cowgirls, and waitresses serving shots of Paradise. We tripled down on the Wisconsin experience when we ordered Ellsworth cheese curds, Friday night fish fry, and New Glarus Spotted Cow.

Our evening reminded me that Minnesota's and Wisconsin's love of lakes is about so much more than just fishing and boating. There is something magical about watching the sun set slowly over a glistening lake, bouncing shards of color off the rippling waves. Each lake nurtures its own little ecosystem—not just of fish, birds, and wildlife that live by the water, but also clusters of lake homes and cabins, farms, and tiny towns.

Lakes and rivers function as economic nuclei for communities in the St. Croix River Watershed. They support recreation, tourism, and higher

A hand-drawn map of Balsam Lake on the wall at Balsam Lake Lodge in Wisconsin.

property values, and also contribute to quality of life for people who live nearby. In 1992, Donald Steinnes, an emeritus professor of economics at the University of Minnesota–Duluth developed an economic model that demonstrated a direct relationship between water clarity (measured by Secchi disk transparency readings) and land values. A later study, conducted by Bemidji State University in 2008, found that Minnesotans are willing to pay up to $267 more per year to fund restoration for lakes that have become impaired.

Unfortunately, many lakes in the region are in danger of being "loved to death" due to farming and development in the surrounding watershed. Communities in Polk and Burnett Counties in Wisconsin have struggled in recent years to address the challenge posed by agricultural companies that wish to establish large, industrial livestock farms, also known as concentrated animal feeding operations (CAFOs). These megafarms can generate millions of gallons of manure per year, much of which is spread on nearby farm fields, contributing to runoff pollution and groundwater contamination. They pose an especially large risk during floods, when overflows can send hundreds of thousands of gallons of manure directly into nearby bodies of water.

Corn and soybean cropland and smaller livestock operations also have a widespread environmental impact on lakes, rivers, wetlands, and streams in the watershed. This includes runoff pollution from nutrient-rich sediment, fertilizer, and manure, as well as the loss of connected habitat corridors for wildlife in the region.

Closer to the Twin Cities metro area, watershed management organizations are working to reverse the impacts of shoreline development on popular lakes such as Big Carnelian, Forest, and the Chisago Chain of Lakes. In 2022, the Minnesota Pollution Control Agency added Lake Jane (Lake Elmo), Bone Lake (Scandia), and eight lakes in the Chisago Chain of Lakes to Minnesota's impaired waters list due to loss of fish and macroinvertebrate diversity resulting from shoreline development. The agency also warned that Big Carnelian (May Township) and Big Marine (May Township/Scandia) were in danger of becoming impaired in the near future if shoreline development continues.

From studying other lakes in the region, we know that small changes (removing trees, shrubs, and perennial plants; adding rock along the water's edge [riprap]; or building homes and driveways) can add up to big ecological impacts over time. As shorelines become increasingly more developed, we start to see shoreline erosion, fewer fish and wildlife, more algae in the water, and diminished water clarity.

As lake-lovers, we're called to do more than just search for supper clubs and sip drinks by the shore. We're called to continually engage as community residents, landowners, food-buyers, and volunteers. If you're lucky enough to own shoreline property, you also play a critical role in helping to protect your lake's health and biodiversity.

To protect local lakes from shoreline degradation, counties and watershed districts have established permit programs that establish rules for shoreline development. Lakeshore landowners should always check with their local government offices first before embarking on any projects such as home additions, clearing trees or shoreline vegetation, grading, or adding riprap.

The Minnesota DNR offers a Score Your Shore tool to self-assess the habitat and health of your lakeshore: www.dnr.state.mn.us/scoreyourshore. Many local government partners offer cost-share incentives to help shoreline owners transition turf and rock-wall shorelines back to a more naturalized landscape with deep-rooted native plants, shrubs, and trees to guard against erosion and provide habitat for fish and wildlife. ◇

Eight Lakes to Visit in the
St. Croix River Watershed

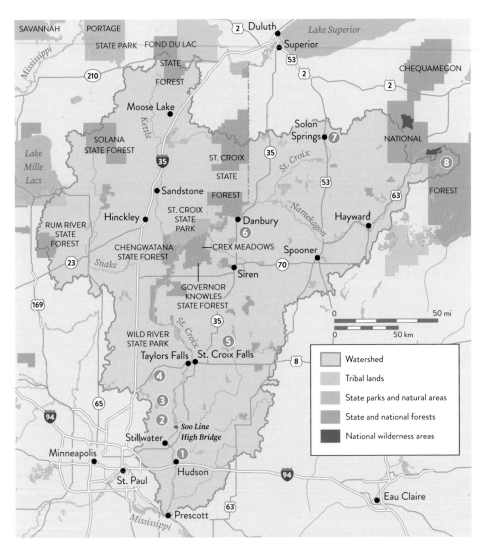

1 Perch Lake,
   St. Croix County, Wisconsin

2 Square Lake,
   Washington County, Minnesota

3 Big Marine Lake,
   Washington County, Minnesota

4 Chisago Lakes Water Trail,
   Chisago County, Minnesota

5 Balsam Lake,
   Polk County, Wisconsin

6 Northern
   Burnett County, Wisconsin

7 Upper St. Croix Lake,
   Douglas County, Wisconsin

8 Namekagon Lake,
   Bayfield County, Wisconsin

Paddling on Perch Lake

① Perch Lake, St. Croix County, Wisconsin

A small, exceptionally clear lake with activities for all ages

Beginner

Sometimes good things come in small packages. This tiny, forty-five-acre lake is a hidden gem with deep, clear water and tree-lined shores. Perch Lake is popular for swimming and scuba and is designated as an "outstanding water resource" by the State of Wisconsin.

I visited Perch Lake for the first time on an early fall day at the beginning of the school year. It had been a long summer—the third in a row that I'd struggled with working full-time without day care—and I was eager to carve out a morning for myself. After watching my son climb aboard his bright yellow school bus, I turned around, loaded the dog and my stand-up paddleboard into my car, and drove over the bridge to Wisconsin.

Though it was a rather gray day with mist rolling in, I was still entranced by the crystal clear water at Perch Lake, as well as its quiet, forested shores. The dog and I paddled across the lake for a

Molly balances on the paddleboard while I paddle across the lake.

while before pausing to wander in the woods. Green light filtered through the maple leaves, and we found mushrooms and aster amid a carpet of pine needles. After a short hike, we paddled back to the boat launch and loaded into the car, just as the mist transitioned to rain.

Perch Lake is most easily accessed from Homestead Parklands, which is a St. Croix County Park. There you can find a beach, as well as picnic areas, a playground, three miles of hiking trails, a fishing pier, and boat rentals for $10 per hour (canoes, kayaks, rowboats, and paddleboards). The park is located at 550 Perch Lake Road, Hudson, Wisconsin 54016. Dogs are allowed in the park but not on the beach. A St. Croix County Park Pass is required, which costs $30 per year or $10 per day. A public boat launch is across from the park at 497 Perch Lake Road.

Birch and aspen line the trails at Homestead Parklands in St. Croix County, Wisconsin.

Square Lake in Washington County is known for its clear, clean water and is popular for swimming and scuba diving.

② Square Lake, Washington County, Minnesota

A popular beach and clear water for scuba and open-water swimming

Beginner

ALONG CAME A LOON AND SWAM UP BESIDE HER

July 4, 2018

I was training for an Ironman triathlon and, despite my best intentions to prevent it from taking over my life, the triathlon had taken over my life. On a typical day, I would get up at 4:45 a.m. to fit in my first workout before starting work at 7 a.m. I did my second workout over lunch, leaving the evening free for gardening, momming, and everything else. In between swimming, biking, and running around the county, I took breaks to write newspaper articles, attend community events, plan workshops for local elected officials, and answer a never-ending stream of emails and phone calls.

This is a long way of explaining why I was swimming across Square Lake at 6:30 a.m. on the morning of July 4th. I woke up determined to fit in a "quick" swim, bike, and run before the Marine on St. Croix parade at noon, a BBQ with friends, and fireworks at night. The funny thing is that I was just one of many people who had also woken up early in the morning to swim in the crystal clear waters of Square Lake that day. At least a dozen other swimmers were there, and some had arrived even earlier than I. The sky was clear, the water temperature was absolutely perfect, and halfway across the lake I popped my head out of the water and discovered a family of loons swimming casually beside me. Yes, I thought, Square Lake is good.

Square Lake is one of about fifteen lakes in Washington County that consistently score A grades in the Metropolitan Council's annual lake water quality report card. Two-thirds of the best quality lakes in the Twin Cities seven-county metro area are located in Washington County. Square Lake, in particular, is known for excellent water clarity, which makes it a favorite destination for swimmers, scuba divers, and beach-loving families from miles around. Why is water quality and clarity so much better in some lakes than in others?

Lake science is actually a lot more complicated than you might think. To begin with, some lakes are shallow, while others are deep. Lake bottoms can be rocky, sandy, or silty, and the different types of rocks and minerals all affect the water differently. Some lakes are groundwater-fed, while others collect rainwater and surface runoff. Lakes can be in a chain, connected by streams and wetlands, or isolated in glacial pockets in the landscape. The number and kinds of fish in a lake affect water quality and clarity, as do the plants and trees that grow around and in the water. Last, but not least, human activities and changes to the landscape impact lakes as well.

Square Lake is ranked in the top 1 percent for water clarity in the North Central Hardwood Forest ecoregion of Minnesota. It has a small watershed in comparison with the lake's size, and receives 70 percent of its inflow from groundwater, 25 percent from precipitation, and only 5 percent from surface runoff. The lake is relatively deep (68 feet), which helps to keep the water clear since there is less chance of sediment on the lake bottom being stirred up by boats, wind, and wildlife. In other words, Square Lake's water quality is partly due to "good genes."

Though Square Lake is one of the cleanest and clearest in the metro area, human activities have still impacted the lake over time. Approximately 25 percent of the land draining to the lake is developed and another 22 percent is farmland. Most of the lake is still buffered by woods and natural vegetation, thanks to careful development along the shoreline.

For years, the Minnesota DNR stocked Square Lake with rainbow trout, until two decades worth of studies by the Carnelian–Marine–St. Croix Watershed District and Square Lake Association showed that the fish were impacting the lake's food web and causing poorer water clarity. Essentially, the trout were eating zooplankton called daphnia, which meant fewer daphnia available to eat algae in the water. There is curly-leaf pondweed in the lake, but so far, the lake has not been infested by Eurasian watermilfoil, zebra mussels, or other aquatic invasives. Through a lot of hard work and careful planning, the watershed district, lake association, DNR, and other partners are maintaining the delicate balance that allows us to love Square Lake without loving it to death.

Most of us don't think about geology, ecoregions, watershed management, or fisheries science when we grab a towel and head to the lake. We paddle an oar, cast a line, dive in, drop anchor, wade around, speed along, skip stones, sit back, and enjoy the view. And every once in a while, we take a break in the middle of the lake to say hello to the loons.

VISITING SQUARE LAKE

There is a large public beach at Square Lake Park, which is usually packed on summer weekends, as well as a fishing pier and public boat launch. Stop by the lake on a summer day, and you'll likely find at least one long-distance swimmer crossing the lake while towing a bright yellow buoy behind. It is a popular location for scuba diving, and Washington County Parks also offers weekly stand-up paddleboard programs.

The park is located at 15450 Square Lake Trail North, Stillwater, Minnesota 55082. No dogs allowed. A Washington County Parks vehicle permit is required, which costs $30 per year or $7 per day. Kayak and stand-up paddleboard rentals are available through an iPaddlePort station; pay with a smartphone, $30–35 for two hours.

Lilies grow in the shallow south bay of Big Marine Lake.

③ Big Marine Lake, Washington County, Minnesota

*Three boat launches and a county park
with beach and playground*

Beginner

Big Marine is a deep lake with exceptional water quality that consistently earns A grades on the Metropolitan Report Card for clean and clear water. Along with good water quality, long stretches of natural shoreline, shallow bays with emergent vegetation, and acres of undeveloped wetland and upland areas surrounding Big Marine Lake ensure good fishing and plenty of wildlife habitat as well. Big Marine is known as one of the best places in the metro area to catch largemouth bass, and there are several rare and endangered species such as Blanding's turtle living near its shores. The lake is 1,800 acres, fifty-nine feet deep, and has three public boat launches.

Gary joins me for a canoe trip on the lake.

There is a public beach at Big Marine Park Reserve at the south end of the lake, as well as a large playground, fishing pier, and public boat launch nearby. The shallow water in the swimming area makes it an ideal beach to visit with younger children. The park is located at 17495 Manning Trail North, Marine on St. Croix, Minnesota 55047. Dogs are allowed in the park but not on the beach or playgrounds. A Washington County Parks vehicle permit is required, which costs $30 per year or $7 per day. The other two public launches on the lake offer free water access.

❹ Chisago Lakes Water Trail, Chisago County, Minnesota

Ten connected lakes with numerous amenities

Beginner

Before European American settlement, more than a dozen lakes in southern Chisago County connected to form one large lake that the Ojibwe people called Kichisaga, meaning "fair and lovely waters." After a rail line was built in the 1880s, the lakes became a tourist destination where people enjoyed fishing, sailing, boating, and passenger steamers. When the railroad closed in 1948, connecting channels between several of the lakes were filled in to make level roadbeds for highways.

Currently, ten lakes in the Chisago Water Trail are connected by navigable channels or short portages across public land. Green, Little Green, Chisago, South Lindstrom, Kroon, South Center, and North Center have public boat launches for motorboats. There are nineteen carry-in access points for canoes, kayaks, and stand-up paddleboards. There are numerous city and county parks throughout the area, some with camping, and there are public swimming beaches on Chisago and South Lindstrom. Together, the ten lakes in the water trail boast more than one hundred miles of shoreline and five thousand acres of water.

To find a map of the Chisago Water Trail and information about activities in the area, go to www.chisagolakeswatertrail.com. Captain Shawn's rents pontoons, fishing boats, and kayaks: www.captainshawnsrental.com.

Aerial view of South Lindström Lake, looking southwest toward Chisago City. Courtesy of Northern Exposure Photography, LLC.

A MARTHA STEWART GUIDE TO LAKE WATER QUALITY

July 1, 2021

"I remember being on this lake seven or eight years ago and just cutting a path through the algae," Jerry Spetzman remarks as we motor across South Lindstrom Lake. Today, the water is so clear that we're able to lower a Secchi disk twelve feet deep into the water before it vanishes from sight. "At the end of that road, there is a sand-iron filter that removes phosphorus from runoff before it goes into the lake," he continues, "and the city park over there has a below-ground filtration practice as well."

Spetzman is the administrator of the Chisago Lake Improvement District (LID), a special-purpose local unit of government that oversees flood prevention and water quality improvement efforts for nineteen lakes and seven thousand acres of surface water in Chisago County. The LID was formed in 1976 to address high water and the flooding of shoreland homes, and now maintains a system of channels and weirs designed to keep lake levels low. For Spetzman, the best part of his job is getting out on the lakes once a month to monitor water quality.

As we move from lake to lake, Spetzman demonstrates how to collect water samples and the various measurements used to evaluate lake water quality. Three variables (water clarity, total phosphorus, and chlorophyll) are combined to create a metric known as a trophic state index. Lakes with a low trophic state index have exceptionally clear water and are considered "oligotrophic." These lakes are most common in cold regions with little to no development, like the Boundary Waters, and they usually have rock bottoms with little muck or sediment.

In contrast, "eutrophic" and "hypereutrophic" lakes have excessive amounts of nutrients, especially nitrogen and phosphorus, and are dominated by algae and aquatic plants. In the middle, mesotrophic lakes are characterized by relatively clear water with enough nutrients to support a healthy food web and abundant fish.

To measure chlorophyll, scientists collect water samples from a few feet below the lake surface and strain it through a filter to collect algae that is suspended in the water. These samples are then sent to a lab for analysis. A few years back, Spetzman began noticing that the color of the algae samples on a white filter corresponded almost perfectly with the lakes' overall water quality. "We started filtering the algae and noticing different colors, and I wondered if that means anything," he says. So, he picked up a few Martha Stewart color charts and began bringing them along on the boat. "Now I've been doing it long enough that I can pretty consistently estimate the water quality tropic index on a lake purely based on the color," he laughs. Samples collected from higher quality lakes will be in the "yellows and creams," while samples from lower quality lakes will be greener.

Barbara Heitkamp analyzes the color of a water sample collected from the lake.

During today's water monitoring trip, Lindstrom Lake and the north basin of Chisago Lake both have clear water with Secchi disk readings of 12–14 feet deep. According to Martha Stewart, the algae samples from both are the color of a chopstick. In the south basin of Chisago Lake, the water clarity is only eight feet deep, and the algae looks more like parchment paper. We find the clearest water in the channel between North Center and Lindstrom Lakes where there are loads of aquatic plants amidst crystal clear water. Here the algae sample is the color of heavy cream.

Thanks to runoff-reduction projects in the surrounding communities, water quality is improving in 100 percent of the lakes for which the Chisago LID has monitoring data. North and South Center Lakes improved enough to be removed from Minnesota's impaired waters list over the winter. "They still aren't pristine," Spetzman explains, "but they crossed the threshold from impaired to non-impaired. Basically, they improved from a D grade to a C."

As water quality has improved, Chisago County lakes are again living up to their Ojibwe name Kichisaga. For Spetzman, that means fewer days boating though green masses of algae, and more days collecting clear water samples with algae in shades of chopstick and cream. ◊

Sunset at Balsam Lake Lodge

⑤ Balsam Lake, Polk County, Wisconsin

Bass fishing, supper clubs, and family-owned resorts

Beginner

Balsam is a 1,901-acre lake in western Wisconsin that is particularly well known for bass fishing. There are five boat landings, one carry-in water access, and several small resorts on and near the lake. Within the nearby Village of Balsam Lake (population 1,000), you can find supper clubs, several bars, an ice cream shop, and a café. A small river called the Balsam Branch connects Balsam Lake to Lake Wapogasset, farther south, and eventually the Apple River.

Balsam Lake operated as a trading post from 1844 to 1854. Settlers later built a dam, lumber mill, boarding house, and schoolhouse on Balsam Lake. At that time the Balsam Branch provided a convenient connection to float logs downriver to other communities in the watershed.

In 1976, the Balsam Lake Protection and Rehabilitation District was established as a special-purpose, local unit of government to manage a wide array of issues impacting Balsam Lake, including aquatic invasive species and water quality. In recent years, the District's work has focused on East Balsam Lake, which has poor water quality in comparison with the rest of the lake and is listed as impaired by the Wisconsin DNR. You can learn more about current projects to protect and restore Balsam Lake at www. blprd.com. To find maps and information about Balsam Lake, head to https://dnr.wi.gov/lakes/lakepages and search for "Balsam."

⑥ Northern Burnett County, Wisconsin

Numerous small lakes: Northwoods, cabins, and camping

Beginner–Intermediate

With more than five hundred lakes, Burnett County is quintessential cabin country. The area is filled with cabins, resorts, supper clubs, and campgrounds, providing plenty of options for places to stay and play. The Wisconsin state record for catching a lake sturgeon using a hook and line was set in Yellow Lake, Burnett County in 1979: the gargantuan fish weighed 170 pounds!

If you're planning a trip to the area, https://burnettcountyfun. com offers information about places to stay, things to do, restaurants, and more. In addition to booking a cabin or campsite, you can also find maps of lakes in the county, get a fall colors report, and even line up an outfitter for a canoe trip on the Namekagon or St. Croix River. The Burnett County Lakes and Rivers Association

Yellow Lake

is a collaborative effort of more than forty individual lake associations that work together to address regional issues such as preventing the spread of aquatic invasive species. Learn more at https://bclra.org.

⑦ Upper St. Croix Lake, Douglas County, Wisconsin

Headwaters of the St. Croix River

Beginner

The Upper St. Croix Lake in Solon Springs is the headwaters of the St. Croix River, which originates in a spring-fed bog northeast of the lake. Before colonial settlers arrived, Native people and French fur traders used a 2.2-mile portage trail to bridge the divide between the Brule River to the north and the St. Croix River to the south. This trail was part of a larger canoe and portage route that connected communities along Lake Superior with those farther south along the St. Croix and Mississippi Rivers. Today, you can still hike this trail to find the place where coldwater springs bubble out of the ground and form the creek that leads to Upper St. Croix Lake.

Upper St. Croix Lake

At 828 acres and 22 feet deep, Upper St. Croix Lake is relatively small, yet locals say it is full of walleye, northern pike, bass, and sunfish and is popular for fishing during both the summer and winter. There are four public landings on the lake, and a swimming beach at Lucius Woods County Park, which is located just south of the village of Solon Springs on the west side of the lake.

Lucius Woods County Park has twenty-nine campsites, a public beach, hiking trails, and picnic areas. The park features an open-air amphitheater, which hosts a popular Music in the Park concert series during the summer. The park is located at 9231 East Marion Avenue in Solon Springs. The village of Solon Spring has art galleries, gift shops, groceries, bars, restaurants, and several other services.

Please note that there are numerous aquatic invasive species in Upper St. Croix Lake. If you are boating on the lake, take extra care when cleaning and draining your watercraft before visiting any other bodies of water.

⑧ Namekagon Lake, Bayfield County, Wisconsin

Headwaters of the Namekagon River

Beginner

Namekagon Lake, located northeast of Cable, is a sprawling 2,897-acre body of water with numerous basins, islands, and peninsulas that forms the headwaters of the Namekagon River. In the Anishinaabe language, the name means "lake abundant with sturgeon." Today, there are no longer sturgeon in the lake, but it is still home to a thriving fishery with muskies, walleye, largemouth bass, smallmouth bass, northern pike, and panfish. Namekagon Lake is one of only three lakes in Wisconsin managed as a trophy muskie lake.

Lake Namekagon is a prime tourist destination and is surrounded by numerous resorts, campgrounds, and outdoor recreational opportunities. There are seven public boat launches on the lake, and it is a popular location for kayaking, canoeing, boating, swimming, and wildlife watching. Off the water, you can enjoy hundreds of miles of hiking, mountain biking, and cross-country skiing trails in the region.

Sunset over Lake Namekagon by Carrie Rolstad. Rolstad writes, "Shared In honor of my dad, James L. Wester, who instilled an appreciation for nature and inspired me to capture its beauty and wonder.".

During a survey in 2010, the Wisconsin DNR identified thirty-three locations in Namekagon Lake with critical habitat that are designated as sensitive areas. The DNR also found forty-five aquatic plant species in the lake and surrounding wetlands, which indicates a more balanced and ecologically rich environment when compared with other lakes in northern Wisconsin.

Unfortunately, Lake Namekagon's popularity has created some growing challenges. One is the introduction of nonnative Eurasian watermilfoil in recent years. This aquatic invader crowds out beneficial native species and diminishes aquatic habitat. Another concern is wake boats, which contribute to shoreline erosion.

The Namekagon Lake Association is a nonprofit organization, established in 1995, that works to preserve and protect the lake and its surrounding watershed. In addition to sponsoring educational programs, the lake association works with the DNR to ensure that boaters clean, drain, and dry their watercraft when traveling between Namekagon and other lakes in order to prevent the spread of aquatic invasive species. You can find more information at https://namakagonlakeassociation.org.

STEWARDSHIP STORY

Saving Bone Lake
June 11, 2018

It's 6:30 p.m. on a Tuesday night, and a small group is gathered inside the Scandia Pizzeria to hear their neighbor Tom Furey talk about water quality in Bone Lake. Twelve years ago, Bone Lake was considered one of the worst lakes in Washington County. The water was murky and phosphorus, algae levels were high, and the Metropolitan Council gave the lake an F on its annual report card. Now, thanks to several large projects led by the Comfort Lake–Forest Lake Watershed District, the lake is on its way to better health and has inched its way up to a grade of B+.

When Furey bought a home on Bone Lake a few years ago, he wondered what he could do to help protect and improve the lake. After learning about cost-share grants to restore shoreline habitat, he began working with the watershed district and Washington Conservation District to redesign his lakeshore landscaping. He also volunteered to join a new program, Minnesota Water Stewards, that trains and empowers volunteers to work on water issues in their communities. Through the program, Furey learned about watersheds, stormwater management, water policy, strategies for engaging friends and neighbors, and landscaping practices to reduce runoff pollution in urban and rural settings. This summer, for his capstone project, he is helping a neighbor with native planting on her property and is also organizing a series of informative

A winter bonfire on Bone Lake. Photograph by Tom Furey.

gatherings for people living on Bone Lake, including a pontoon tour and the pizza night in town.

Freshwater Society developed the Minnesota Water Stewards program as a way to help amplify the impact of conservation districts and watershed management organizations in Minnesota. Stewards receive fifty hours of free training through a combination of online instruction, in-person classes, and hands-on, outdoor activities. After becoming certified, water stewards provide twenty-five hours per year of volunteer support to their watershed organizations, helping with outreach, education, and community engagement efforts.

A similar program, known as St. Croix Watershed Stewards, is hosted by the North Woods and Waters of the St. Croix Heritage Area. Thirty-two watershed stewards were trained through the program in 2017–18 and continue to volunteer in their Wisconsin and Minnesota communities.

Though water stewards all share a passion for protecting water resources, their interest areas, capstone projects, and volunteer efforts are quite diverse. Down the road from Scandia in Marine on St. Croix, water steward John Goodfellow developed a community forestry plan and worked with neighbors to build a gravel bed tree nursery to propagate trees for reforestation projects.

In Woodbury, stewards Joan Nichols and Susan Goebel created a planting plan and helped to design interpretive signs and lessons for two new outdoor classrooms at Lake Middle School and Middleton Elementary School. Nichols's husband, Nathan Zerbe, developed a habitat improvement plan for Marsh Creek Preserve and recruited volunteers to help remove buckthorn during the summer. In Lakeland, Sally Arneson planted native plants to stabilize an eroding ditch near the St. Croix River and, in Cottage Grove, Cole Williams restored a stretch of shoreline property along the Mississippi River.

In addition to helping local partners to extend their limited resources, the Water Stewards programs offer area residents a meaningful way to make new friends and get involved in their communities. To learn more about Minnesota's Water Stewards program or apply to join, go to https://minnesotawaterstewards.org. Since 2013, Freshwater Society has certified more than four hundred water stewards in Minnesota. The St. Croix Watershed Stewards program is not currently accepting new applications but may in the future as funding becomes available. Email info@northwoodsandwaters.org to learn how to get involved in that program. ◊

A coldwater stream flows through the Buffalo Skull tract at Standing Cedars Community Land Conservancy in western Wisconsin.

Rivers and Streams

More than thirty rivers and streams flow to the St. Croix River, creating a vast network of living water that is dynamic and ever-changing. Included among these tributaries are rivers such as the Snake (Minnesota, 104 miles), Namekagon (Wisconsin, 101 miles), Kettle (Minnesota, 83 miles), and Apple (Wisconsin, 77 miles) that cross multiple counties and are large enough for kayaking and canoeing. There are also numerous smaller streams, especially on the Minnesota side of the St. Croix, that travel mere miles before ending their journeys in the river that unites them.

Due to geology and human influence, the tributaries of the St. Croix River have vastly different personalities. The Kettle and Snake Rivers are known for their challenging rapids, whereas the Apple River's wide, flat water beckons to groups of lounging lolly-gaggers, who float down the river on inner tubes, drinking beer.

Rivers such as the Apple, Willow, Kinnickinnic (Wisconsin), and Sunrise (Minnesota) that flow through agricultural areas carry a disproportionately large amount of sediment and nutrients due to runoff and erosion from farm fields and drainage ditches. In the wilder, upper reaches of the watershed, rivers such as the Totogatic (Wisconsin) and Lower Tamarack (Minnesota), which are surrounded by forests, remain mostly pristine as a result.

Though they might not always show up on maps, the small streams within the St. Croix River Watershed are actually quite fun to explore. In the springtime, groundwater-fed seeps and springs along the river are filled with skunk cabbage and marsh marigold, and offer the first signs of life returning after a long, cold winter. There are also dozens of waterfalls within the riverway, ranging in size from tiny trickles to raging torrents that freeze solid like ice castles in the winter.

Whether you're a thrill-seeker, looking for whitewater adventure, or a weekend day-tripper chasing waterfalls, the St. Croix region is a great place to dip your toes in the water and enjoy nature for a while.

Tributaries and Waterfalls in the St. Croix River Watershed

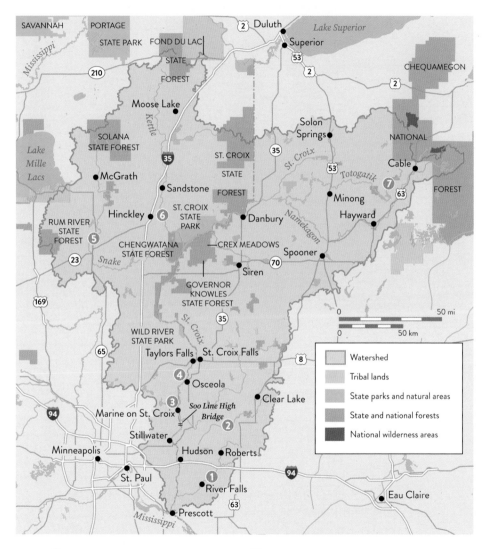

1. Kinnickinnic River:
   Roberts to River Falls, Wisconsin
2. Willow River:
   Clear Lake to Hudson, Wisconsin
3. Mill Stream:
   Marine on St. Croix, Minnesota
4. Cascade Falls: Osceola, Wisconsin

5. Snake River:
   McGrath to Chengwatana
   State Forest, Minnesota
6. Kettle River: Moose Lake to
   St. Croix State Park, Minnesota
7. Totogatic River: Cable to
   Namekagon River, Wisconsin

Amber Adam paddles a kayak on the Kinnickinnic River near River Falls, Wisconsin.

1 Kinnickinnic River: Roberts to River Falls, Wisconsin

Spring-fed, coldwater stream popular for trout fishing and kayaking

Intermediate

Though its full name is Kinnickinnic, most people call this 22-mile long gem "The Kinni." Starting near Roberts, Wisconsin, in a groundwater-fed wetland that is also a nesting site for trumpeter swans, the Kinni and its tributaries support one of the highest densities of brown trout in the country and it is popular for fly fishing and kayaking.

The Lower Kinni courses through a deep gorge, plunging more than 70 feet before it meets the St. Croix River. In addition to trout, the Kinni is also home to three endangered mussel species: Higgins' eye, spectaclecase, and snuffbox.

The Kinnickinnic River Land Trust works to protect the Kinni and its surrounding watershed and has developed a public recreation map that shows river access points and public lands within the watershed: www.kinniriver.org.

In recent years, the community of River Falls grappled with the question of whether to remove two dams located within the city. The dams disrupt fish migration, create artificial lakes along the riverway, and can cause water temperatures to rise by more than 4°F, enough to prevent trout from reproducing. Removal, however, could send accumulated sediment downstream, causing major impacts as well.

The city voted in 2019 to remove Powell Falls Dam by 2026, followed by the Junction Falls Dam in 2035–40. A nonprofit organization called the Kinni Corridor Collaborative was formed to bring together the technical and financial resources for removal.

After a flood in 2020 severely damaged the Powell Falls Dam, The Wisconsin Department of Natural Resources awarded the city $1 million toward dam removal. The Federal Energy Regulatory Commission approved delicensing of the dam in February of 2022; later that year the city approved a contract with the U.S. Army Corps of Engineers to conduct a feasibility study for removal of both dams and full ecological restoration of the Kinni.

② Willow River:
Clear Lake to Hudson, Wisconsin

Hilly trails and a spectacular waterfall at Willow River State Park

Beginner–Intermediate

The Willow River flows seventy miles from southern Polk County to North Hudson, Wisconsin, passing through Cylon Marsh Wildlife Area, Betterly Waterfowl Production Area, and Willow River State Park along the way.

Once upon a time, the Willow flowed free and unfettered to the St. Croix River. After settlers arrived, a series of dams were constructed in 1848 and 1854 to power mills in the region. As a

result, the Willow now ends in a 289-acre lake known as Lake Mallalieu.

In 1967, the State of Wisconsin purchased three hydroelectric dams and 2,800 acres of land surrounding the Willow River upstream of Lake Mallalieu to create Willow River State Park. Eventually, the Wisconsin DNR removed the middle (Willow Falls) and upper (Mounds Plant) dams in 1992 and 1997, respectively, which restored Willow Falls and the Willow River Gorge back to a natural state.

The third dam, Little Falls Dam, is still in operation and was recently reconstructed by the Wisconsin DNR in 2019. The dam is no longer used to generate electricity but does create a 172-acre reservoir, known as Little Falls Lake, which is popular for swimming, fishing, canoeing, and kayaking.

Portions of the Willow River's main stem and the North and South Forks of the Willow are Class II and Class III trout waters. There are public boat ramps on Lake Mallalieu in North Hudson and at Little Falls Lake in Willow River State Park, as well as eight carry-in access points along the river for canoes and kayaks. To find maps of the river, paddling itineraries, and information about towns and recreational opportunities along the Willow River, go to www.willowriverwatertrail.org. Willow Kayaks (willowkayaks. com) provides kayak rentals and shuttling service along the river.

The 2,800 acres of rolling hills in Willow River State Park make for great hiking and trail running, and there is a campground with 150 sites, several picnic areas, a beach, and a nature center. If you only see one thing while you're there, make sure it's the spectacular waterfall along the Willow River on the east side of the park. Rock terraces branching out beneath the falls make it easy to wade and swim, and there is a cute bridge crossing the river near the waterfall. The Hidden Ponds Nature Trail is wheelchair-friendly, and the park also offers accessible campsites and an accessible fishing pier.

A Wisconsin State Park vehicle permit is required at Willow River State Park, which costs $28 per year or $8 per day for Wisconsin residents, or $38 per day or $11 per day for out-of-state visitors. The main entrance is located at 1034 County Highway A, Hudson, Wisconsin 54016.

Waterfall at Willow River State Park

TRYING FOR TROUT

What is it about trout that makes them so alluring? Is it their beauty? Is it the way that they fight? Do people like them just because they taste good? Though walleye may hog the limelight when it comes to Minnesota and Wisconsin fishing, talk to any experienced angler and it's clear that trout are something special. Based on my own experience, I have a hunch that the passion is inspired as much by the places where trout can be found as it is by the fish themselves.

If you're looking for any old fish, you can probably find one in all but the most lifeless and polluted of ponds. Trout, however, only flourish in pristine habitats. The majority of trout lakes in Minnesota are located in the northeastern corner of the state, not coincidentally, in some of the wildest and most beautiful locations. Trout streams can be found throughout the driftless area of northeast Iowa, southeast Minnesota, southwest Wisconsin, and northwest Illinois where the landscape is comprised of wooded hillsides and craggy valleys, and plentiful cold-water springs team with native brook trout and wild brown trout. Because trout and the insects that they rely on for food—stoneflies, mayflies, and caddisflies—are so sensitive to pollution and increases in water temperature, trout by necessity require pretty places to live.

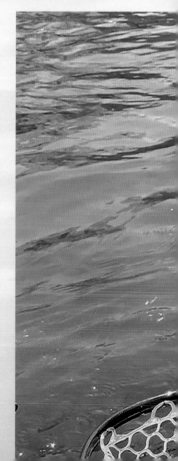

Ten years ago, I had the pleasure of joining the Kiap-TU-Wish chapter of Trout Unlimited for their annual banquet and learned a little bit more about this citizen group's efforts to protect and improve local coldwater resources for trout and other wildlife. Established in 1972, the Kiap-TU-Wish chapter includes nearly 250 members from western Wisconsin and east-central Minnesota who are working to protect and restore the Kinnickinnic, Willow, Apple, and Rush Rivers. In particular, the Kinnickinnic River is known as one of the most beautiful and productive trout streams in the state of Wisconsin.

Through monitoring, the Kiap-TU-Wish chapter has documented the impacts that stormwater runoff from the River Falls area has had on the Kinnickinnic River, and this research has helped to demonstrate the need for development and redevelopment rules to protect the river from further harm. They have also taken the lead on stream habitat restoration projects on the Willow, Kinnickinnic, and Rush Rivers, as well as Parker, Tiffany, Eau Galle, and Pine Creeks.

In 2012, the Wisconsin DNR purchased 2.5 acres of land along the Kinnickinnic, just west of River Falls, which is known as the Red Cabin Site. There, Trout Unlimited is leading restoration efforts along a 1,700-foot stretch of river (approximately one-third of a mile) that will restore natural habitat for fish and the insects that they eat.

When I picture an angler fishing for trout, they are standing in waders near a bend in the stream someplace wooded and wild. A healthy trout stream or lake is nature at its finest, and that, I think, is the true allure of the trout.

Learn more about the national Trout Unlimited organization at www.tu.org. Find more information about projects led by the Kiap-TU-Wish Chapter here www.kiaptuwish.org. ◊

Brown trout are stocked into the Kinni and other local streams.

NIBI WATER WALKS

On March 1, 2013, Sharon Day started walking and she didn't stop for a long time. Every day for two months, she and four other "Water Walkers"—Deon Kirby, Ira Johnson, Beth Brent, and Barb Baker-Iarush—walked beside the Mississippi River, all the way from Minnesota to Louisiana. During their journey, several hundred people joined the walkers for some of the distance, offered them lodging at night, or provided them with food. The group walked to draw attention to the peril that the Mississippi River faces due to pollution and, just as important, they walked to remember their connection to this great river and giver of life.

Water Protectors stand near the St. Croix River during an advocacy and awareness-raising event in 2020.

"When we spend time respecting and thanking the water for keeping us alive, it becomes impossible to abuse it," says Day, who is an enrolled member of the Bois Forte Band of Ojibwe and executive director of the Indigenous Peoples Task Force. In the Anishinaabe culture, women have cared for the water, *nibi*, since time immemorial, and believe that it is the blood of Mother Earth. Because women also give life, they are the keepers of the water. Over the past decade, Day has led more than two dozen Nibi Walks and has traversed the length of the Mississippi and Ohio Rivers, as well as several tributaries in the St. Croix River Watershed, including the Kinnickinnic, Willow, and Kettle.

I come from the world of marathons and triathlons where four-hour events are supported by water stops and finish line goodies, sheriff patrols to guard busy intersections, and volunteers shouting encouragement along the way. Yet Sharon Day is a grandmother, and her companions are ordinary people. During their Nibi Walks, they walk every day, through snow, rain, wind, and sun, without corporate sponsors and in everyday clothes. At times, they follow scenic roads that are surrounded by nature and beauty. At others, they follow busy highways that pass through industrial wastelands. In these places, the walkers are dwarfed by the human-built landscape—four small figures, moving slowly along the shoulder of the road.

"The rivers that we walk have been all over the United States," Day explains. "I usually select a river because it is under an imminent threat or, in the case of the Mississippi River, it is highly polluted. Often people or organizations reach out to me to request a walk."

In 2019, North Woods and Waters of the St. Croix Heritage Area reached out to Day to suggest a Nibi Walk along the Willow River. The walk was delayed due to Covid, but eventually happened in 2021. "I went there ahead of time and found the headwaters, which was in a farmer's field," she told me. "It was a beautiful walk. We followed along a path instead of the road when we went through Willow River State Park. On the other side of the park, the path wasn't very discernable, and the walkers got ahead of the guide, but we eventually came back together and found the river again." The Willow River Nibi Walk was cosponsored by the Friends of the Willow River and Kinnickinnic State Parks and the Clear Lake Earth Day Committee, as well as North Woods and Waters.

Day ends each of her Nibi Walks with a loving message to the water that might also be a healing prayer for all people. "This is how you started off; this is how we wish for you to be again. Remember that at one time you were pure and clean at the source."

Learn more about or join upcoming Nibi Walks at www.nibiwalk.org. ◊

St. Croix River near the Mill Stream in Marine on St. Croix

③ Mill Stream: Marine on St. Croix, Minnesota

Historic site of the first commercial sawmill on the St. Croix River

Beginner

If you've grabbed a bite to eat at the Brookside Bar and Grill in Marine on St. Croix, you've probably noticed that the restaurant has a unique claim to fame: a stream runs right through the middle of the building! The Mill Stream originates in William O'Brien State Park and flows downhill, across Minnesota Highway 95, and through the Brookside, before cascading down a waterfall to the St. Croix River. This tiny stream gave rise to the first commercial sawmill on the St. Croix River and now attracts history buffs and nature lovers from around the region.

During Marine's Art & Nature camp in 2021, I led a group of grade-school children on a nature scavenger hunt that included searching for aquatic macroinvertebrates and other critters in the Mill Stream and St. Croix River (macro—meaning you can see them with your eyes; invertebrate—meaning they have no internal skeletons). During an hour of muddy, sloppy fun, the kids discovered a wide assortment of mussels, frogs, leeches, and insect larva, including species such as caddisfly larva and hexagenia mayfly nymphs (giant burrowing mayfly) that are only found in high quality, clean streams.

Scientists conduct macroinvertebrate surveys on streams to create Index of Biological Integrity (IBI) scores that function much like grades on a report card. According to Mike Isensee, administrator for the Carnelian–Marine–St. Croix Watershed District, Mill Stream received an IBI score of B in 2022. The district hopes that water quality improvement efforts will bring that grade up to an A over the next decade.

In fall of 2021, the watershed district finished work on a multistage Village Center Revitalization project, completed in partnership with the City of Marine on St. Croix. The project includes two new stormwater basins, a pretreatment basin, and two wetland restoration projects, constructed to treat polluted runoff from Minnesota Highway 95 before it flows into Mill Stream. Together with gully and ravine stabilizations in town, the retrofits are expected to keep an estimated 22–27 pounds per year of phosphorus out of Mill Stream and the St. Croix River.

A wooden path leads upstream to a small waterfall.

The Marine Village Revitalization project has benefitted from a $224,000 United States EPA 319 grant and a $97,600 Minnesota Clean Water grant, which were awarded to Carnelian–Marine–St. Croix Watershed District. Isensee emphasizes the high level of partnership between the city, watershed district, and other governmental partners that allowed the project to move forward seamlessly. Community volunteers were also integral. "We've had four planting events so far, and volunteers have planted about eight thousand plants," says Isensee.

The district is also engaging student volunteers to continue monitoring macroinvertebrate populations. Beginning in 2022, high school biology students from St. Croix Prep work with Washington Conservation District staff to collect and analyze aquatic macroinvertebrates in Mill Stream as part of a volunteer stream monitoring program. With hope, these populations will continue to flourish as water quality in the stream improves.

④ Cascade Falls: Osceola, Wisconsin

A large and easily accessible waterfall

Beginner

Cascade Falls is a twenty-five-foot waterfall in Osceola Creek located at the south end of town behind the Watershed Café. A long staircase leads down to the base of the waterfall, and you can use a rock trail with boardwalks to follow the creek to the St. Croix River.

Charlie stands at the bottom of Cascade Falls.

"In the field of geomorphology (the study of how the Earth changes), waterfalls are an example of a knickpoint—a point in a river's channel where there is a sudden and marked change in slope, or steepness," explains Barbara Heitkamp, a watershed educator with the Lower St. Croix Watershed Partnership. "Knickpoints can be static and stay in one place, or they can move as the environment around them changes. They can move quickly, or slowly—accelerate, or decelerate. They can be large, or small, but at every scale, knickpoints represent points of transition and change in a river channel."

The structure at Cascade Falls is an undercutting knickpoint, which means it is continually eroding and moving farther away from the St. Croix River.

Cascade Falls is most alluring because it is so close to the main road. If you'd like to spend a little more time along the river, you can combine a trek down to the waterfall with a hike along the 1.5-mile Falls Bluff Loop, which combines the Cascade Falls, Eagle Bluff, and Simenstad Trails and offers panoramic views of the St. Croix River below. The village of Osceola has installed LED lighting at Cascade Falls so that tourists can enjoy the waterfall at night.

Cascade Falls is located in Wilke Glen at 101 North Cascade Street, Osceola, Wisconsin 54020. The Watershed Café at the top of the hill serves farm-to-table food and is open Wednesday through Sunday.

⑤ Snake River: McGrath to Chengwatana State Forest, Minnesota

A Minnesota State Water Trail through a deeply forested landscape

Advanced

The Snake River flows 104 miles from Solana State Forest to the Chengwatana State Forest, passing through the communities of McGrath, Mora, Grasston, and Pine City before eventually reaching the St. Croix River. It is a designated State Water Trail that features numerous rapids and falls, as well as a beautiful, forested landscape.

*Muskrat in winter at
Chengwatana State Forest*

Though you might imagine that the river's name comes from its sinuous pathway, the name is actually a translation of the Ojibwe word *Kanabec*, which the Ojibwe once used to describe the Dakota people who lived farther upriver. The Snake River also passes through Kanabec County.

The uppermost portion of the river, McGrath to Snake River State Forest, and lowermost portion, Pine City to the St. Croix River, are for experienced whitewater paddlers only. Between Silver Star Road and County Road 3, the upper Snake is dotted with rapids and falls that range from Class I–IV, depending on water levels. Below Cross Lake in Pine City, the river tumbles again, dropping 136 feet in its last twelve miles, through a series of Class I–III rapids.

If you're merely hoping for a leisurely paddle in a canoe or kayak, stick with the stretch between Mora and Pine City, where the Snake River is gentle and relatively free of rapids. If you're interested in fishing, the Snake River is home to walleye, northern pike, smallmouth bass, catfish, and even the legendary sturgeon.

In the upper portion of the Snake River, you can find forest thick with birch, aspen, oak, maple, ash, and elm. There are numerous granite outcrops there, and you might be lucky enough to see white-tailed deer, black bears, gray and red fox, beavers, muskrats, otters, bobcats, coyotes, and minks. Between Mora and Grasston, the river remains wooded, but this transitions to farmland east of Grasston. Eventually, as the Snake approaches the St. Croix River in Chengwatana State Forest, the trees return again.

I spent a week in a cabin along the Snake River the year that I began writing this book. It was winter and the nearby Chengwatana Forest was desolate, save for the muskrat that appeared in the middle of the trail one afternoon, apparently as an omen to warn me that my son and I would soon be sick with Covid. If you're looking for quiet and solitude, the Snake River could be the place for you.

To learn more about the Snake River and download a map for navigation, visit www.dnr.state.mn.us/watertrails/snakeriver. Two outfitters in the area offer gear rental and shuttling services.

Hard Water Sports, located at 511 Main Street, Sandstone Minnesota 55072, offers guided whitewater rafting trips on the Snake River, as well as canoe, kayak, and camping gear rental. The company also serves the Kettle and St. Louis Rivers: http://hard watersports.com or 651-302-1774.

Snake River Outfitters, located in Pine City, Minnesota, offers canoe and kayak rental and shuttle service, as well as guided twenty-two-foot "Big Canoe Adventures" and overnight camping trips: http://snakeriveroutfittersmn.com or 612-718-0125.

The fifteen-mile Snake River Canoe race takes place each May and has since 1981. If you'd care to float your boat at high speed, you can learn more about the race at https://vasaloppet.us/snake-river-canoe-race.

While you're in the area, the Snake River Fur Post in Pine City is an interesting half-day activity. The site is managed by the Minnesota Historical Society and includes a visitor center, a historic fur post and Ojibwe camp, and 1.5 miles of trails: https://www.mnhs.org/furpost. The Fur Post is open Fridays and Saturdays from June through the end of September.

⑥ Kettle River: Moose Lake to St. Croix State Park, Minnesota

One of the best whitewater rivers in the Midwest

Advanced

The eighty-mile Kettle River starts just north of Moose Lake, Minnesota and flows through General Andrews State Forest, Banning State Park, St. Croix State Park, and the Chengwatana State Forest before uniting with the St. Croix River. It is one of six

Kettle River in St. Croix State Park

state-designated Wild and Scenic Rivers in Minnesota and is known as one of the best whitewater rafting destinations in the Midwest.

The river is named after the kettles in and around the lower Kettle River that were formed when swirling water and rocks scoured rounded holes in the sandstone. These same geologic formations can be seen at Minnesota's Interstate State Park. Though the river is exceptionally clean, you might be surprised to notice that it is brown like root beer. That's because the Kettle originates in bogs and slow-moving streams in Carlton County where the water takes on a brown hue from the tannins in decomposing plants and trees.

The forests surrounding the Kettle River are filled with black spruce, fir, birch, aspen, maple, ash, elm, and pine. As in other parts of the upper watershed, these are second-growth forests that have regenerated since the 1800s logging era. As it passes through Banning State Park, there are towering cliffs rising one hundred feet above the river and sixteen miles of Class II to IV rapids that are created by the river tumbling over boulders and through rocky narrows.

The stretch of river through Banning State Park and Sandstone should only be attempted by experienced whitewater paddlers. There are dangerous undercut walls and ledges throughout Banning State Park that can trap kayaks and swimmers, and the river changes dramatically depending on the water levels. Even if

Kettle Lake near the headwaters of the Kettle River in Fond Du Lac State Forest

you are experienced, always scout this stretch ahead of time. For the last seven miles of the Kettle River, as it flows through St. Croix State Park and the Chengwatana State Forest, there are rapids as well, though these are smaller and more easily navigated by canoe or kayak. Most of the rest of the river is smooth and easy to paddle.

By late summer, the Kettle River slows to a trickle, and it can become impossible to travel by canoe or kayak, especially in the upper reaches. In recent years, a coalition of mining companies has been studying mineral deposits in the Kettle River headwaters area. While no mines have been proposed yet, this could be a concern for the river in the future.

To learn more about the Kettle River and download a map for navigation, visit www.dnr.state.mn.us/watertrails/kettleriver. Two outfitters in the area offer gear rental and shuttling services.

Hard Water Sports, located at 511 Main Street, Sandstone Minnesota 55072, offers guided whitewater rafting trips on the Kettle River, as well as canoe, kayak, and camping gear rental. The company also serves the Snake and St. Louis Rivers: http://hard watersports.com or 651-302-1774.

Swiftwater Adventures, located at 22 East Riverside Road, Esko, Minnesota 55733, offers guided wilderness and whitewater rafting trips on the Kettle River from May through June. The company also serves the Cloquet and St. Louis Rivers: www.swiftwater mn.com or 218-451-3218.

⑦ Totogatic River: Cable to Namekagon River, Wisconsin

An eighty-mile tributary of the Namekagon with excellent water quality and beautiful scenery

Advanced

The first challenge you'll encounter when exploring the Totogatic River is figuring out how to pronounce its name. There are two official spellings for the river, Totogatic and Totagatic, and six different pronunciations, depending on who you talk to and what town you're in. "At one point in time, the U.S. Postal Service actually wrote to four different cities along the river to inquire as to its official spelling," laughs Kathy Bartilson, the former supervisor of

Autumn rapids on the river. Photograph by Kathy Bartilson.

the DNR water quality program in northwestern Wisconsin. "All of the post offices said they spell it Totogatic with an o, but in the official federal river designation, it is still spelled with an a."

The second challenge will be figuring out how to explore this wilderness treasure. "This is a wild river to be paddled carefully," Bartilson cautions. "There are four dams along the way and water levels are unpredictable and flashy. Furthermore, there are only a few established landings, with no bathrooms or easy parking."

Nonetheless, the Totogatic River is a wild and beautiful river with numerous gifts to offer.

The name Totogatic comes from an Ojibwe word meaning "boggy river" or "place of floating bogs." It is one of the few remaining wilderness streams in Wisconsin and was designated as a Wild River in 2009. This designation permanently protects the Totogatic from development and new impoundments in the future and also prohibits landowners along the river from cutting trees and removing vegetation.

The river originates in Totagatic Lake in Bayfield County and flows seventy miles through mostly forested land until it reaches

LIVING DINOSAURS
ROAM THE RIVERWAYS

Sturgeon are sometimes referred to as living dinosaurs because they have lived in the Great Lakes region for an estimated 136 million years. In fact, the name "Namekagon" is actually derived from the Ojibwe word *Namekaagong-ziibi*, which means "river at the place abundant with sturgeons."

Though full-grown lake sturgeon can be eight feet long and three hundred pounds, they are gentle giants with soft mouths and whiskered snouts. Environmental historian Nancy Langston describes them as "little Dyson vacuum cleaners that have evolved to suck up crustaceans and mollusks and crabs." In addition to being huge, sturgeon also live very long lives. A typical male lives to be fifty-five years old, while females can live eighty to 150 years.

When white settlers first arrived in Minnesota and Wisconsin, sturgeon were so abundant that they tangled fishing nets and toppled boats. In less than one hundred years, however, these settlers had almost driven the sturgeon to extinction by overfishing. They sold sturgeon eggs as caviar and piled their bodies along shorelines to dry, before stacking them like cordwood and burning them to fuel steam ships.

By 1920, the St. Croix, Namekagon, and Kettle Rivers were three of the only remaining rivers in Minnesota and Wisconsin where sturgeon still survived.

Eventually, the commercial sturgeon fishing craze came to an end and new harvest rules were enacted, but sturgeon still struggled to rebound within riverways due to newly constructed dams. Even today, a dam built on the Namekagon River near Trego in 1927 blocks upstream travel for fish and prevents them from breeding and spawning.

In the 1990s, state and tribal partners in Minnesota and Wisconsin began monitoring sturgeon populations and working to improve their habitat. After a decade of tracking, fisheries managers with the Minnesota DNR estimated that there were around 350 sturgeon living in the Kettle River, the majority of which are year-round residents. This is unique, because most sturgeon spend most of their lives in lakes and only return to rivers to spawn.

The Minnesota DNR also led research on sturgeon tracking in the Mississippi, St. Croix, and Chippewa Rivers. After implanting forty-seven fish with transmitters between 2013 and 2017, fisheries staff observed that the sturgeon swim freely between the three rivers and travel distances of fifty to one hundred miles. An estimated five thousand sturgeon live in the Lower St. Croix River now.

In the Namekagon River, the Wisconsin DNR stocks fingerling sturgeon each year, and you can find these giant fish throughout the river below the Trego dam. Most recently, Wisconsin DNR staff have also found several sturgeon upstream of the dam and in the Trego Flowage.

Sturgeon spawning in the wild. Photograph by James Pintar/Adobe Stock.

Today, the future of sturgeon in the St. Croix River Watershed appears bright. Within the Kettle River subwatershed, dams were removed from the Kettle in 1995 (Sandstone) and the Willow in 2021. A third dam, located on the Grindstone River in Hinckley, may also be removed in the future.

Sturgeon fishing is prohibited in the Kettle and Namekagon Rivers but is allowed, with strict regulations, in the St. Croix River. In the Upper St. Croix, sturgeon fishing is catch-and-release only, year-round. In the Lower St. Croix, anglers can harvest one fish per calendar year during a designated time in the fall. A special tag from the Minnesota or Wisconsin DNR is required.

As for records, the largest sturgeon caught in Minnesota since the DNR began keeping track was seventy-eight inches long and weighed 120 pounds. It was caught by Darren Troseth and John Kimble in the St. Croix River near Bayport on February 9, 2019. In Wisconsin, John J. Procai caught a record-sized sturgeon in Yellow Lake, Burnett County, on September 22, 1979. The fish was seventy-nine inches long and weighed 170.5 pounds. Yellow Lake is connected to the St. Croix River by a short tributary called the Yellow River. Both of these record-sized fish were released back to the water and may still be swimming somewhere in the St. Croix River Watershed today. ◊

the Namekagon River, just upstream from the Namekagon Bar-rens. During its journey, the river passes through Nelson Lake (Sawyer County), the Totogatic Wildlife Area and Colton Flowage (Washburn County), and the Minong Flowage (Douglas County). The free-flowing reaches of the Totogatic River are designated as "wild," while these four flowages are excluded.

"I feel like we're really lucky to be living so close to the Holy Trinity of rivers—St. Croix, Namekagon, and Totogatic," says Bartilson. In addition to spending many years of her professional career working to protect the Totogatic, she has also explored al-most every mile of the river and its surrounding landscape.

The Totogatic River is home to more than twenty-three species of greatest conservation need, including numerous rare and en-dangered mussel species. The forest along the river in Washburn County is designated as a "quiet woods," and is a wonderful place to hike and enjoy nature without auditory intrusions from cars or ma-chinery. There are also numerous special places along the river—wild rice and waterfowl at Totagatic Lake, alternating sections of wide water and narrow canyons, and a wide and slow-moving swamp at the end of the river.

According to Bartilson people refer to this locally as "The Great Dismal Swamp." When she testified before the Wisconsin House in favor of giving the Totogatic a Wild River designation she disagreed. "I can call it great. I can call it a swamp, but I can't call it dismal because it's really quite beautiful."

If you're interested in paddling a portion of the Totogatic River by canoe or kayak, Bartilson recommends starting at the Minong Flowage, which is located roughly five miles north of Wisconsin Highway 77 and six miles east of U.S. Highway 53, and then float-ing southwest to the Namekagon. It is more easily navigable than upper portions of the river but can still be a challenge due to the current and riffles, as well as numerous obstacles.

Over the years, the state and several counties have purchased numerous parcels of land along the Totogatic River to protect them from erosion and logging. One example is a 259-acre parcel in Washburn County in the Town of Chicog that was placed into permanent land protection in 2015. The land has 2.5 acres of river frontage and is now managed by the Wisconsin DNR.

Toward the end of her career at the DNR, Bartilson received a photograph in the mail from a man who had visited the Totogatic

River in 1960. When he asked if the river still looked the same, she responded by sharing a photograph of her and her son standing on the same rock in the same stretch of river. "He told me that it took his breath away to know that he could go back to that same rock if he wanted to and see that nothing had changed."

To learn about the Totogatic River, visit https://dnr.wisconsin. gov/topic/lands/totogatic. If you can find a copy, the book *Canoeing the Wild Rivers of Northwest Wisconsin* offers detailed trip reports and maps for the Brule, Eau Claire, Totogatic, Clam, Namekagon, St. Croix, and Yellow Rivers.

Wetlands

If you take more than three steps to the left or the right while you're touring in the St. Croix River Watershed, you'll likely end up in a wetland. Wetlands exist along the edges of lakes, rivers, and streams, as well as in low-lying areas where rain and melting snow gather. Some wetlands hold water throughout the year, while others, called ephemeral wetlands, are only wet in the spring or after large rainstorms.

A lily-covered wetland near Hayward, Wisconsin

STEWARDSHIP STORY

Lending a Helping Hand to Afton's Trout Brook

A coldwater stream flows through the hills of Afton Alps and Afton State Park, bringing life to a valley in the woods. Over the past 150 years, Trout Brook has weathered the rise and fall of logging in the region, decades of farming, and several human-made alterations designed to make way for parking lots, roads, buildings, and ski slopes. In recent years, South Washington Watershed District has worked with Great River Greening, Vail Resorts (Afton Alps), and Minnesota DNR to complete a large-scale restoration project designed to return tiny Trout Brook to good health.

The landscape in Afton and Denmark Township features deeply carved valleys amid steep, wooded hills. The same hills that make Afton Alps a great place to ski also create unique habitats. Groundwater flows out of the bedrock and into Trout Brook year-round, and the stream helps to sustain native brook trout, turtles and frogs, migratory birds, and even fox and badgers. After passing through Afton Alps, Trout Brook flows through Afton State Park to the St. Croix River.

When European American settlers first mapped the area in 1848, the Trout Brook stream corridor was entirely forested, with prairie found only near the headwaters (located just east of Manning Avenue today). Over the next one hundred years, however, settlers from Germany and Sweden converted much of the landscape to farm fields. Eventually, in 1960, three local farm families combined three hundred acres of land to create Afton Alps. Construction began in 1960 and the ski hill opened on December 21, 1963, with thirty-seven guests in attendance. Five years later, the state purchased adjoining land, which eventually became Afton State Park. Today, the park includes 1,702 acres of land along the river with trails and hike-in camping.

Over the years, government and nonprofit partners have worked to restore habitat and reduce runoff pollution within the St. Croix River corridor and along its tributaries. As part of a larger study conducted in 2013, Washington Conservation District identified several potential projects to improve water quality in both the St. Croix River and Trout Brook, including within Afton Alps and Afton State Park.

The stream was rerouted from an artificial channel back to its natural, meandering course, and several additional features were added to improve habitat and reduce erosion. The wiggles in the stream create different types of habitat that fish need: deep pools with slow-moving water; shallow riffles with fast, turbulent water running over rocks; and

Charlie wades in Trout Brook, just downstream from Afton Alps.

runs with deep, fast water and little or no turbulence. Wood logs help to anchor the stream bank and reduce erosion. Project partners also re-created the natural floodplain so that sediment settles out along the banks of the stream instead of in the center. As a result, fertile soil carried by floodwater can nourish plants along the water's edge instead of burying fish spawning areas.

"When the DNR first conducted a fish survey on Trout Brook in the early 1990s, they only found a few trout," explains Mark Nemeth, a trout habitat specialist with the Minnesota DNR. Now, says Nemeth, you can find anywhere from 150 to 1,100 fish per mile in Trout Brook, depending on where you sample.

In addition to supporting trout, stream restoration efforts have also created better habitat for smaller fish, including sculpin, white suckers, creek chubs, brook sticklebacks, and pearl dace, and biological surveys show a healthy array of aquatic invertebrates in the stream—larval insects such as mayflies, dragonflies, caddisflies, stoneflies, and craneflies.

Funding support for the Trout Brook restoration work has come from the Minnesota Clean Water Fund, Lessard-Sams Outdoor Heritage Council, Lower St. Croix Watershed Partnership, and South Washington Watershed District. ◇

Wetlands provide critical services to humans and wildlife. Along the edges of rivers, streams, and lakes, they provide flood protection and reduce shoreline erosion. Some wetlands collect surface water from rain and melting snow and allow it to soak into the ground, replenishing groundwater supplies. Others bring cool, clean groundwater to the surface of the land, creating unique habitats for plants and animals.

Approximately 43 percent of threatened and endangered plant and animal species in the United States live in or depend on wetlands. Wetlands provide habitat for spawning fish, migrating waterfowl, breeding frogs and turtles, and insects such as dragonflies. Some of the species of concern found in St. Croix wetlands include plants, such as fernleaf false foxglove, kittentails, creeping juniper, and American ginseng; and animals such as red-shouldered hawks, Blanding's turtles, eastern hognose snakes, American brook lampreys, milk snakes, and Louisiana waterthrush. Though Minnesota and Wisconsin have lost roughly half of their original wetland acreage since European settlement, there are still many places to find and explore unique wetlands in this region.

Wetland Types

Six main categories of wetlands are in the St. Croix River Watershed: bogs, shallow and deep marshes, shallow open water, shrub and wooded swamps, seasonal basins, and wet meadows.

BOGS

Bogs are common in the northern St. Croix River Watershed. These quaking forests grow in soggy, acidic, and nutrient-poor soils, where layers of peat accumulate over time to form a giant sponge-like surface. Tamarack trees are often found growing in bogs. These beautiful conifers feature needles that turn gold and drop in the fall like a deciduous tree. Tamaracks can live to be more than three hundred years old. Bogs are also home to sphagnum moss and carnivorous plants such as pitcher plants and sundews.

SHALLOW AND DEEP MARSHES

A familiar wetland type to most people, marshes are most easily identified by their cattails, which appear rather like corndogs

Boardwalk across a bog in northern Washington County at the now-closed Warner Nature Center.

Charlie and Molly wade in a rainy marsh at Standing Cedars Community Land Conservancy.

on six-foot-tall stems. Other plants common in marshes include bulrush, spikerush, arrowhead, pickerelweed, and smartweed. Deep marshes are often found along the edges of lakes and rivers and may contain wild rice, as well as pondweed, naiad, coontail, watermilfoil, waterweed, duckweed, water lily, and spatterdock. Marshes are bird magnets and are usually filled with the songs of red-winged blackbirds, ducks, and sometimes even sora.

SHALLOW OPEN WATER

Smaller than a lake but wetter than a marsh, these wetlands are three to eight feet deep and are often managed as shallow lakes or ponds. Though they don't usually support large populations of fish, they provide great habitat for frogs, turtles, muskrats, beavers, and birds.

SHRUB AND WOODED SWAMPS

These are found along the edges of lakes, rivers, and streams. Shrub swamps are usually filled with alder, willow, and dogwood.

Grandfather and grandson look for frogs in the shallow water along the edge of Long Lake in Stillwater, Minnesota.

Marsh marigold and skunk cabbage in spring at Standing Cedars Community Land Conservancy

A seasonal wetland at Willow River State Park

Wooded swamps tend to feature tamarack, northern white cedar, black spruce, balsam fir, balsam poplar, red maple, and black ash.

SEASONAL BASINS

Some wetlands are only wet for portions of the year, after heavy rains or when the snow melts in the spring. These seasonal, or ephemeral, wetlands provide critical habitat for insects and amphibians whose eggs might otherwise provide a tasty meal for fish. Numerous species of dragonflies, frogs, and salamanders have adapted their life cycles to make use of seasonal wetlands; by the time the water dries up in the summer, these amphibious creatures have already gone through metamorphosis and are able to live on land.

WET MEADOWS

Another common wetland type within the St. Croix River Watershed are wet meadows. In these places, the soil is wet throughout the year, but there is no standing water. Wet meadows often form a transition zone between open water and dry upland areas. The plants that grow in these locations include grasses, sedges, and flowers such as spotted Joe-Pye weed and white turtlehead.

Ironweed blooms in the wetland at William O'Brien State Park.

500 FROGS A CROAKING

April 6, 2020

On the third week of coronavirus my true love gave to me, five hundred frogs a croaking, four (dozen) calling birds, three rich fens, two mourning doves, and a partridge in the Great Plains.

It is Saturday, which means two days of rest, away from video conferences, working remotely, homeschooling, and tending home. So, we run away and hide in the Wisconsin woods. Though the sun is shining, the thermometer has barely cracked 30 degrees. To improvise a scarf, my son heads back to the car, grabs a spare pair of pants, and wraps them around his neck.

We've got our bag packed with all of the essentials: water, trail mix, peanut butter crackers, and tissues. For entertainment, I also brought a camera, binoculars, two nature journals, and a box of colored pencils. We have nowhere in particular to go, nothing to do, and no intention of returning home before the sun begins to set.

The farther we walk, the easier it is to imagine that the modern world never actually existed. There are no roads, no cars, no phones, and no computers. Instead of planes overhead, we hear the warbled cries of sandhill cranes in flight. We find an old wooden pole growing out of the base of a tree like an extra trunk. Was there a house here long ago? Address number 760 on a long-forgotten road? The skunk cabbage down

A wood frog hides in duckweed.

near the river smells fabulously putrid. Up on the ridge, five hundred frogs a croaking are singing as if this is the very first day that has ever been created.

Approximately half of all frog species and one-third of all salamander species in North America lay their eggs in ephemeral wetlands, which usually exist only in the spring or after heavy rains. The upper Midwest is dotted with prairie potholes that formed when glaciers retreated thousands of years ago, leaving behind a pockmarked landscape with low areas that collect water from rain and melting snow. These areas also provide habitat for migrating birds and insects such as dragonflies.

As we stand beside one such wetland, we can hear at least three different kinds of frogs. The wood frogs sound like an army of angry ducks. Their squawks intensify every time my son approaches the edge of the water. In the midst of the commotion, we can also hear high-pitched spring peepers and raspy ribbitting chorus frogs. My son pokes the water with a cattail frond and finds gelatinous blobs filled with thousands of eggs. More frogs will soon appear.

Here at Standing Cedars Community Land Conservancy, the frogs have hopped happily for hundreds of years. Out in the rest of the world, it's not always easy being green. Amphibians are vulnerable to pollution from fertilizers and pesticides because they have porous skin that can absorb chemicals in water. These chemicals are especially deadly in

A baby American toad fits on the tip of my finger.

the spring and early summer when frogs are laying eggs and tadpoles are hatching. Like other wildlife, frogs also battle the relentless spread of agriculture and development.

If you live near a lake or wetland, you can help to create healthier habitat for frogs by leaving an unmowed buffer of vegetation around the edges of soggy woods and seasonal wetlands. Limit the amount of chemicals you use on your lawn and gardens, and consider planting native plants along the water's edge. Good plants for lake and wetland edges include sedges, blue flag iris, swamp milkweed, joe-pye weed, cardinal flower, black-eyed Susans, and ferns. It's also nice to leave a few fallen trees and logs in the water to provide shelter for the frogs, as well as a place to bask in the sun.

By late afternoon, the sun is high in the sky and its rays are luxuriously warm. I lay my pack on the ground and my body on the warm, yellow prairie. The dog and child are happily chasing frogs and teasing cattails. I close my eyes and steal just a few more minutes of this peaceful wild. ◊

A *green frog rests in the shallow water of a sandbar in the St. Croix River.*

A *gray tree frog attempts to camouflage with the trees.*

Five Places to Explore Wetlands in the St. Croix River Watershed

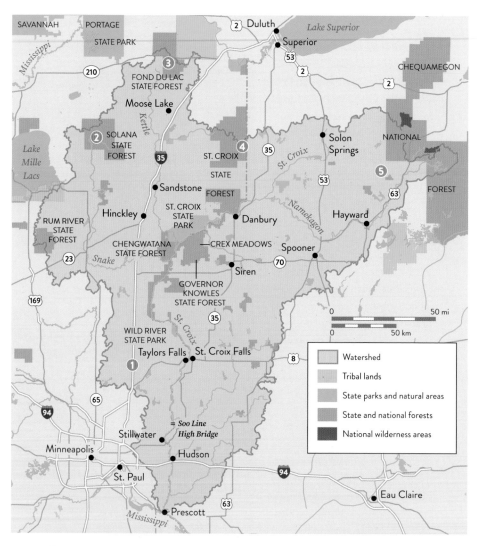

① Carlos Avery Wildlife Management Area, Anoka and Chisago Counties, Minnesota

② Solana State Forest, Minnesota

③ Fond Du Lac State Forest, Minnesota

④ Black Lake Bog—Pine County, Minnesota, and Douglas County, Wisconsin

⑤ Totagatic Lake Wildlife Area, Cable, Wisconsin

Fluffy white clouds decorate the sky above one of the many marshes at Carlos Avery Wildlife Management Area in Minnesota.

① Carlos Avery Wildlife Management Area, Anoka and Chisago Counties, Minnesota

Excellent bird-watching and a popular location for hunting and fishing

Intermediate

On the border of Anoka and Chisago Counties in Minnesota, Carlos Avery Wildlife Management Area (WMA) has twenty-four thousand acres of protected land, about two-thirds of which are marshes and shallow ponds. You can also find sedge meadows and wooded swamps in the WMA.

The Main Unit of the Carlos Avery WMA is 17,400 acres, located west of Interstate 35 near Columbus and Wyoming. The 7,000-acre Sunrise Unit is located east of Interstate 35 in Chisago County near Stacy.

A network of dirt and gravel roads runs through the refuge, which is perfect for a scenic drive or touring on a gravel bike. Visitors can park on the side of the road anywhere within the WMA or at one of the numerous designated pull-off parking spots. The South Road in the southwest section of the WMA is closed to motor vehicles from March 1 through August 31 every year.

A rainbow in the forest over ferns

Carlos Avery WMA is located within the Anoka Sand Plain, a unique ecological region 1,960 square miles in size that has thousands of shallow wetlands, miles of rivers and streams, and the largest concentration of oak savanna in the Midwest. The lands here once lay at the bottom of a glacial lake, and they remain flat and sandy today, with a shallow water table that feeds numerous wetlands, shallow lakes, and connected streams.

When my son and I visited Carlos Avery WMA on a sunny August day, we were both beguiled by the maple and birch forest sprinkled throughout the refuge. At one location, we pulled over to wander into the woods and found a lush carpet of ferns,

Pennsylvania sedge, and large leaf aster. That day, the sun streamed down through the leafy canopy, imbuing the forest with a sense of magic.

We crept through the woods on our hands and knees, searching beneath mushrooms for toads and hiding fairies. We tried continuing onward into a nearby marsh that was fringed by arrowhead and water lily but had to turn back when the mud threatened to swallow us whole.

Carlos Avery is a popular location for hunting, fishing, and bird-watching. Waterfowl and deer hunting seasons are open September through December, with turkey hunt-

Fly agaric mushroom on the forest floor

ing in October. Be sure to wear blaze orange or pink if you visit the WMA during these months. People also visit the WMA to hunt for squirrels, woodcock, pheasant, ruffed grouse, rabbits, and black bear during their designated hunting seasons. Hunting licenses from the Minnesota DNR are required.

Fishing is most popular near the dams in the Sunrise Unit. There are boat launches on North Sunrise Pool and South Sunrise Pool. There are also three carry-in canoe access sites in the Sunrise Unit and one carry-in access site at Pool 8 in the Main Unit.

The WMA is also an Audubon Important Bird Area and an eBird Hotspot. More than 270 species of birds have been recorded in the area, including black terns, American bitterns, trumpeter swans, northern harriers, sandhill cranes, rough-legged hawks, and northern shrikes.

Three State Wildlife Sanctuaries within the WMA, totaling 4,600 acres, are closed to the public. The WMA headquarters is located at 5463 West Broadway Avenue (County Road 18), Forest Lake. It is 6.5 miles west of Interstate 35.

Sun streams through the trees at Shire in the Woods, which offers cabin rentals and nature retreats in Solana State Forest. Photograph by Michael Bonnette.

➋ Solana State Forest, Minnesota

Forested wetlands and ATV trails

Advanced

In the remote and undeveloped northwestern portion of the St. Croix River Watershed, Solana State Forest and Fond Du Lac State Forest in Minnesota are two locations where you can explore forested wetlands.

Solana State Forest is located in the southeastern corner of Aitkin County and contains the headwaters of the Snake River. Slightly over half of the area within the forest is wetland. The two best ways to explore here are by ATV along the Soo Line or Solana Loop Trails or by canoe or kayak on the Snake River Water Trail.

White Pine Township, located within Solana State Forest, was a bustling lumber community in the late 1800s and early 1900s until a fire destroyed the James McGrath sawmill in 1925. In the wake of the fire, McGrath sold 3,400 acres of his land to the State of Minnesota. During the following decade, a group of World War I veterans and their families lived on and attempted to farm the land here. Soon the settlers moved on and White Pine became a ghost town.

The Soo Line railroad removed its tracks from the burned-down mill and closed down the nearby train stations. In 1989, the railroad sold its entire 130-mile corridor from Genola to Duluth to state and local government, and the tracks were removed to create the Soo Line Trail. The Solana Loop Trail offers a scenic fifteen-mile detour off the main trail through the State Forest.

Today, the Solana State Forest includes 68,141 acres of forested wetlands with black spruce, tamarack, and white cedar in the wet, lowland areas; maple, oak, ash, and basswood grow in the drier upland sections. The forest is home to deer, black bear, ruffed grouse, wild turkey, woodcocks, gray wolves, bobcats, beavers, fishers, snowshoe hares, otters, minks, muskrats, trumpeter swans, and eagles.

There are no campgrounds in the Solana State Forest, but dispersed camping is permitted. If you are not a resident of Minnesota, you'll need a nonresident trail pass to operate an all-terrain vehicle (ATV), off-highway motorcycle (OHM), or off-road vehicle (ORV) on the trails. Visit the Minnesota DNR website to find maps and information about Solana State Forest: www.dnr.state.mn.us/state_forests.

If you'd like to visit the Solana State Forest but aren't up for an unsupported wilderness camping experience, Shire in the Woods offers cabin rentals and nature retreats. The 120-acre property includes five miles of groomed trails for biking, hiking, snowshoeing, and cross-country skiing, and there is also a screened-in gazebo, wood-burning sauna, rose garden, labyrinth, beaver pond, frog and turtle pond, tree swings and hammock, and outdoor fire pit. Shire in the Woods is located at 14044 220th Street, McGrath, Minnesota 56350. More information can be found at https://shireinthewoods.com.

Forest and wetlands in the remote Fond Du Lac State Forest, Minnesota

③ Fond Du Lac State Forest, Minnesota

*Alder-willow brushlands and peat bogs
with shallow wild rice lakes*

Advanced

Located on the border of Carlton and St. Louis Counties, Fond Du Lac State Forest covers 64,505 acres of land, including the Kettle Lake Wildlife Management Area. There is a large network of ATV trails here, as well as trails for hiking and cross-country skiing. There is also carry-in canoe access to Kettle Lake. The property borders on the Fond Du Lac Indian Reservation and contains the headwaters of the Kettle River.

Though it is remote and appears untouched, the land within the Fond Du Lac State Forest has changed dramatically since European colonization. Between 1916 and 1920, settlers dug a ditch system to drain the wetlands and cleared about one-third of the forest so that people could build houses and farm the land. In 1918, a large portion of the land burned during the Great Cloquet Fire, and settlers continued to clear the land with periodic fires until the 1930s. After less than a decade, the majority of settlers abandoned their holdings and the tax-delinquent land was transferred to the counties. Today, the Minnesota DNR manages 70 percent of

DISPERSED CAMPING

If you're accustomed to camping at state and national parks or even places like the Boundary Waters Canoe Area Wilderness, dispersed camping might be a foreign concept. The Minnesota DNR describes dispersed camping as "a wilderness experience for campers who enjoy camping far from others and do not need any amenities." The key here is that dispersed camping happens in locations where there is no designated campground. As such, there are also no bathrooms, pit toilets, water pumps, fire grates, trash cans, or picnic tables.

Dispersed camping is allowed in most state and national forests within Minnesota and Wisconsin and is also permitted in many county forests and federal wilderness areas. The rules vary from one site to the next but tend to have the same basic guidelines in common. In Minnesota State Forests, you must be at least one mile outside a designated campground and cannot camp at parking lots or trailheads. Campers should also be at least one hundred feet away from lakes, rivers, and streams. You may not camp in the same location longer than fourteen days in the summer or twenty-one days in the fall, winter, and spring.

When participating in dispersed camping, it is also important to practice Leave No Trace principles. Look for an open area, such as a natural clearing, meadow, or recently logged land, and avoid cutting trees or disturbing vegetation when you set up your campsite. For campfires, only collect dead wood that is lying on the ground. Bury human waste and carry out all trash. The biggest benefit to dispersed camping is that it is free and requires no reservations. Simply show up in the forest with supplies and a sense of adventure, and you'll be ready to camp. ◊

the Fond Du Lac State Forest, with the rest under county, corporate, and private ownership.

There are no campgrounds in the Fond Du Lake State Forest, but dispersed camping is permitted. If you are not a resident of Minnesota, you'll need a nonresident trail pass to operate an all-terrain vehicle (ATV), off-highway motorcycle (OHM), or off-road vehicle (ORV) on the trails. Visit the Minnesota DNR website to find maps and information about Fond Du Lac State Forest: www.dnr.state.mn.us/state_forests.

Tamarack and black spruce at Black Lake Bog Scientific and Natural Area. Minnesota DNR. Photograph by Kelly Randall.

④ Black Lake Bog—Pine County, Minnesota, and Douglas County, Wisconsin

Deep wilderness with rare plants and animals—extremely inaccessible

Super Advanced

Black Lake Bog is comprised of 1,414 acres in the Nemadji State Forest of Pine County, Minnesota, and 2,009 acres in Douglas County, Wisconsin. It contains large swaths of high-quality bog and fen wetlands and is home to rare plants, as well as timber wolves, moose, pine marten, lynx, yellow-bellied flycatchers, and the ground-nesting short-eared owl.

As amazing as this location is, it is almost completely inaccessible to humans. On the Minnesota side of the Black Lake Bog, the only access is from the Gandy Dancer State Trail. The trail is remote and there is virtually no cell signal available. It is fifteen miles between the two nearest road crossings on the north and south end of Nemadji State Forest. On the Wisconsin side of Black Lake Bog, there are no roads or trails at all.

If you're intimidated by the thought of a deep-wilderness experience in the Black Lake Bog (and you should be!), there is a smaller and much more accessible bog in Woodbury, Minnesota, just outside the eastern edge of the St. Croix River Watershed.

TIPTOEING THROUGH THE TAMARACK NATURE PRESERVE

Beginner

You might not expect to find an ecological wonder in the middle of Woodbury, but Tamarack Nature Preserve is not only the southernmost tamarack wetland in Minnesota, but is also both a rich fen and a poor bog. Hydrologically, it is located just outside the St. Croix River Watershed, in an area that eventually drains to the Mississippi River.

Unlike other conifers, tamarack trees change color and lose their needles in the fall.

The Tamarack Nature Preserve (TNP) is a 169-acre city park in Woodbury with soft trails winding through woods and a unique boardwalk over the wetland. In 2019, the city upgraded the boardwalk to allow for better safety and Adopt-A-Park volunteers helped to create a new map and wayfinding signs, as well as numerous other tools to better connect visitors with the site.

Recently, Tamarack Nature Preserve was featured in *Natural History Magazine* in an article by Robert Mohlenbrock, professor emeritus of plant biology at Southern Illinois University. Upon touring TNP, Mohlenbrock was surprised to find that the wetland has characteristics of both a fen and a bog. He writes, "A bog is acidic and receives its water from rain that usually falls into depressions. Bogs are nutrient-poor for plant growth. Fens, on the other hand, receive their water from the ground where water flows over calcareous material, such as limestone or dolomite. Fens are rich in nutrients, such as calcium and magnesium, and are alkaline. In the Tamarack Nature Preserve, both bog species and fen species intermingle with each other."

Some of the plants characteristic of bogs that can be found in TNP include poison sumac, bog willow, winterberry, and tamarack trees.

Boardwalk in fall at Tamarack Nature Preserve in Woodbury, Minnesota

As the name implies, poison sumac contains the same oils present in poison ivy and oak and can cause a severe allergic reaction if touched. Its leaves are quite different from those of the common staghorn sumac, and the plants have white berries instead of red.

During his visit, Mohlenbrock also found numerous plants that are usually found only in nutrient-rich, alkaline fens. Some of these include Riddell's goldenrod, bulblet-bearing water hemlock, white turtlehead, spotted Joe-pye weed, Kalm's lobelia, and American black currant.

Unlike most wetlands in the area, the plants and trees at Tamarack Nature Preserve grow out of layers of peat that

Wild calla in the tamarack bog

float on top of groundwater, creating a quaking forest that is impossible to walk across (hence the need for a floating boardwalk). Peat forms when plants and trees in waterlogged areas die and only partially decompose, leaving layers of rich material that build up and compact over time.

Over the past two decades, the Ramsey–Washington Metro Watershed District has worked with the city and volunteers to implement numerous projects in and around Tamarack Nature Preserve to protect this unique habitat from invasive species and water pollution. Examples include a pond-like treatment system at the edge of the park that captures sediment and pollutants from road runoff, as well as rain gardens and vegetated swales in neighborhoods surrounding the preserve.

Tamarack Nature Preserve is free and open to the public year-round. The park is located north of Valley Creek Road, off Tower Drive. To learn more about Tamarack Nature Preserve, go to https://www.tamarack naturepreserve.org. ◇

⑤ Totagatic Lake Wildlife Area, Cable, Wisconsin

One of the most productive wild rice lakes in northern Wisconsin

Intermediate

Located in the northeastern portion of the St. Croix River Watershed, Totagatic Lake Wildlife Area in Bayfield County, Wisconsin, is an excellent place to find shallow open water and marsh wetlands. The 1,400-acre property is one of the most productive wild rice lakes in northern Wisconsin and is also a popular destination for waterfowl hunting. Wild rice production and harvesting are monitored closely by the Great Lakes Indian Fish and Wildlife Commission.

To get there, take U.S. Highway 63 south from Cable approximately 2.5 miles to Leonard School Road. Go west on Leonard School Road to a T-intersection with Cable Sunset Road. Go south on Cable Sunset Road and continue following it south, then west. It will turn into Totagatic Lake Road, which ends at the boat landing of Totagatic Lake and at the Wildlife Area.

Wild rice at Totagatic Lake. Photograph by Kathy Bartilson.

WHERE FOOD GROWS ON WATER

September 17, 2022

It's 7 a.m. on a Saturday in September and the fog is thick. I'm driving down the road in the middle of absolute nowhere, dodging massive flocks of wild turkeys that race across the road and swarm open fields around every bend. At one point, I stop my car to watch the largest herd of white-tailed deer I've ever seen leap and prance across the road, fawns skittering along beside their mothers on slender legs.

I'm in northern Minnesota near the Mississippi River, driving to meet a group of Water Protectors and Anishinaabe (Ojibwe) people for a day of harvesting wild rice. My friend Giiwedin, whom I met through TikTok, invited me a week ago and I jumped at the opportunity. He is an enrolled member of the St. Croix Chippewa Indians of Wisconsin but grew up on the Leech Lake Reservation in Minnesota. Later in the day, we'll drive south to the Moose Horn and Kettle Rivers, in the St. Croix River Watershed, to harvest and process the rice.

In the world of watershed protection and restoration, we like to remind people that water ignores jurisdictional boundaries. Though rivers are often used to mark boundaries between counties, states, and countries, their tributaries stretch out like capillaries across the land. The heart and lungs power the same body. So, too, do the lakes, wetlands, rivers, and streams within a watershed.

Giiwedin and his friend canoe across the Moose Horn River.

In a similar way, people and animals cross boundaries as well, migrating across cities, watersheds, and even continents. I arrive at the Welcome Water Protectors camp and join a circle that includes Indigenous people from tribes in Minnesota and Wisconsin, as well as visitors from as far away as Borneo, South Africa, and Senegal.

The Water Protectors are working to protect lakes, rivers, and drinking water from contamination caused by mining, oil pipelines, and other threats. "We are coming together, all colors, just as the creator predicted, to protect the water," says Charlotte, an Anishinaabe woman from Michigan.

We begin by smudging sage and offering tobacco to the fire to cleanse our minds and offer thanks and prayers to Mother Earth. "Hundreds of years ago, our people lived on the east coast," explains Charlotte. "Then a prophet had a vision that we should move west to the place where food grows on water. Now, Anishinaabe live throughout the Great Lakes region in Michigan, Wisconsin, Minnesota, and Canada."

Wild rice, known as *manoomin* in the Anishinaabe language, is actually a grass that grows in marshlands along the edges of rivers, lakes, and streams. At one time, it grew throughout Minnesota and Wisconsin, including in the Twin Cities and Milwaukee. Today, 30 percent of the historical rice beds have been lost due to shoreline development, dredging, and the construction of dams and weirs that artificially control water levels.

A painted sign at the Welcome Water Protectors camp in northern Minnesota

Even so, wild rice grows in lakes, rivers, and flowages throughout Minnesota and northern Wisconsin. "Wild rice has sustained us over the generations and protected us from famine," says Carol, an Anishinaabe woman from Wisconsin. "It is so important that we protect the water to preserve the wild rice and the sturgeon. These are gifts from the Creator that keep us alive."

"When we harvest *manoomin*, we are practicing our given rights," emphasizes Tania, who lives on the Leech Lake Reservation in Minnesota. "This right to harvest food was not 'given to us' by white people. It is a fundamental right we have retained as Anishinaabe people."

Within the St. Croix River Watershed, the land known as Minnesota and Wisconsin today was taken by the U.S. government through a series of treaties with Dakota and Ojibwe people in 1837, 1842, and 1854. Through these treaties, the tribes ceded land to the United States in exchange for payments of cash and goods and the creation of permanent reservations. The tribes also retained the right to hunt, fish, and gather food from land and waters within the ceded territories.

Giiwedin and I get ready to go wild ricing on the Moose Horn River in Minnesota.

"Manoomin is the only plant mentioned in any treaties between the United States and Native peoples," my friend Giiwedin explains. "The 1837 treaty guarantees us a right to manoomin forever."

Ready to Harvest

After breakfast and conversation, our group divides into cars and forms a caravan to drive south to Moose Horn River, which flows through the city of Moose Lake, Minnesota. On the way, we pass the Rice Lake National Wildlife Refuge, the Rice River, and a sign marking the boundary of the 1854 ceded territory. In town, there are several restaurants and bait shops, a taproom for Moose Lake Brewing Company, and a gas station advertising wild rice for sale. This is not a day that moves in a hurry. Though our group first gathered at 8 a.m., it is nearly 1 p.m. when we arrive at the river's edge.

Here, new people meet us with canoes, long wooden push poles, and shorter wooden sticks known as "knockers." We'll use the poles to propel ourselves through the wild rice beds and the knockers to gently bop the grass until the seeds fall off into our boats. Surprising to me, they advise us to chew gum and wear eye protection to guard ourselves from the wild rice seeds that tend to get stuck in your mouth, nose, and eyes when you are ricing.

After offering tobacco to say thank you to the river, the women in our group lead us in praying and singing to the water. Then, we break off into groups of threes, climb into canoes, and head down the river to find the rice.

It is important to note that wild rice is as much a part of the living ecosystem as it is food for people to eat. According to the Wisconsin DNR,

Paddlers heads out to collect wild rice.

Birds fly through the wild rice stands.

a stand of wild rice can produce more than five hundred pounds of seed per acre, and these seeds provide a nutrient-rich source of food for migrating waterfowl, including mallards, blue-winged teals, ring-necked ducks, and wood ducks. Wild rice is the most important food for mallards during the fall migration.

Wild rice beds are also filled with aquatic and terrestrial insects, a reality that becomes immediately obvious to us as soon as we're among the grass, with spiders, inchworms, and beetles tumbling into our laps. These insects feed blackbirds, bobolinks, rails, and wrens. The birds lift into the air as we approach in our canoe before settling again a few feet deeper in.

The wild rice that grows in Minnesota and northern Wisconsin—*Zizania palustris*—is an annual plant that grows from seed each year, so it is critical to avoid overharvesting. "Don't worry if some of the rice falls into the water when you're knocking," Giiwedin advises our group before we head out, "because it will seed itself and grow new plants next year."

After an hour or two of harvesting, the amount of wild rice in the bottom of our canoe seems embarrassingly small. We count ourselves lucky, though, when a canoe downriver from us overturns and dumps three people into the water. We paddle over to help them out of the river and then head back to shore to meet up with the larger group. The next step from here will be to bring the seeds to the ricing camp to be cleaned, dried, parched, winnowed, and then stored for the winter ahead.

When the seeds of wild rice are ripe, they turn from green to purple or brown and fall easily when tapped with a knocker.

Wild rice in a pile at the bottom of our canoe

Protecting Wild Rice

Because of its cultural and ecological value, the Water Protectors and others are working to protect wild rice from the impacts of mining, development, logging, and other threats. In Minnesota, the Pollution Control Agency recently worked with the U.S. Environmental Protection Agency (EPA) and tribal nations to update water quality standards for sulfate to better protect wild rice. Proposals to open sulfide-ore mines to extract copper and nickel have sparked vicious public debate and legal battles during the most recent decade.

James Rasmussen, a policy analyst with Great Lakes Indian Fish and Wildlife Commission (GLIFWC), says the tribes are also beginning to research possible impacts of perfluorinated alkylated substances (PFAS) on wild rice. PFAS is a chemical compound that was used to manufacture products such as nonstick pans and Scotchgard in the 1950s and 1960s and has since contaminated groundwater aquifers in Washington County, Minnesota. In 2022, the Minnesota Pollution Control Agency determined that PFAS had made their way to the St. Croix River and can now be found in the tissue of fish that live in the river. Rasmussen worries that the same could happen to wild rice.

Toward the end of my wild rice adventure, I am driving down a muddy dirt road in the Fond Du Lac State Forest, hoping that my Prius won't get stuck. It is early evening when I arrive at the rice camp that the Water Protectors have set up near Kettle Lake. There is a tipi with a warm fire burning inside and the people there teach me how to carve a piece of wood into a wild rice knocker. I have to leave before they begin to process the rice but stay long enough to enjoy a warm cup of potato stew and share a few stories.

A woman named Ashes tells us that her work with Indigenous people and the Water Protectors has made her reevaluate what it means to be a good treaty partner. "Treaties do not grant Indigenous people with special rights," she says. "They acknowledge rights that have always existed. What the treaties do is provide rights to the occupiers who live here now."

I leave for the drive home with a swirl of thoughts and emotions racing through my mind, much like the turkeys in the fields that crossed the road that morning. I feel gratitude for the people I've met and the experience that we shared, but also a sense of responsibility to care for and protect the water from harm.

Wild Rice Harvest: Rules and Regulations

Wild rice harvesting in Minnesota and Wisconsin is strictly regulated. In Minnesota, the wild rice season runs from August 15 to September 30, and people who are not tribal members must purchase permits from the Minnesota DNR. Harvesting is only allowed between 9 a.m. and 3 p.m. and is prohibited in National Parks and National Wildlife Refuges, except when authorized by special permits. It is illegal to harvest with machines or mechanical equipment. To learn more and purchase a permit, go to www.dnr.state.mn.us/regulations/wildrice.

In Wisconsin, only Wisconsin residents are allowed to harvest wild rice, and a permit from the Wisconsin DNR is required. Wisconsin also requires tribal members to get a free permit before harvesting wild rice outside reservation lands. Unlike in Minnesota, there is no designated wild rice season. On some of the lakes regulated by GLIFWC, ricing is only permitted after a notice is posted on-site and online. Date-regulated lakes within the St. Croix River Watershed include Pacwawong Lake in Sawyer County (part of Namekagon River) and all county and state-owned wild rice beds within the Minong Flowage in Douglas County (part of the Totogatic River). Learn more at https://dnr.wisconsin.gov/topic/wildlifehabitat/rice.html.

All wild rice waters within the boundaries of Indian Reservations are managed by the respective tribes. These lakes and rivers are typically only available to tribal members.

Indigenous-led Organizations
Working to Protect Water

Welcome Water Protectors is based in northern Minnesota and organizes to protect water from threats related to mining and oil pipelines: welcomewaterprotectors.com.

Honor the Earth is a nonprofit organization that creates awareness and support for Native environmental issues across the United States and Canada: https://honorearth.org.

Great Lakes Indian Fish and Wildlife Commission (GLIFWC) represents eleven Ojibwe tribes in Minnesota, Wisconsin, and Michigan who reserved hunting, fishing, and gathering rights in the 1836, 1837, 1842, and 1854 treaties with the United States government: https://glifwc.org. ◊

STEWARDSHIP STORY

Restoring Farm Fields to Wetlands in Isanti County
September 2, 2021

We've scrambled over the hills, through the woods, and into a giant field of radish and turnip greens where Isanti County landowner Dave Medvecky is leading us in deeper to view a wetland restoration currently underway. It feels more or less like we're walking through a giant bowl of salad.

Medvecky tells us that the land here was heavily pastured during the drought of the 1930s. Later, when water levels returned to normal, the landowners constructed lateral ditches to drain wetlands on the property and keep it available for farming. Since purchasing the land, he has been working to restore habitat and incorporate sustainable farming practices such as planting cover crops on the areas still in production.

Staff from Isanti Soil and Water Conservation District and the Lower St. Croix Partnership talk with Dave Medvecky, a farmer working to restore wetland on his property.

Wetlands provide critical services to humans and wildlife. Along the edges of rivers, streams, and lakes, they provide flood protection and reduce shoreline erosion. Some wetlands collect surface water from rain and melting snow and allow it to soak into the ground, replenishing groundwater supplies. Others create unique habitats for plants and animals. Despite these many benefits, Minnesota lost nearly half of its wetland acreage to farming and development during late 1800s to mid-1900s.

One goal of the Lower St. Croix Watershed Partnership, a joint effort led by seventeen local government partners in Minnesota, is to restore one thousand acres of wetlands in high priority locations within Anoka, Chisago, Isanti, Pine, and Washington Counties, in order to increase resiliency against flooding and provide natural treatment for water flowing downstream to the St. Croix River. Dave Medvecky's project in Isanti County will restore approximately thirteen acres of wetlands that have been lost to farming for nearly a century.

As we continue walking across his property, Medvecky points out a sedge meadow, which contains many of the native plant species he hopes to see established in the newly restored wetland basins. Before excavating these basins, he worked hard to remove invasive, nonnative reed canary grass, so that the native plants will have room to grow. He also constructed large berms to block ditches on the property so that water will be held back and drain more slowly when it rains. The radishes and turnips are an annual crop, planted to hold the soil in place and prevent erosion until he is able to seed the area with deep-rooted, native plants later this fall.

In addition to restoring large wetlands on his land, Medvecky has also worked with the U.S. Fish and Wildlife Service to create smaller, vernal pools in woodland areas to provide habitat for frogs and salamanders. These shallow wetlands fill with water in the spring and are usually dry by June.

Today, the remaining wetlands in Minnesota are protected by state and federal law. In general, these laws prohibit draining, filling, or otherwise altering wetlands. Landowners are also required to get permits for all projects that impact wetlands, including driveways, culverts, new construction, and home additions. Some cities and watershed districts require landowners to preserve buffers of unmowed vegetation around wetlands to protect wildlife habitat and reduce runoff pollution. ◊

UNIQUE GEOLOGIC FORMATIONS

I USED TO THINK THAT ROCKS WERE BORING, BUT NOW I AM FASCInated by the geologic stories in the rocks, cliffs, rivers, and lakes around our region. Take the St. Croix River as an example. According to Justin Tweet, a paleontologist with the American Geosciences Institute, the river valley was formed by a failed continental rift that almost split the land apart 1.1 billion years ago. In other words, if things had gone differently, there would be more dividing Minnesota and Wisconsin than just a Vikings–Packers rivalry.

When this rift opened, lava flowed up into it and formed the dark, black basalt rocks that can now be found in the Taylors Falls–St. Croix Falls area, as well as at Banning State Park. Later, during the Cambrian and Ordovician periods, 540 to 443 million years ago, the continents were arranged differently, and an ocean covered most of what is now Minnesota and Wisconsin. Over time, the sand at the bottom of this prehistoric ocean compacted to form layers of sedimentary rock called sandstone. The shells, coral, algae, fecal matter, and other organic debris on top of the sand eventually solidified into limestone and is where we find marine fossils today.

Much, much more recently in geologic time, a series of glaciations swept through Minnesota in several waves from two million to fourteen thousand years ago. As the glaciers melted and receded, they created most of the lakes, rivers, and groundwater aquifers that we see in our present landscape. The glacial rivers also

Sandstone layers at Crystal Spring Scientific and Natural Area in Minnesota

carved through sandstone on the earth's surface to create steep bluffs like what we see along the St. Croix River today.

Some of the water from glaciers soaked down into the ground and filled empty pore space in the sandstone layers deep below. This groundwater is continually replenished by rain and melting snow and forms the aquifers that we use for drinking water today. Groundwater aquifers also feed coldwater trout streams; deep, clear lakes; and seepage swamps throughout the St. Croix River Watershed. While rocks form the literal foundation for every inch of the St. Croix River Watershed, a few locations along the river and its tributaries are known for cliffs and unique geologic formations.

Sandstone cliffs at the St. Croix Boom Site north of Stillwater

Four Places to Find Unique Geology in the St. Croix River Watershed

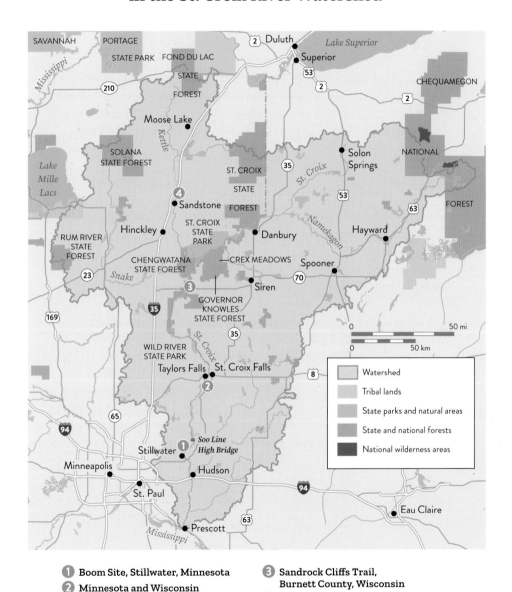

1. Boom Site, Stillwater, Minnesota
2. Minnesota and Wisconsin Interstate State Parks
3. Sandrock Cliffs Trail, Burnett County, Wisconsin
4. Banning State Park, Sandstone, Minnesota

① Boom Site, Stillwater, Minnesota

*Tall sandstone cliffs, groundwater springs,
logging history, and ample graffiti*

Intermediate

The St. Croix Boom Site is located on the Minnesota side of the river, just north of Stillwater, and includes a public boat launch at River Mile 25, as well as a wayside, picnic area, and historical site at River Mile 26. Park at the picnic area and follow a steep staircase down to the river to explore the sandstone cliffs, groundwater springs, and beach below.

My personal favorite technique for getting to the bottom of the stairs in the winter is to sit down on my snow-pant-covered bottom and let gravity be my guide. Three quick seconds later, you'll be down at the beach and ready to explore, as long as you don't die along the way.

Though the geology at the Boom Site is truly amazing, you may be dismayed by the copious amounts of graffiti and litter that you find there. Even so, the Boom Site is still one of my favorite places to visit on the St. Croix River, and I've come to accept and grudgingly appreciate the graffiti as part of the story of this place. It is worth noting that the cliffs here were covered in Native American pictograms when white settlers first arrived in the early 1800s.

When you visit the Boom Site, please carry out your garbage and refrain from adding to the already abundant graffiti. If you approach your visit with a bit of humor and the eye of an art critic, you might better enjoy your experience.

RATING GRAFFITI
AT THE ST. CROIX BOOM SITE

May 2, 2021

The first piece of graffiti artwork that I see looks like a toilet paper roll with a giant eyeball that is wearing a crown. It's a nice use of color, though I'm not really sure what it is. It's very visible, so I rate it 6/10.

A frozen waterfall at the northern boundary of the Boom Site

The second is actually quite sweet. "Your'e my sun, moon and stars," the painter has written, with a flourish of sunshine and a crescent moon against midnight blue paint to illustrate the sentiment. The apostrophe is in the wrong place, so I have to take off a point for that. 5/10.

The third reads simply "[Cat] Power." It's not very artistic, but I am a feminist, so I give it 6/10.

Next, I approach my favorite of the bunch, a whirling dervish carved into the soft sandstone. It must have taken a long time to carve, and it is very pretty, even though I cringe at the assault on this sandstone cliffside built from an ancient ocean. Nonetheless, it's a solid 10/10.

The fifth one is an eyeball. Obviously. It is brightly colored and had decent execution, so I rate it 7/10.

The final artistic creation I visit is not actually graffiti but rather an abandoned handmade outdoor altar that's been built at the base of a silver maple. It comes complete with still burning candles—no people in sight—and a cross made of sticks. I rate this 14/10, for creativity and creepiness factor.

LOGGING ERA HISTORY

During the logging era, from 1856 to 1914, the St. Croix Boom was the primary location where logs from the river were sorted and processed before being sent to lumber mills to become lumber. The first boom site on the river was actually built in 1851 near Osceola. Five years later, Isaac Staples, Martin Mower, and several other investors bought out all but one of the St. Croix Boom Company's previous owners and built a second boom site just north of Stillwater, which immediately became the more successful of the two.

The National Park Service describes the historic boom along the St. Croix River as "a complex series of piers, pilings and floating booms (log fences) that extended for miles of river, creating log channels, navigation channels, sorting gaps, and holding pens for moving and organizing the vast quantities of timber that floated out of the watershed." During the logging era, there was also a settlement above the river for rivermen that worked on the boom.

When the St. Croix Boom closed in 1914, the pilings and crib woods were quickly removed and sold. Within three short years, the river again flowed free and there were virtually no signs left of the industrial logging past.

EXPLORING THE BOOM SITE TODAY

To explore the beach and cliffs along the river, follow the stairs down from the wayside parking lot. At the bottom, you'll find a shady grove with sand and trees. Turn right to find a small human-made cave, which will likely be filled with litter and smoke stains. There is a thin stretch of beach along the base of the cliff that you can follow for quite a distance in either direction.

The sandstone here is the remnant of an ancient sea that once covered the land in this part of the world five hundred million years ago. This sandstone actually underlies the entire St. Croix River Watershed but is usually buried beneath soil and glacial till. Because the sandstone is porous, it holds water from rain and melting snow. At the Boom Site, you can see water from these aquifers seeping out from the base of the cliffs and into the St. Croix River, even in the middle of the winter.

If you visit the Boom Site in winter, it is possible to see small fish and even mudpuppies (a type of salamander) swimming in the open water near these groundwater springs. Be careful walking on the river during the winter, as the ice cover can be unpredictable and unstable. Though the Boom Site is popular, be aware that it is not a particularly accessible location. The only bathroom is a satellite located in the parking area at the top of the bluff, and this is usually removed during the winter. The stairs down to the river are steep and flanked by a decrepit railing, and the unoffi-

Mudpuppies are the only salamanders in the St. Croix River Watershed that are fully aquatic.

cial footpaths along the river's edge are steep and slippery. Take special caution during the spring when river levels are high, and after rainstorms, when portions of the bluff can become unstable and collapse.

Minnesota's Interstate State Park is well known for its basalt cliffs and pothole formations.

❷ Minnesota and Wisconsin Interstate State Parks

St. Croix Dalles and Centennial Bedrock Glade, potholes, rock climbing

Beginner

Unlike the sandstone cliffs at the St. Croix Boom Site, the cliffs at the Minnesota and Wisconsin Interstate State Parks are made of basalt that was formed by ancient lava flows. When glacial Lake Duluth emptied ten thousand years ago, the meltwater carved a path through this basalt and created the gorge that you see today. Known as the St. Croix Dalles, this segment of the St. Croix River has dramatic cliffs and piles of boulders, known as talus slopes.

The most unique glacial features on display at the Interstate State Parks are cylindrical potholes, which were formed by sand and small stones swirling in the current of the same glacial river

Minnesota's Interstate State Park is well known for its basalt cliffs and pothole formations.

that carved the basalt cliffs. Some of these potholes are small, while others are as large as six feet wide and twelve feet deep. The cliffs and potholes at Minnesota Interstate State Park are easily accessible from a series of short, easy trails, including a half-mile, wheelchair accessible trail from the picnic area. On the Wisconsin side of the river, the trail system is more robust and offers several miles of hiking with steep hills and dramatic scenery.

The rocky landscape at both parks supports rare plant communities that can't be found in other parts of the St. Croix River Watershed. There are polypody ferns, fragile ferns, rusty woodsia, mosses, and lichens. Within the dry forest that surrounds the cliffs and boulders, there is red cedar, basswood, white pine, and oak; with big bluestem, blueberry, sumac, long-leaved bluets, bearberry, and poverty oats grass growing beneath.

The Centennial Bedrock Glade State Natural Area, located within Wisconsin Interstate State Park, is a rare natural community in Wisconsin, created by the hot, dry conditions and thin soil of the glade. Plants here include a diverse assemblage of lichens and dry prairie plants, including the prairie fameflower, a succulent endemic to the upper Midwest. The woodland surrounding the glade is filled with miniature oaks.

Though both parks are very popular, exercise caution when hiking and scrambling on the rocks and boulders. Unfortunately, accidents occur here almost every year due to people climbing or exploring too close to the edge.

Minnesota Interstate State Park is located just south of Taylors Falls and offers camping, river access, canoe rental, and four miles of hiking trails. The park is located at 307 Milltown Road, Taylors Falls, Minnesota 55084. A Minnesota State Park vehicle permit is required, which costs $35 per year or $7 per day. Dogs are allowed, but must be kept on a leash at all times. Learn more about the park at www.dnr.state.mn.us/state_parks/interstate.

Wisconsin Interstate State Park is located just south of St. Croix Falls and offers camping, river access, nine miles of hiking trails, and 12.5 miles of cross-country skiing and snowshoeing trails. The park is also the westernmost end of the thousand-mile-long Ice Age National Scenic Trail. There is a swimming beach with a beach house at Lake O' the Dalles. The park is located at 1275 State Highway 35, St. Croix Falls, Wisconsin 54024. A Wisconsin State Park vehicle permit is required, which costs $28 per year

Moss in early spring

or $8 per day. Dogs are allowed, but must be kept on a leash at all times. Learn more about the park at https://dnr.wisconsin.gov/topic/parks/interstate.

ROCK CLIMBING

Minnesota Interstate State Park is one of the most popular locations in the state for rock climbing and is one of only four Minnesota State Parks specifically designated for climbing activities. The park has traditional climbing and bouldering areas. No permanent anchors of any type are allowed. Climbing permits are required for all group and individual climbers at Interstate State Park. These permits are free and must be renewed each year.

Devil's Lake Climbing Guides offers organized climbing trips at Interstate State Park. Learn more at 608-616-5076 or www.devils lakeclimbingguides.com. Mountain Project also gives information about climbing areas and routes at Minnesota Interstate State Park: www.mountainproject.com.

Climbing permits are not required at Wisconsin Interstate State Park and there are no designated climbing areas in the park.

LICHENS ABOUND

Do you like lichen? Lichen forms through a symbiotic relationship between fungus and algae or bacteria and is most often found growing on the sides of rocks and trees, including the boulders at Minnesota and Wisconsin Interstate State Parks.

Lichen comes in all different colors and textures, but there are three main kinds. The first, crustose, looks like it was spray-painted on the surface of rocks and trees. The second one, foliose, has a more leaf-like structure. The third, fruticose, is basically an all-out village with structures that look like itty-bitty trees growing among moss and mushrooms.

Lichens can have really funny names, such as fairy barf, pixie dust, sidewalk firedot, pitted beard, and British soldier. If you're a casual lover of lichens, like me, you can use the iNaturalist app to help identify the species of lichens that you find while exploring the St. Croix River Watershed. And Lichenportal.org has a comprehensive online catalogue of lichens found in North America.

Lichen-covered boulder

Lichens form through a symbiotic relationship between fungus and algae and come in many different colors and growth formations.

Winter sunset over the St. Croix River at the Sandrock Cliffs trail in Burnett County, Wisconsin.

③ Sandrock Cliffs Trail, Burnett County, Wisconsin

A pine-fringed view of the St. Croix River

Beginner

It is winter and the riverway is silent and white. As the dog and I run along the ridge at Sandrock Cliffs Trail, the only sounds I hear are the *thwap, thwap, thwap* of snow flying off the backs of my snowshoes and the steady pitter-patter of Molly's paws beside me. The setting sun filters through pine needles above and casts a warm glow on the frozen landscape surrounding us.

Sandrock Cliffs Trail is located along the St. Croix River, five miles west of Grantsburg, Wisconsin. The five-mile trail system has parking access along Wisconsin Highway 70 in the south and Tennessee Road in the north. There are walk-in campsites on top of the cliffs at the north end of the trail, as well as a canoe and kayak landing and paddle-in campsite along the river below. There is also a boat ramp at the southern parking lot. The campsites are free and are first come, first served.

From the Wisconsin Highway 70 parking lot, you can also walk south along the river, under the highway, to reach the St. Croix Family Campground at Governor Knowles State Forest. From there, you can enjoy dozens of miles of backpacking trails with access to free canoe-in and hike-in campsites along the river. The sandstone cliffs here are similar to those farther south at the St. Croix Boom Site, but with fewer visitors and in a pine-filled forest setting.

④ Banning State Park, Sandstone, Minnesota

Towering walls of sandstone, raging rapids,
and remnants from a historic quarry

Beginner

Banning State Park is located in Sandstone, Minnesota, and is a popular destination for hiking, kayaking, and rock climbing.

The Kettle River tumbles and roars through the park, chiseling a deep valley into the bedrock sandstone, with towering walls that rise forty to one hundred feet above the water below. The park is a favorite destination for whitewater kayaking and features sixteen miles of Class I–IV rapids, with names including Blueberry Slide, Mother's Delight, Dragon's Tooth, and Hell's Gate. There are also seventeen miles of hiking trails that traverse over, around, and through the rocky landscape.

The Kettle River in winter at Banning State Park

CRUSHING STONE
DISCOVER THE BANNING QUARRY

In the early 1900s, the Banning quarry ran out of high quality stone and turned to manufacturing crushed stone to stay in business. Rocks were dumped down from the railroad track to be loaded by hand into the crusher. A bucket conveyor carried the stones from under the crusher to the sorting screen and bins, built high above these concrete. Once screened and sorted by size into storage bins, the stone emptied into a rail car waiting below.

From 1892 to 1905, this location was the site of a sandstone quarry that was named after William L. Banning, the former president of the St. Paul and Duluth railroad. During its operation, a small town named Banning surrounded the quarry as well. After the most valuable sandstone was removed, the quarry closed down, and the railroad removed its tracks. Within a decade, the people had left as well, and Banning became a ghost town. In 1963, the State of Minnesota bought the land and transformed it into a state park.

Most people who visit Banning explore the park on foot, along the numerous hiking trails. From the picnic area parking lot, a short (150 yards) handicap accessible trail leads to Teacher's Overlook, with views of the Hell's Gate rapids below. The Quarry Loop trail follows the Kettle River and passes the historic ruins of the sandstone quarry. From the southernmost point on the trail, continue on to the Hell's Gate trail to get up close to the river's largest rapids.

The Wolf Creek Trail runs along the top of the bluff until it eventually reaches a small, twenty-foot waterfall, where the spring-fed Wolf Creek meets the Kettle River. If you continue south toward Robinson Park, there is a two-hundred-foot-deep cave in the bluffs along the trail that is filled with ice most of the year. It is closed to the public to protect the little brown bats, big brown bats, and Keen's myotis bats that live in the cave. On the north end of the park, the Skunk Cabbage Trail goes through low-lying wetlands where you can find marsh marigold and skunk cabbage in the spring.

Banning State Park offers thirty-three campsites, one camper cabin, and a tent-only group camp for up to fifty people. The park is located just north of Sandstone off Minnesota Highway 23. A Minnesota State Park vehicle permit is required, which costs $35 per year or $7 per day. Dogs are allowed, but must be kept on a leash at all times. Climbing permits are required for all group and individual climbers at Banning State Park, except for within the Robinson Park climbing area, just north of Minnesota Highway 123. There are four public access points to the Kettle River within Banning State Park—three with trailer-in access and one that is carry-in only. Learn more about the park at www.dnr.state.mn.us /state_parks/banning.

Remains of the former sandstone quarry can be seen when hiking along the trails.

A dramatic wall of ice cascades down the side of a cliff along the river.

STEWARDSHIP STORY
Join the Landscape Revival
May 5, 2015

When he starts kindergarten in two years, the young baby oaks we planted last week will still be shorter than he is. They'll continue growing slowly, maybe a foot each year, so that they'll finally be taller than he is by the time he gets his driver's license, though still too skinny for him to carve his initials alongside another's in a heart. By the time the oaks are sturdy and tall enough for me to sit and rest my back against, he may already have kids of his own. Perhaps I'll bring them to visit the trees and gather up acorns to bring home and plant in their yard.

Many, many years from now, when his grandchildren have grandchildren of their own, those trees that we helped to plant on Arbor Day 2015 will finally stand tall and proud with gnarled limbs and massive canopies, roots anchored deep in the prairie. By then, no one will remember who planted the trees or know that we patted the soil beside each seedling, whispering words of encouragement, "Grow big little buddy."

My son Charlie is so much like me in all the best and worst ways. He is loud and outgoing, never stops talking, and approaches most things in life with great enthusiasm. My husband and I get along fabulously, but he is not a natural outdoorsman, so I'm stealthily working to train Charlie as my outdoor nature companion who can explore prairies, woods, and streams with me. Sometimes we share magical experiences and other times the afternoon ends with me carrying a kid and a dog through knee-deep snow for a short eternity while everyone, including the dog, cries.

Charlie also loves stories. In fact, we have two full-sized bookshelves full of books in his room, including many from my and my parents' childhoods. When he was three years old, Charlie became obsessed with Dr. Seuss's *The Lorax*. After reading it for the first time, he wanted to read it again. And again. And then again. And each time we read it, he got more and more worked up. Soon he was up and pacing around the room waving his arms in the air. "If anyone tries to cut down a tree, I will tell them, 'No! You can't do that. Trees give us oxygen. We need trees.' If they try to cut down a tree, I... I... I... I'm not going to be their friend anymore!"

Hiking through Nor Olson's restored prairie in Stillwater Township, Minnesota, during a workshop organized by the Washington Conservation District.

After that, *The Lorax* became a big part of our lives. Charlie began reciting the story, verbatim (at age three!) while I was out in the garden. We'd be walking in the woods, and he would see a tree stump, and the next thing I knew he would be popping out of it announcing, "I am the Lorax. I speak for the trees!" We went to the Franconia Sculpture Garden and there was a children's play sculpture that looked just like the Onceler's house. Soon, Charlie was leaning out a window from up above, calling, "Catch, Mom! It's a truffula seed—the very last one in the world."

Around that time, the South Washington Watershed District began working with Great River Greening to organize volunteers for a tree planting event in southern Woodbury in the watershed district's conservation corridor. I told Charlie about it, saying, "Charlie! We're going to plant trees—truffula trees! Just like in *The Lorax*."

When the day came, it was cold and rainy and actually rather miserable, but he was thrilled. He brought his shovel and a bucket to collect worms, and he took it upon himself to personally bring good tidings and cheer to every single volunteer around us.

And here's the deal—I think most of us have participated in some volunteer planting event or Earth Day clean-up, and we wonder, "Is this really making any difference?" Because it's easy to get overwhelmed by the scale of the environmental problems we face in our world. Seeing the event through Charlie's eyes, however, made me recognize what a big deal it actually was.

Do you remember the last lines in *The Lorax*? "UNLESS someone like you cares a whole awful lot, nothing is going to get better. It's not."

There we were, planting trees with two hundred other volunteers, and Charlie was seeing firsthand that all those people DO care, and we ARE doing something. He was learning that people can work together to fix problems in life. And it wasn't just volunteers: there were watershed district managers and county commissioners rolling up their sleeves and planting trees. Charlie learned that our decision-makers—the people in charge—also care and take action.

Jenn Radtke helps Charlie and Linnea plant trees at an Arbor Day event cohosted by South Washington Watershed District and Great River Greening.

Research from the field of community-based social marketing has demonstrated that "doing something" actually changes your internal perception of who you are. So, if you pick up litter, you start to think of yourself as the kind of person who does things like that. Someone who plants a tree at a volunteer event starts to think of themselves as the kind of person who cares about the environment, and that bleeds over into other decisions they make and actions they take in life.

In the St. Croix River Watershed, people aren't just planting trees and prairie; they're coming together as a community to make a difference in the world. Envision those oak trees in Woodbury one hundred years from now. Think about the birds that will nest in their branches, the fox that will den beside their roots, and the shade those trees will provide.

I don't know if Charlie will remember the 2015 Arbor Day planting event when he's an adult. What I do know is that he'll grow up thinking, "We're the kind of people who care a whole awful lot. We're the kind of people who work together to fix problems in our world." We're the kind of people who plant trees.

Getting Started

Through actions large and small, individuals and organizations in the St. Croix River Watershed work to restore native landscapes lost to farming and development, and to protect the wildlife and waters of the region.

Here are some of the many ways that you can be part of the movement.

Volunteer: Adopt a drain; attend a planting or clean-up event in your community; help lead programming at a park or nature center in your area; become a river guide, trail guide, or project leader with Wild River's Conservancy; or become a water steward, master naturalist, or master gardener.

Put on your gardening gloves: Plant a native wildflower garden, a rain garden, a prairie, a tree, or even a forest. The following resources can help you get started:

Blue Thumb—Planting for Clean Water: www.BlueThumb.org

My St. Croix Woods: www.mystcroixwoods.org

Minnesota Department of Natural Resources:
www.dnr.state.mn.us/backyard

Wisconsin Department of Natural Resources:
www.dnr.wisconsin.gov

Wisconsin County Land and Water Conservation Departments

Minnesota County Soil and Water Conservation Districts

Donate to organizations that protect and restore water quality and habitat in the watershed:

Wild Rivers Conservancy of the St. Croix and Namekagon:
https://wildriversconservancy.org

Kinnickinnic River Land Trust: https://kinniriver.org

Kiap-Tu-Wish Chapter of Trout Unlimited: www.kiaptuwish.org

Wild Ones—St. Croix Oak Savanna Chapter:
https://stcroixoaksavanna.wildones.org

Prairie Enthusiasts—St. Croix Valley Chapter:
www.theprairieenthusiasts.org/st_croix_valley

St. Croix 360: www.stcroix360.com

Support restoration projects led by government partners: Attend community input meetings, send emails, and make phone calls. Participate in your local environmental commission or citizen advisory committee. Talk to your neighbors, and vote for local, state, and federal representatives who care about the environment and are willing to both pass protective legislation and fund restoration work. ◊

Jacob, Charlie, David, and
Rosemary head into the prairie.

Part II

EXPLORE THE OUTDOORS

THE FIRST YEAR THAT MY HUSBAND, GARY, AND I began dating in college, I spent the summer working at a wildlife park in northern Wisconsin. While there, I lived out my childhood dreams of holding and petting nearly every type of animal that lives in North America—rabbit, fox, porcupine, black bear, prairie dog, great horned owl, bull snake, kestrel, and more. I was bitten, scratched, peed and pooped on, and generally regarded with disdain by every one of those animals. In the evenings, I slept alone in a camping trailer in the forest, and during my free time I hiked at nearby parks and rode my bike on country roads.

Midway through the summer, when Gary came to visit for the first time, I eagerly drove him to the nearest trail, assuming that he would love hiking just as much as I did. Within our first hundred yards on the trail, he had already emptied an entire bottle of Deep Woods Off as he sprayed a cloud of insecticide into the air in an attempt to vanquish all gnats within ten feet. After half a mile, he pleaded to cut the hike short and return to the car. "Maybe we aren't meant for each other after all," I worried, as I reluctantly turned and headed back.

●●●

We all enjoy nature differently. Depending on your style, your dream day might include hanging out at the beach and swimming in Square Lake ... or paddling a canoe or kayak down the St. Croix River ... or boating with friends on Lake Namekagon ... or peeping at fall colors along the St. Croix Scenic Byway ... or cross-country skiing at William O'Brien State Park. In Part II of this book, I offer practical advice for nature-based activities in the St. Croix River Watershed during all four seasons, along with suggestions for enjoying nature specifically with children, with seniors, or as a solo adventurer.

OUTDOOR NATURE ACTIVITIES FOR SPRING, SUMMER, AND FALL

Biking

I LIKE TO RIDE MY BIKE. FAST. IF YOU SEE ME PEDAL BY WHILE YOU'RE on a ride of your own, I'll pretend that I don't see you as I spin the crank just a little bit faster to be sure that I stay in the lead. Yes, we're racing. No, you aren't going to win.

One summer day, while riding the country roads in Washington County, I spotted a bike approaching from the opposite direction just as I was turning to head south toward Pine Point Regional Park. As I rounded the corner, I hit the gas and pedaled harder knowing that the other bike was probably close behind. Perhaps he'd seen pigtails sticking out from beneath my helmet and thought it would be easy to catch a girl. Little did he know that I am quick like a rabbit, flying fast across a field.

I continued riding hard for three miles until suddenly, just as I had settled in for a final push toward home, I spotted what appeared to be a smooth black rock in the center of the road. I slowed, swerved in toward the dotted yellow line and scooped up a painted turtle that was slowly inching its way across the road. As I turned to deposit the turtle safely in the grass at the other side, a bike

Prepping to fish at Wild River State Park

A group of kids from the St. Croix Valley Athletic Association head out on the mountain bike trails at Whitetail Ridge in River Falls, Wisconsin.

streaked past me on the shoulder of the road. Once again, the tortoise beats the hare.

Where to Bike

If you are a road cyclist like me, Washington and Chisago Counties in Minnesota and St. Croix County, Wisconsin, provide many opportunities for riding on wide, paved shoulders and quiet country roads. The St. Croix River Watershed also features six paved, off-road bike trails and numerous locations for mountain biking.

Bike networks, including roads and trails

Minnesota State bicycle map: www.dot.state.mn.us/bike/state-bike-map.html

Wisconsin State bicycle map: https://wisconsindot.gov/Pages/travel/bike/bike-maps/state.aspx

The Sunrise Prairie Trail follows Forest Boulevard north from Wyoming to North Branch in Chisago County.

Off-road paved trails

St. Croix Loop Trail—five and a half miles between Minnesota and Wisconsin near Stillwater

Gateway and Brown's Creek State Trails—twenty miles from Stillwater to St. Paul, Minnesota

Hardwood Creek and Sunrise—Prairie State Trails—twenty-six miles from Hugo to North Branch, Minnesota

Swedish Immigrant Regional Trail—twenty-mile, multiuse trail developed through the Chisago Lakes Area, Minnesota

Willard Munger State Trail: seventy miles from Hinckley to Duluth, Minnesota

Off-road gravel trails for biking

Stower Seven Lakes State Trail—fourteen miles between Dresser and Amery, Wisconsin

Gandy-Dancer State Trail—southern segment: forty-seven miles from Centuria to Danbury, Wisconsin

Mountain biking

Close to the Twin Cities metro area:

White Tail Ridge, River Falls, Wisconsin—five miles, singletrack

Lake Elmo Park Reserve, Lake Elmo, Minnesota—fourteen miles, multiuse

Sunfish Lake Park, Lake Elmo, Minnesota—five miles, singletrack

Valley View Park, Oak Park Heights, Minnesota—three miles, singletrack

Farther out:

Willard Munger State Trail at St. Croix State Park, Minnesota—twenty-one miles, multiuse

Chequamegon Area Mountain Bike Association—
130 miles of trails plus 200 miles of mapped gravel
routes near Hayward, Seeley, Cable, Namekagon,
and Bayfield, Wisconsin—https://cambatrails.org

Birding

Birds sing to river,
I finally stop talking,
And hear the song too.

Wild Wings on the St. Croix River

July 5, 2016

Balancing in the water on one leg, I push off and climb into the
kayak behind him. He is a bundle of movement and energy, never
resting and never quiet. His child-sized paddle bumps mine on almost every stroke, splashing water into our laps.

Trumpeter swans on the St. Croix River in winter. Photograph by Gordon Dietzman.

"Let's stop there and explore!"

"No, we just stopped ten minutes ago."

"Let's stop there and explore!"

"No, we just stopped eleven minutes ago."

Then, we round a bend into a backwater channel and suddenly he is calm. He tucks his oar into the nose of the kayak and leans back against my chest. A great blue heron flies up from the tall grass along the river's edge, barely clearing our heads.

"Is this an ancient place?" he asks dreamily. "Did people live here long ago?"

I tell him about the American Indian tribes who live near the St. Croix, and how they once moved from place to place with the changing seasons, catching fish from the river and harvesting wild rice in places where it grew. I tell him that the river is eternal—it existed before glaciers covered the land and it exists here again today.

Finally, I stop talking too and only birds' sweet melodies dance in the summer air.

Birds of the St. Croix River Watershed

The St. Croix River Watershed is home to 240–280 species of birds, including sixty species classified as species of greatest conservation need. While a handful of birds (about twenty species) stay in the region year-round, the vast majority are migratory species that are best spotted in the spring, summer, and fall. Bird-watching is particularly exciting during the spring and fall migrations. It is possible to see birds anywhere in the watershed, but bird-watching is especially popular in a few particular locations:

Carpenter Nature Center, Hastings, Minnesota— Carpenter has an active bird-banding program and leads regular birding hikes. You can also meet raptors that live year-round at the center due to injuries: https://carpenternaturecenter.org

Lower St. Croix River—There is a great blue heron rookery on an island near the St. Croix Boom Site and you can also see swans on the water in the winter. The largest great blue heron rookery on the river is located between Osceola and William O'Brien State Park.

A great blue heron perches on the boardwalk at Lake McKusick in Stillwater.

**Carlos Avery Wildlife Management Area,
Minnesota**—270 species of birds have been recorded in the
WMA, including black terns, American bitterns, trumpeter
swans, northern harriers, sandhill cranes, rough-legged
hawks, and northern shrikes.

Upper St. Croix River—Stevens Creek Landing is a
good spot to see northern shrikes. The forests along
the riverway between State Highway 70 and the Snake
River Landing are filled with warblers during the spring
migration. Look and listen for Baltimore orioles, barred
owls, and wood thrushes between St. Croix State Park and
Thayers Landing.

Crex Meadows Wildlife Area, Wisconsin—280 species
of birds have been recorded in the WMA. Visit during
the spring or fall to see thousands of sandhill cranes:
www.crexmeadows.org.

Namekagon Barrens, Wisconsin—sign up in January
to see sharp-tailed grouse on their leks in the spring:
www.namekagonbarrens.org

Namekagon River, Wisconsin—look for northern boreal species such as white-throated sparrows between Namekagon Dam Landing and Phipps Landing. You can also find pied-billed grebes and American coots at the Namekagon Dam Landing.

Bald eagles are common along the entire riverway.

Protecting Neotropical Migrants

There are a handful of year-round avian residents—owls, grouse, woodpeckers, chickadees, nuthatches, cardinals, robins, and sparrows, but the vast majority of bird species in Minnesota and Wisconsin migrate south in the fall and return in the spring, using the St. Croix and Mississippi Rivers as a migratory corridor to reach the Gulf of Mexico and points farther south. Birds referred to as neotropical migrants overwinter in Mexico, Central and South America, and the Caribbean Islands. These include songbirds, such as warblers, thrushes, tanagers, and vireos; shorebirds; some species of raptors; and several species of waterfowl.

Tropical Wings is a nonprofit organization that supports neotropical migratory birds through a Sister Parks Agreement between fifteen national parks in the upper Midwest of the United States and seven national parks in Costa Rica. In the St. Croix National Scenic Riverway, Tropical Wings hosts spring and fall migration events at Phipps Center for the Arts in Hudson and Carpenter Nature Center in Hudson and Hastings. The organization also awards grants of up to one thousand dollars to individuals, businesses, and organizations in the St. Croix River Watershed to preserve and restore bird habitat: https://tropicalwings.org.

Bringing Birds to Your Backyard

If you enjoy watching birds in your yard, try planting native flowers, shrubs, and trees to provide year-round food and habitat. Trees and shrubs with berries, such as wild cherry, wild plum, hawthorn, highbush cranberry, and winterberry provide a source of food for birds such as robins that overwinter in Minnesota and Wisconsin.

Native plants also attract native insects, which are the primary food source for songbirds during the spring, summer, and fall.

Good bird-friendly options for properties in the St. Croix River Watershed include hackberry, nannyberry, pagoda and red osier dogwood, hazelnut, hawthorn, wild plum, black cherry, white pine, red maple, and white oak.

Boating

There are many opportunities for boating on the St. Croix River and inland lakes.

To find information about boating in Minnesota, including rules and watercraft registration, visit www.dnr.state.mn.us/boating. For information, rules and registration in Wisconsin, head to https://dnr.wisconsin.gov/topic/Boat.

Minnesota and Wisconsin laws require one U.S. Coast Guard–approved, properly sized, and easily accessible life jacket for each person on the boat. In Minnesota, all children under ten are required to wear an approved life jacket when the boat is moving. In Wisconsin, children thirteen and younger are required to wear life jackets.

Boating on the St. Croix River near Stillwater

Preventing the Spread of Aquatic Invasive Species

Aquatic invasive species (AIS) such as Eurasian watermilfoil, curly-leaf pondweed, zebra mussels, and flowering rush inhabit a small number of lakes and rivers within the St. Croix River Watershed. These nonnative plants and animals disrupt aquatic food webs and cause environmental and economic damage.

Once introduced, AIS typically spread quickly and are expensive and nearly impossible to remove. To prevent the spread of AIS, Minnesota and Wisconsin laws require all boaters to clean and drain boats, trailers, and other equipment after coming out of the water, and to dispose of unwanted bait, including minnows, in the trash.

Along the St. Croix River, upstream watercraft travel from below the Arcola High Bridge is prohibited in order to prevent zebra mussels in Lake St. Croix from spreading farther north into the river.

If you'd like to volunteer to help conduct AIS monitoring, watercraft inspections, or public education, sign up for one of the training programs offered through Project RED (https://wisconsin rivers.org/project-red) or Minnesota AIS Detectors (https://maisrc. umn.edu/ais-detectors).

Camping

Camping on the St. Croix and Namekagon Rivers

North of U.S. Highway 8, riverside campsites are free, available on a first-come, first-served basis and do not require a permit or reservation. Between U.S. Highway 8 and the Arcola High Bridge, a free annual camping permit from the National Park Service is required. For detailed information on camping rules and campsite locations, visit www.nps.gov/sacn/planyourvisit/camping.htm.

State Parks with Campgrounds

Afton State Park, Minnesota

Willow River State Park, Wisconsin

William O'Brien State Park, Minnesota

A tent in the woods on a hot summer day

Interstate State Park, Minnesota

Interstate State Park, Wisconsin

Wild River State Park, Minnesota

St. Croix State Park, Minnesota

Banning State Park, Minnesota

Moose Lake State Park, Minnesota

Other Parks with Campgrounds

St. Croix Bluffs Regional Park, Lake Elmo Regional Park—Washington County, Minnesota

Allemansrätt Park—Lindstrom, Minnesota

Ojiketa Regional Park—Chisago City, Minnesota

Governor Knowles State Forest, Wisconsin

Willow River Campground—General C. C. Andrews State Forest, Minnesota

Namekagon Lake Recreation Area, Wisconsin

Learn to Camp

The Minnesota DNR's "I Can Camp!" programs are a great way to try camping for one or two nights before committing to buying equipment of your own. The DNR provides tents, air mattresses, firewood, cookstoves, cooking gear, and most other basic camping equipment, and sends out a packing list prior to the program. Choose from one-night, two-night, or backpacking programs. In the St. Croix River Watershed, one-night programs are held at Afton, William O'Brien, Interstate, Wild River, and St. Croix State Parks. Backpacking programs are held at Afton. Learn more at www.dnr.state.mn.us/state_parks/ican/camp.html.

Canoes and kayaks at Lake Alice in William O'Brien State Park

Canoeing, Kayaking, and Stand-up Paddleboarding

Picture, if you will, a woman serenely paddling down the St. Croix River on a stand-up paddleboard with a boy and a dog balanced on either end. The sun is warm, the water is calm, and all is right with the world. Level: Expert. Total time to complete: five hours.

Instructions

STEP 1: Pack your car the night before. (No, you don't need a truck.)

STEP 2: Drop off two bikes and two helmets at the takeout, William O'Brien State Park.

STEP 3: Drive to Log Cabin Landing in Scandia. Inflate stand-up paddleboard. Climb aboard with kid and dog. Paddle.

STEP 4: Stop at a partially submerged island to play for a while.

STEP 5: Paddle the remainder of the way to William O'Brien. Deflate stand-up paddleboard and stash gear in the tall grass.

STEP 6: Climb aboard the two bikes. Grab dog leash. Pedal back to the car with dog running alongside. Do not fall off your bike.

STEP 7: Drive back to William O'Brien to pick up stashed gear.

STEP 8: Celebrate a successful journey!

Canoe, Kayak, or Stand-up Paddleboard: Which Vessel Is Right for You?

CANOE

A canoe is the best option if you are planning a multi-day trip, want to bring kids or dogs out on the water, or are worried about balance and agility. On the flipside, they are heavy and hard to transport and generally require two people to paddle.

KAYAK

A kayak will allow you to be more nimble and explore shallow inlets and backwaters that might not be accessible to canoes. If you anticipate doing most of your water exploration solo, then a kayak is likely the best option. They are lighter than canoes but still require some effort to transport. There is limited storage.

SUP

Stand-up paddleboards (SUPs) are another good option for solo explorations, and can be a quick, fun way to get out on the water. They come in a variety of styles. Inflatable SUPs are the easiest to transport and can fit into even the smallest car when deflated. There is virtually no storage, and they move slower than canoes and kayaks, so they're best suited for short trips of five miles or less. SUPs require a fair amount of balance and agility. If you practice, it's possible to bring kids and dogs along on an SUP as well. Just be prepared to fall in occasionally.

Since acquiring an inflatable paddleboard of my own a few years ago, I've become an SUP evangelist for a number of reasons. First, they are great for small cars. You can easily fit two inflatable SUPs rolled up in a back seat or trunk and there is no need to purchase a roof rack or tie-downs. Use a pump to inflate them once you've arrived on site, and then let the air out again when it's time to head back home.

Gary and Charlie join me for a canoe trip on the St. Croix River near Scandia, Minnesota.

Second, you can sit, stand, kneel, lie, and even do yoga on them so you won't get sore from sitting in the same position all day. I've also found SUPs to be extremely versatile. You can paddle into shallow backwaters that are inaccessible to canoes, and they're light enough to pick up and carry across islands and shallow water, almost without breaking a sweat.

If you have good enough balance to stand while paddling, the extra height will help you to see down into the water better and you'll likely notice more fish and turtles than you do while sitting in a canoe or kayak.

Finally, they look cool.

Charlie and Gabe play on an SUP in the river.

Rules and Regulations

In Minnesota, canoes, kayaks, and paddleboards longer than ten feet must be licensed through the Minnesota DNR: www.dnr. state.mn.us/licenses/watercraft. Wisconsin does not require licenses for nonmotorized watercraft.

Shuttle Services and Watercraft Rental

On the National Park Service website, you can find information about private companies offering shuttle services; canoe and kayak rental; and guides for fishing, hunting, and paddling trips within the St. Croix Riverway: www.nps.gov/sacn/planyourvisit/ goodsandservices.htm.

You can also find outfitters operating on the Kinnickinnic, Willow, and Apple Rivers in Wisconsin, as well as the Snake and Kettle Rivers in Minnesota.

Learn to Paddle

The Minnesota DNR's "I Can Paddle!" program is designed especially for first-time paddlers. Learn how to canoe, kayak, or plan a canoe camping trip. Classes are offered on evenings and weekends throughout the summer in Minnesota State Parks and include all of the equipment you'll need, including canoe, kayak, paddles, and life jackets. Learn more at https://www.dnr.state.mn.us/state_parks/ican/paddle.html. Find how-to videos and classes through the American Canoe Association: https://americancanoe.org/.

Join a Guided Paddle with Wild Rivers Conservancy of the St. Croix and Namekagon

Wild Rivers offers day trips and overnight kayaking excursions on the St. Croix and Namekagon Rivers with experienced staff who can help you to navigate the riverway and learn about the wildlife, geology, and cultural history of the watershed. To learn more, visit www.wildriversconservancy.org/learn-explore/paddle-adventures.

Fishing

It's 8 a.m. and I need to write an article about bee lawns and send it to the newspaper by noon. So of course, I make a quick TikTok about goats and buckthorn instead.

Now it's 8:30 a.m. and I look at Charlie. Poor kid's got no camp this week and all his friends are busy, so he'll probably be lying on the couch watching YouTube until nightfall.

No way. I've got a plan.

So, we grab the dog—she's giving me a guilt trip—and pack my computer and a fishing pole to head to the nearest lake in town. Easy peasy, right?

We head out the door, and look! A flyer on a light post says that some guy is selling night crawlers on Sherburne Avenue, only ten blocks out of our way. We walk there, but he's sold out, so now we have to go another two blocks to the corner store to get some corn—$0.59.

Charlie heads out to the fishing pier at William O'Brien State Park.

We're drenched in sweat by the time we get to Lily Lake, but it's all good because Charlie catches several bluegills, and two sets of moms drop off more kids with fishing poles while we're there.

Molly the dog hunts for frogs, I write about bee lawns, and I send the article to the newspaper at 11:49 a.m.

Easy peasy, fish 'n' beezies!

●●●

It was the summer of 2021 when my son Charlie, then age nine, became obsessed with fishing. In fact, I don't think it's much of an exaggeration to say that fishing saved us that year as we navigated yet another summer of Covid with no day care and only a few weeks of camp.

Some days, he and neighbor Gabe would grab their poles and head to Lily Lake or the St. Croix River, both within walking distance of our house. On others, we'd make a break for it in the afternoon and head to William O'Brien State Park, Square Lake, or Big Marine, where I would run or swim while he fished and while he fished and chatted with others fishing from the piers.

Whether you grew up fishing, or have never held a pole in your life, there are literally hundreds of places to develop your own fishing stories in the St. Croix River Watershed. Elsewhere in this book I offer recommendations for popular fishing and boating lakes, as well as fly-fishing rivers and streams. Here are additional resources to help you make the most of your fishing adventures.

Licenses and Rules

Fishing licenses are required in Minnesota and Wisconsin for everyone sixteen and older. In Minnesota go to www.dnr.state.mn.us/fishing for information about fishing, licenses, rules, and seasons. In Wisconsin, go to dnr.wisconsin.gov/topic/Fishing.

Learn to Fish

The Minnesota DNR "I Can Fish!" programs teach the basics of fishing, from casting to fish identification, and provide all of the equipment you'll need for a two-hour class. Every participant gets a small tackle box to take home. Learn more at www.dnr.state.mn.us/state_parks/ican/fish.html.

The MinnAqua program provides in-depth fishing education and lesson plans for educators and youth group leaders: www.dnr.state.mn.us/minnaqua/index.html. Wisconsin DNR offers a similar program: dnr.wisconsin.gov/topic/Fishing/anglereducation/index.

Trout Unlimited conducts fishing education through its Trout in the Classroom program mntu.org/trout-in-the-classroom and offers fly-fishing mentorship for older youth and adults through its Foster the Outdoors program. The Kiap-TU-Wish Chapter of Trout Unlimited hosts free fly-fishing clinics for ages twelve and up at the Kinnickinnic River in River Falls.

Where to Fish

Information about any lake in Minnesota or Wisconsin can be found at www.dnr.state.mn.us/lakefind or https://dnr.wisconsin.gov/topic/Lakes.

Minnesota's Fishing in the Neighborhood program (FiN) makes it easy to go fishing in the Twin Cities metro area, with loaner tackle and poles and maps of lakes with shore fishing access. In the St. Croix River Watershed, FiN lakes include Coon (Anoka County);

Silver (Ramsey County); and St. Croix, Elmo, Demontreville, Lily, Northland, McKusick, Square, Big Marine, and Alice (Washington County). More info at www.dnr.state.mn.us/fishing/fin.

In Wisconsin, the DNR offers suggestions for good locations to go fishing with kids in every county: https://dnr.wisconsin.gov/topic/Fishing/anglereducation/takekidsfishing.

Good rivers for fishing in the St. Croix River Watershed include the Apple, Kinnickinnic, Kettle, Namekagon, Snake, St. Croix, and Willow.

More than sixty species of fish call the St. Croix River home, including everything from American eel to sturgeon, paddlefish, and giant flathead catfish. "Be prepared for anything," advises the Minnesota DNR.

Is It Safe to Eat the Fish?

When the Minnesota Pollution Control Agency (MPCA) released its draft list of impaired lakes and rivers in November 2021, many local anglers took notice. Included in the list are twenty-six water bodies that were found to have high levels of perfluorinated alkylated substances (PFAS), also known as the "forever chemical." The St. Croix River and seventeen metro area lakes are on the list, leading many people to ask, "Is it safe to eat the fish?"

The short answer is, it depends.

Minnesota has one of the most extensive fish monitoring programs in the United States, and the Minnesota Department of Health (MDH) maintains a long list of fish consumption advisories for rivers and lakes that have been impacted by toxic chemicals, including mercury, PCBs, and PFAS. It can take months or even years of regularly eating fish for a person to accumulate dangerous levels of toxins, so you shouldn't worry if you went fishing a few times last summer and ate the fish that you caught. The consumption advisories are intended to provide guidance on how often you can safely eat fish from impaired lakes and rivers without getting sick.

Mercury from the atmosphere is, by far, the leading source of water pollution that leads to fish consumption advisories in Minnesota. The element is released into the atmosphere during industrial processes, including gold and iron mining and burning coal for electricity. Once in the air, mercury "falls out" onto our landscape and ends up in water and fish. There are 1,608 lakes and rivers in Minnesota that are listed as impaired due to too much mercury, including some of the most pristine lakes in northern Minnesota and within the Boundary Waters. Wisconsin lists 146 lakes and rivers, most of which are located in the northernmost portion of the state, which have elevated levels of mercury and PCBs.

It can be particularly dangerous for pregnant women and children to be exposed to mercury. Mercury puts newborns at risk for learning disabilities and may also affect a child's behavior. In adults, the first symptoms of mercury poisoning include loss of coordination and a burning or tingling sensation in the fingers and toes. Because mercury bioaccumulates as it travels up the food chain, mercury levels are highest in large walleye, northern pike, and other predatory fish.

In contrast with mercury, scientists are less sure about the long-term health impacts of PFAS. In some studies, higher levels of PFAS in a person's body were associated with higher cholesterol, changes to liver function, reduced immune response (i.e., making vaccines less effective), thyroid disease, and increased kidney and testicular cancer. The latest information also indicates that fetuses and infants are more vulnerable to the chemicals.

Data collected by the Minnesota Pollution Control Agency shows that PFAS concentrations in fish can be eight thousand times higher than in the surrounding environment, so it can be dangerous to eat fish caught from impaired lakes, even if the PFAS concentrations in the water are relatively low. For this reason, the Department of Health has issued DO NOT EAT advisories for fish caught in Lake Elmo and five other smaller nearby lakes in central Washington County where PFAS contamination is most pervasive.

When developing the 2022 impaired waters list, the MPCA caught and sampled fish from eighty lakes around the state, focusing on the locations where people most often fish and the species that they catch. In each of these lakes, the researchers sampled fifteen fish total (five each of species from predator, rough fish, and panfish groups) and analyzed the fish tissue to measure mercury, PCB, and PFOS levels.

Taking all of this into consideration, the Minnesota Department of Health and Wisconsin DNR offer the following consumption advisories for lakes and rivers in the St. Croix River Watershed.

Rivers

Kettle (mercury)—eat no more than one meal per month of channel catfish

Snake (mercury)—eat no more than two meals per week of crappie

St. Croix (mercury and PCBs)—eat no more than one meal per month of white bass (above Stillwater) and buffalo and catfish (below Stillwater). There are currently no consumption advisories related to PFOS.

Lakes

Aitkin County, Minnesota

Big Pine Lake, Hazelton Township (mercury)—eat no more than one meal per week of small walleye and one per month of walleye larger than twenty inches

Anoka County, Minnesota:

Martin, Linwood Township (mercury)—eat no more than two meals per week of sunfish

Bayfield County, Wisconsin

Tahkodah Lake, Cable (mercury)—eat no more than one meal per week of panfish and one meal per month of walleye (pregnant women and children should eat no more than one meal per month of panfish and should not eat walleye)

Carlton County, Minnesota

Eddy, Barnum Township (mercury)—eat no more than one meal per week of small northern pike and one per month of northern pike larger than twenty-four inches

Hanging Horn and Little Hanging Horn, Barnum Township (mercury)—eat no more than one meal per week of cisco, crappie, and small walleye, and one meal per month of northern pike and walleye larger than thirteen inches

Moosehead, Moose Lake (mercury)—eat no more than two meals per week of crappie and one per month of walleye

Chisago County, Minnesota

Kroon, Lindstrom (mercury)—eat no more than two meals per week of bullheads

Douglas County, Wisconsin

St. Croix Flowage (mercury)—eat no more than one meal per week of black crappie (no more than one per month for pregnant women and children)

Pine County, Minnesota

Bass, Pine Lake Township (mercury)—eat no more than one meal per week of bullheads

Cross, Pine City (mercury)—eat no more than two meals per week of yellow perch

Grindstone, Dell Grove Township (mercury)—eat no more than two meals per week of rainbow smelt

Sturgeon, Windemere Township (mercury)—eat no more than one meal per month of walleye

Tamarack, Sandstone (mercury)—eat no more than one meal per week of sunfish (no more than one per month for pregnant women and children)

Upper Pine, Pine Lake Township (mercury)—eat no more than one meal per week of crappie

Polk County, Wisconsin

Pipe Lake, Johnstown (mercury)—eat no more than one meal per month of largemouth bass (pregnant women and children: do not eat)

Washington County, Minnesota

Big Carnelian, Stillwater Townshjp (mercury)—eat no more than one meal per week of bullheads (no more than one per month for pregnant women and children under fifteen years)

Big Marine, May Township/Scandia (mercury)—eat no more than two meals per week of bullheads, and one meal per week of crappie and small walleye (no more than one per month for pregnant women and children). All people should eat no more than one meal per month of walleye larger than twenty-one inches.

Demontreville, Lake Elmo (PFOS)—eat no more than two meals per week of crappie and one meal per week of sunfish.

Eagle Point, Elmo, Horseshoe, Rest Area Pond, Tartan Pond, West Lakeland Ponds (PFOS)—all species— DO NOT EAT.

Jane, Lake Elmo (mercury)—eat no more than one meal per week of bullhead, sunfish, and small pike (no more than one per month for pregnant women and children) and one meal per month of large pike greater than twenty-one inches (pregnant women and children: do not eat large pike).

Olson, Lake Elmo (mercury)—eat no more than two meals per week of bullheads (no more than one meal per month for pregnant women and children).

There are more stringent guidelines for women who are pregnant or may become pregnant and children younger than fifteen years that apply to both fresh-caught (anywhere in Minnesota or Wisconsin) and store-bought fish.

To find current fish consumption advisories for all lakes and rivers in Minnesota and Wisconsin, see www.health.state.mn.us/communities/environment/fish for Minnesota and, for Wisconsin, dnr.wisconsin.gov/topic/Fishing/consumption.

Will Steger (in center with tan backpack) joined me in leading a Sierra Club hike at Afton State Park in 2005.

Hiking and Trail Running

Two roads diverged in the wood, and so I took one on the first day and the other on the second.

On the third day, I cut a path through the prairie. There, I found aster in shades of pink, purple, and white, cloaked in dogwood, with a garland of Virginia creeper.

By then, a fourth day had passed, and I no longer recalled the way out of the wood.

Ages and ages hence, they will wonder whatever became of that girl with the red hair who liked to talk so much.

I went off into the prairie on a beautiful fall day. And that was what made all of the difference.

Jay Riggs and Tim Foss explore the forest in May Township Conservation Area, Minnesota.

Where to Hike in the St. Croix River Watershed

It would take pages to list every state park, county park, nature center, and wildlife refuge in the St. Croix River Watershed where you can hike. Even if you visit every location highlighted in the first half of the book, there will still be more places to hike and more nature to see.

If you're looking for a multiday hiking experience, two great options pass through the watershed:

Ice Age National Scenic Trail: This trail begins at Interstate State Park in Wisconsin and continues more than one thousand miles to Potawatomi State Park on Lake Michigan. The trail is primarily an off-road hiking and backpacking trail, though a few sections are wider, multiuse trails. The Ice Age Trail Alliance has extensive information about the trail and resources for hikers. www.iceagetrail.org.

North Country National Scenic Trail: Stretching 4,800 miles from North Dakota to Vermont, the North Country National Scenic Trail is the longest in the U.S. National Trails System. It enters the St. Croix River Watershed just west of Solon Springs, Wisconsin, and then continues east through the Chequamegon National Forest before heading north into Michigan's Upper Peninsula. Find information about the trail through the North Country Trail Association. https://northcountrytrail.org.

Join a Guided Hike

North Woods and Waters of the St. Croix Heritage Area offers a online community calendar (www.northwoodsandwaterslynx.org) where you can find guided hikes at parks and nature centers in the St. Croix watershed.

Hunting

Hunting is a time-honored tradition for many families in Minnesota and Wisconsin.

Hunting in Minnesota

To find information about hunting in Minnesota, including regulations, season dates, licenses, and a list of public lands where hunting is allowed, visit www.dnr.state.mn.us/hunting. The Minnesota DNR offers licenses and firearm safety training for youth and also operates a program called Becoming an Outdoors Woman, which offers classes on hunting, fishing, and other outdoor skills. Hunting licenses are available for bear, deer, elk, grouse, mourning dove, pheasant, prairie chicken, small game, waterfowl, and wild turkey.

Hunting in Wisconsin

To find information about hunting in Wisconsin, including regulations, season dates, licenses, and a list of public lands where hunting is allowed, visit https://dnr.wisconsin.gov/topic/Hunt. The Wisconsin DNR also offers hunter education and safety classes for youth and adults. Hunting licenses are available for bear, deer, elk, birds and small game, and wild turkey.

Matt Downing and his daughter head out for an early morning hunting trip. Photograph by Aaron DeRusha.

Wear Blaze Orange or Pink to Stay Safe during Hunting Season

If you'll be exploring the outdoors in November and December in areas where hunting is permitted, be sure to wear blaze orange, blaze pink, or other brightly colored clothes to ensure that you can be seen from a distance and through brush.

Conservation and Hunting

Hunters contribute large amounts of annual funding toward conservation and wildlife management via licenses, stamps, excise taxes on hunting equipment and ammunition, and access fees. Numerous conservation organizations work to protect and improve habitat for game species. Among the most active organizations in the St. Croix River Watershed are:

Pheasants Forever: www.pheasantsforever.org

Quail Forever: quailforever.org

Wisconsin Sharp-tailed Grouse Society:
www.wisharptails.org

Ducks Unlimited: www.ducks.org

Leaf–Peeping (Fall Colors)

Minnesotans and Wisconsinites have a long list of favorite fall pas-
times, including football, apple picking, and corn mazes. Perhaps
most popular of all is an activity known as "leaf-peeping." During
the fall, deciduous trees change from green to yellow, orange, red,
and brown, creating a colorful tapestry along roadways, shorelines, and trails.

Why Do Leaves Change Color?

The green color that we see in plant leaves is caused by a pigment
called chlorophyll. Plants also have carotenoid compounds, which
create yellow and orange pigments, but those pigments are usually overpowered by the chlorophyll during the spring and summer.

Fall colors on the water at Pine Point Regional Park near Stillwater, Minnesota

A feather, birch bark, and fall leaves create a still life masterpiece.

When days shorten and temperatures get cooler in the fall, chlorophyll is broken down faster than it is produced. As a result, the green fades and these other colors are gradually revealed. During the fall, some plants and trees create an additional pigment called anthocyanin, which creates red and purple hues as well.

Sugar maples and red maples turn orange and red, while silver maples, which grow in floodplain areas, turn yellow. Oaks can be brown or deep red. Shrubs that turn red include staghorn sumac and dogwood. Birch, aspen, and hickory leaves turn yellow. Most conifers keep their needles all year round, but the needles of tamarack trees turn golden yellow and drop in the fall like leaves on deciduous trees.

Don't Forget the Prairies!

In September and October, late-blooming flowers such as bottle blue gentian, sneezeweed, goldenrods, and asters flash ostentatious shades of purple and yellow amid waves of red and gold grasses. The autumn prairie is a beauty to behold!

When and Where to See Fall Colors

The best time to see fall colors in the St. Croix River Watershed is late September to mid-October.

To plan your leaf-peeping adventures, check out the Minnesota DNR Fall Color Finder (www.dnr.state.mn.us/fall_colors) or Travel Wisconsin Fall Color Report (www.travelwisconsin.com/fall-color -report), which are both updated weekly to show when different regions of the two states are approaching, at, or past peak color for fall leaves.

The prairies are beautiful in fall when asters are blooming and grasses change color.

Rock Climbing

If you're an adrenaline junkie and love the idea of clinging to the side of a giant wall of rock, there are a few great places to visit in the St. Croix River Watershed.

Connie Taillon ascends the wall at Interstate State Park. Photograph by Steve Hack.

Interstate State Park, Minnesota—this is one of the most popular locations in Minnesota for rock climbing and has areas specifically designated for climbing activities. Climbing permits are required for all group and individual climbers at Interstate State Park. These permits are free and must be renewed each year.

Interstate State Park, Wisconsin—unlike on the Minnesota side of the river, this park does not have designated climbing areas. Nonetheless, it is still a popular climbing location. No permits are required.

Banning State Park, Minnesota—like Interstate, Banning also has areas specifically designated for climbing activities. Climbing permits are required for all group and individual climbers, except for those in the Robinson Park area.

Robinson Park, Sandstone, Minnesota—this city park borders Banning State Park and is popular for rock and rock wall climbing year-round. It hosts the Sandstone Ice Festival each winter, when, in preparation for this unique event, the city uses hoses and sprinklers at the top of the cliff to create massive icicles that climbers can scale using ropes. These walls of ice remain a natural attraction for the rest of the winter.

To practice safe climbing:

Take classes to learn rock climbing skills, or join a guided climb. Only climb within your ability level.

Make a plan that accounts for weather, and study your route ahead of time. Bring a first aid kit and plan ahead for what to do if someone gets injured.

Double-check your anchors, knots, harnesses, and all other safety equipment including fixed gear before climbing.

Wear a helmet to protect yourself from falling rocks or a fall of your own.

Rosemary, Charlie, and David wade in Lake Alice at William O'Brien State Park.

Swimming

In the United States today, most lakes and rivers are clean enough to swim, fish, and play in, without risk from industrial pollution or dangerous bacteria and viruses. Forty-five years ago, before the Federal Clean Water Act was passed, factories were allowed to discharge toxic chemicals and industrial waste directly into lakes, rivers, and oceans, and many cities dumped raw sewage into the water as well. Famously, the Cuyahoga River in Ohio actually caught on fire in 1969 because it was so contaminated—and it wasn't even the first time the river had burned!

Today, thanks to more than fifty years of clean water regulations, it is safe to swim in most lakes and rivers within the St. Croix River Watershed. In fact, some of the lakes here boast spectacular water quality.

To practice safe swimming:

> Look for and obey posted beach closures.

> Look for signs of poor water quality, such as algal blooms, green water, or water that smells like rotten eggs or sewage.

> Avoid swimming near pipes that drain into lakes or streams, especially after rainstorms.

> Avoid stirring up sediment and muck along the edges of lakes and rivers.

> Wear a life jacket when swimming in deep water or rapids in the St. Croix and other rivers where currents can be unpredictable and dangerous.

> Stay out of flooded rivers and streams.

Top swimming lakes in the St. Croix River Watershed, within one hour of the Twin Cities:

> Perch Lake, Wisconsin

> Square Lake, Minnesota

> Big Marine Lake, Minnesota

WINTER
IN THE
WATERSHED

TWENTY YEARS AGO, I ATTENDED A WORKSHOP FOR NATURALISTS on one of those January weekends when the temperatures plummet to twenty below and barely creep above zero during the day. We lodged in bunkhouses like kids at a summer camp and arrived with mukluks, snow pants, mittens, and wooly hats, ready to brave the cold.

Sometime around midnight on our first night at camp, two state park naturalists knocked on our door and whispered urgently that it was time to go look for owls. With a mixture of reluctance and excitement, we bundled up and headed into the woods.

Crunch, crunch, crunch, crunch. We kept our flashlights off and voices low so that the only sound was the scrunch of snow beneath bundled toes. Eventually, our group leaders motioned to us to spread out and sit silently with our backs against the trees.

Obediently, I sat in the snow with my back against a maple, my every breath creating a puff of crystals in the frozen air until my scarf and hat were covered in a glittering glaze of frost. I had never experienced the woods this way before, and I felt giddy, as if I was learning a great secret that no one else knew.

Suddenly, a low hooting sound broke the nearly absolute silence. I was excited, until I realized that it was one of the naturalists, imitating a great horned owl. From the other side of a hill, I heard his partner hooting back. Silence. Waiting. One man hoots, the other replies. More silence. More waiting.

Standing Cedars Community Land Conservancy: Buffalo Skull in winter

Barred Owl. Photograph by Jessie Thiel.

Then, just when I thought that I couldn't possibly sit silently freezing in the woods for another minute, a series of low hoots floated down from the tree branches directly above me—a real and actual owl. A second owl answered from a nearby tree, one hundred feet away. Hoot. Double hoot. Silence and sparkling breath. Hoot. Double hoot. It was a magical night in a dark, frozen forest with a lullaby of owls in the air.

●●●

If you are like most people who live in Minnesota and Wisconsin, winter comes in phases each year. In November and December, there is a sense of euphoria when the first snows arrive. It falls from the sky like magical fairy dust, coating land and trees until the world outside looks like the little villages we place on our hearths throughout the holidays.

During the early winter, each week brings a new and exciting "first." There is the first week we go sledding, the first time we put on skis, and the first time the ice is thick enough to walk across the lake.

Sometime around late January or early February, our collective mood begins to sour, and we enter into the second phase of winter, which often feels interminable. It is tempting to stay indoors until the sun returns and grass is green again. In the St. Croix River Watershed, however, winter lasts too long to spend the whole time indoors.

Whether you love winter or hate winter, I promise that you will feel happier and healthier if you spend at least a little time outdoors each day. Furthermore, winter offers smaller crowds and unique outdoor adventures throughout the St. Croix River Watershed.

Strap on skis or snowshoes. Drill a hole in the ice to search for fish or wander into the woods and find yourself an owl. Remember, if you choose not to find joy in the snow, you will have less joy in your life but still the same amount of snow.

Frost clings to seedheads in the prairie on a dazzling New Year's morning.

What to Wear in Winter

One of the most common mistakes people make in the winter is to overdress for aerobic activities like running, skiing, or snowshoeing. If you will be out for an hour or less, I recommend wear-

Kids and dads bundle up to go sledding: Charlie with friends Jasper and Louis, and dads Chris and Carmen.

ing light layers of wool or moisture-wicking fabric that cover your skin but won't trap in heat or cause you to sweat.

If you'll spend several hours outside, the temperatures are colder, or you'll be sitting or standing still, bulk up with heavier clothes such as wool socks, warm boots, snow pants, parka, mittens, hat, and potentially even a scarf or balaclava.

Footwear

The best investment you can make toward a happier winter is wool socks and quality winter boots. Warm toes make all the difference between an enjoyable outdoor adventure and a miserable freezefest.

If you have only one pair of winter boots, look for a good all-around boot like a Sorel that will keep your feet warm and dry in a variety of conditions. Other boots to consider adding to your winter wardrobe include Bogs (for muck and slush) and mukluks (for snow and deep cold).

For snow running, hiking, or snowshoeing, I prefer mukluks, which are warm but super lightweight. They have soft soles and feel like giant slippers. I've had my Steger Mukluks for twenty years, wear them three to four days a week throughout the winter, and they're still going strong.

Another essential for winter footwear is a pair of strap-on ice cleats. Pull these on over your boots when walking on icy sidewalks and trails or heading out on a frozen lake.

Winter woods at William O'Brien State Park

Pants

For outdoor activities, start with an under layer of soft, close-fitting fabric—long underwear or leggings. Depending on the temperatures and your activity level, you'll want to add either lightweight or heavy winter pants over these. Look for wool or synthetic fabrics instead of cotton and avoid wearing jeans.

Jacket

If you'll be skiing or snowshoeing, wear a lightweight, warm jacket to block the wind. If you'll be sitting, standing, or walking slowly, choose a warmer parka or winter jacket to stay warm.

Accessories

I'm honestly embarrassed to admit how many pairs of mittens, gloves, hats, and scarves I own. If you spend a lot of time outdoors in the winter, chances are that your winter wardrobe looks the same.

Mittens are hands-down the warmest option for your fingers, though you'll likely need a few pairs of lightweight gloves for driving, skiing, or other activities that require manual dexterity. Most

people find that they need different weights of hats and scarves for various activities and temperatures. If you live in Minnesota or Wisconsin, these winter accessories will eventually become your only form of fashion.

Now that you're bundled up like the kid in *A Christmas Story* and ready to head outdoors, here are a few suggestions for ways to explore the beauty of winter in the St. Croix River Watershed.

Light layers are perfect when skiing on a warm winter day.

Ice Fishing

Somewhere in the Frozen North

March 23, 2006

On a cold and snowy day in March, eleven people parked three cars at the end of a desolate stretch of road off the Gunflint Trail, loaded one snowmobile with eleven unusually large and awkwardly shaped packs, called to their four dogs bounding wildly in and out of the woods, and set off for a three-day adventure in the Boundary Waters Canoe Area Wilderness (BWCAW)—located in northern Minnesota on the border with Canada, and not within the St. Croix River Watershed.

We had planned to snowmobile our gear to the edge of the wilderness area and then split into two separate groups to hike in on snowshoes. Only half a mile down the trail, one of the guys in our group went head over heels on a patch of ice and gave himself a nasty concussion. After a somewhat heated debate over what to do, we decided to strap our clumsy friend into the snowmobile and send him back to civilization. My friend Lynn, a true martyr, volunteered to forgo her weekend in the frozen wilderness in order to drive him to the hospital.

With our group now whittled down to nine people with nine large packs, four dogs with four smaller packs, and zero snowmobiles, we hiked onward into the BWCA.

It was my second time winter camping but a first for my dog, Cocoa, and she was overjoyed. Within ten minutes, however, she had already managed to lose her pack, which carried a three-day supply of dog food and two portable bowls. Likely, a lucky fox or wolf dined in style that evening.

The rest of the weekend proceeded rather uneventfully. We drilled holes in the ice to fish and caught a steady supply of delicious lake trout for our dinners. Cocoa had the time of her life, pushing the limits of her stamina by exploring every nook and cranny of the lake's shoreline and logging an estimated fifty miles of running a day. Meanwhile, the other three dogs lazed around camp and occasionally wrestled.

Without a doubt, the highlight of our trip was the "big fish" that my friend Amber caught on our second day in the wilderness. That day, we had hiked to another nearby lake where brook trout

Charlie practices ice fishing during a program sponsored by Wild Rivers Conservancy of the St. Croix and Namekagon and Minnesota Trout Unlimited.

were rumored to swim. Upon arrival, the men of the group immediately set to work drilling holes and dropping their lines. My friend Amber and I were more interested in making lunch, which was followed by chocolate (a necessity for winter camping), and a tasty beverage. By the time we finally drilled holes and dropped our lines, the boys had been at it for nearly two hours without a single bite.

An hour later, the sunlight was starting to fade and, with a feeling of resignation, the boys began making plans to return to camp. Amber and I, still happily sipping our beverages and having nearly forgotten that the goal of the excursion was to catch fish, were suddenly awakened from our reverie by a sharp tug on her pole. We looked down and saw an enormous brook trout swimming just below the now-frozen hole.

With excitement, the men swarmed around us and began frantically chipping away at the ice. Finally, after much yelling and great fanfare, they heaved a behemoth brook trout out of the lake. Amber and the fish proudly posed for photographs and the boys gathered round to share in the glory of the catch.

We returned to our cars two days later, nine people with nine packs, fours dogs with three packs, and one extremely large brook trout, wrapped in a black plastic bag.

It was your typical ice fishing adventure.

Information and Rules

If you've never gone ice fishing, the Minnesota DNR offers great advice on where to go, how to dress, what gear to use, and which fish to look for: www.dnr.state.mn.us/gofishing/learn-ice-fish.html.

Fishing licenses are required in Minnesota and Wisconsin for everyone sixteen years of age and older. In Minnesota go to www.dnr.state.mn.us/fishing for information about fishing, licenses, rules, and seasons. In Wisconsin, go to dnr.wisconsin.gov/topic/Fishing.

Ice Safety

People talk about lakes "turning over" in the fall as the oxygen- and nutrient-rich surface water cools, sinks, and begins mixing with the water below. Lake turnover is an important ecological phenomenon that enables fish to survive in deeper water and under the cover of ice.

Eventually, once all of the water in a lake has cooled to 39°F, the molecules on the surface begin to spread out and crystalize. Ice will form first at the edge of a lake and then gradually spread inward. Once the entire surface of a lake is covered, the ice thickens and forms an insulating layer. In this way, the water below remains a constant temperature even when the air above drops below zero.

In general, ice is safe to walk on when it is at least 4 inches thick. It needs 5–7 inches to support snowmobiles, 8–12 inches for cars, and 12–15 inches to support trucks. Because snow creates additional weight on top of the ice, you should double the above numbers for snow-covered lakes. Avoid ice near streams, springs, bridges, and culverts, and take extra precaution on frozen rivers where currents can cause unpredictable freeze patterns.

Try Ice Fishing with Wild Rivers Conservancy of the St. Croix and Namekagon

Each winter, the Wild Rivers Conservancy offers dozens of free ice fishing programs on lakes around the St. Croix River Watershed. Participants learn fishing regulations, how to use ice fishing equipment, how to identify species of fish, and how to help keep local lakes and rivers clean. The program is supported by the National Park Foundation's Junior Angler grant program. To find a list of upcoming events, head to https://wildriversconservancy.org.

Skiing

Several years ago, I developed a winter survival strategy, which is to carry skis and snowshoes in my car throughout the winter so that anytime I am driving past a park and have thirty minutes to spare, I can jump out, throw them on my feet, and trod off into the forest.

Cross-country skiing is a great workout but also a quiet way to enjoy nature during the winter. There are trail systems throughout the St. Croix River Watershed and many parks and nature centers rent skis and snowshoes. If you'd prefer more fast-paced action, there are also several downhill ski hills within the region.

Cross-country Skiing Etiquette

The two styles of cross-country skiing are classic (also called Nordic) and skate-style. Classic skiing is a lot like walking, with a little bit of glide added. When trails are groomed for classic skiing, there will be two long parallel tracks in the snow that look sort of like railroad tracks. Skate skiing is more like speed skating with skis. People who practice this style of skiing do so on the left side of the trail, to avoid damaging the track set for Nordic skiers.

Cross-country skiing at Pine Point Regional Park

Cross-country ski trails are almost always one-way trails, so it's important to pay attention to signs. Most important, never, ever walk or snowshoe on groomed ski trails. It damages the trail, and you will receive the ire of any skier who passes by.

Cross-country Rules and Information

In Minnesota, anyone older than sixteen is required to carry a signed ski pass while skiing on groomed trails in state parks, state forests, and grants-in-aid trails. Purchase a pass and find information about ski trails around the state: www.dnr.state.mn.us/skiing.

In Wisconsin, ski passes are also required for many trails. Find information about trails around the state, as well as a link to purchase a state trail pass at https://dnr.wisconsin.gov/topic/parks/recreation/skiing.

The Birkie trail system and some county parks also require users to purchase a pass that is separate from the state trail passes.

Cross-country Ski Trails in the St. Croix River Watershed

Birkie Trail: The American Birkebeiner Trail System offers more than sixty-two miles of skiing on groomed trails near Cable, Wisconsin. Birkie Trail ski passes are required from December to March. During the last week in February, the Birkie hosts North America's largest cross-country ski marathon, with a 50k skate-style race and 55k classic-style race, in addition to numerous shorter events. The Birkie attracts skiers from forty-nine states and twenty-seven countries. www.birkie.com/trail.

State and local trails:

Minnesota State Parks: Afton, William O'Brien, Wild River (ski rentals available), St. Croix, Moose Lake.

Wisconsin State Parks: Kinnickinnic, Willow River, Interstate.

Trails within one hour of the Twin Cities:

Minnesota: Lake Elmo Park Reserve, Sunfish Lake Park in Lake Elmo, Brown's Creek Park in Stillwater, Pine Point Regional Park, St. Croix Bluffs Regional Park, Jackson Meadow in Marine on St. Croix, Irving and John Anderson County Park in North Branch

Western Wisconsin: New Richmond Golf Club, Stower Seven Lake Trail in Balsam Lake, Balsam Branch Trails in Amery

Northern Watershed: To find a full list and map of cross-country ski trails in the northern watershed, visit www.skinnyski.com. Search by trails in Central Minnesota and Northwest Wisconsin. Skinnyski also has information about trails across Minnesota, Wisconsin, Michigan, Iowa, Illinois, North Dakota, South Dakota, and southern Canada.

William O'Brien State Park is home to the St. Croix Valley Ski Club, a nonprofit volunteer club that teaches cross-country skiing to kids ages three to fourteen.

Downhill Skiing

Feeling the need for speed? There are three downhill ski areas in the St. Croix River Watershed.

Afton Alps in Minnesota borders Afton State Park. Operated by Vail Resorts, the ski area has worked with South Washington Watershed District in recent years to restore the natural stream corridor for Trout Brook to improve aquatic habitat. Afton Alps is also involved with numerous other environmental initiatives: www.aftonalps.com.

Trollhaugen is located in Dresser, Wisconsin, and offers skiing, tubing, and a ski team. During the summer, there is an adventure park, challenge course, and zip lining: www.trollhaugen.com.

Wild Mountain in Minnesota is located just south of Wild River State Park. It offers skiing and tubing, as well as a water park in the summer. Wild Mountain manages its hills as prairie habitat and supports many environmental

Molly and I had the prairie to ourselves on a late afternoon in winter at Belwin Conservancy in Afton, Minnesota.

initiatives, including electric snowmobiles: www.wildmountain.com.

Snowshoeing

"What is that over there?"
"It's the wild," said the mole. "Don't fear it."
"Imagine how we would be if we were less afraid."

—Charlie Mackesy, *The Boy, the Mole, the Fox, and the Horse*

Two days after my son and I read *The Boy, the Mole, the Fox, and the Horse* together, it suddenly occurred to me that it was possible to walk across the river from Minnesota to Wisconsin. We borrowed my husband's truck, so as not to get stuck at the bottom of a snowy hill, and headed north past Marine on St. Croix with two pairs of snowshoes, a dog in a parka, and snacks. The snow on the river was perfectly flat and glittered in the sun as if someone above had poured a giant bottle of white glitter onto the Earth. When we got to the other side of the river, we sat on a fallen tree for a while to gaze at the view and howl to the wolves. The scene looked exactly like Mackesy's illustration of the wild. It was beautiful and perfect, and we had it all to ourselves.

Snowshoes offer the alluring possibility to explore new destinations within familiar locations during the winter. With snowshoes on, you can walk across a frozen wetland, create a *Family Circus* trail within the woods, or even hike across the river to another state.

If you've never tried snowshoeing before, you might be surprised at how difficult and tiring it can be. It's easy to get a good workout during a relatively short hike, and if you try to jog in them, as I occasionally do, you'll quickly find yourself gasping and out of breath.

Picking the Right Kind of Snowshoe

Historians believe that snowshoes originated in Central Asia and may even have been used by humans who crossed the Bering Strait to North America during the most recent Ice Age.

In more recent times, Indigenous people in North America crafted numerous different variations on the basic snowshoe design, using ash or birch for the frame and deer, caribou, or moose hide for the lacing. Alaskan and Ojibwe snowshoes are the longest

The modified bear-claw style snowshoes are small enough to navigate through woods and fallen trees and have metal claws at the bottom to grip on hills and icy trails.

(4–5 feet) and best suited for very deep snow. Huron snowshoes are slightly shorter (4 feet) and have a rounded front that makes for easy walking in open areas—lakes, rivers, marshes, and fields. Bear paws are the smallest and allow for best maneuverability on woods and hills.

Modern snowshoes are built with lightweight metal, plastic, and other synthetic materials and most offer a variation on the bear-paw design. Buy bigger snowshoes if you'll spend most of your time up north where the snow is deeper and smaller snowshoes if you plan to use them mostly around the Twin Cities and southern St. Croix River Watershed. Most modern snowshoes also have cleats on the bottoms, which help in icy conditions and on hills.

Where to Go Snowshoeing in the St. Croix River Watershed

One major appeal to snowshoeing is the ability to walk anywhere, without needing to follow a trail. In fact, because so many parks groom their hiking trails for skiing in the winter, it can be difficult to find trails where snowshoeing is allowed. The nice thing about walking in the snow is that you'll create your own Hansel and Gretel trail as you go, so it is relatively easy to find your way back out of the woods when it's time to go home.

These parks offer snowshoeing trails and rentals:

Carpenter Nature Center, Minnesota and Wisconsin campuses. Snowshoe rentals available for special programs.

Minnesota State Parks: Afton, William O'Brien, St. Croix. Snowshoe rentals available.

Wisconsin State Parks: Willow River and Kinnickinnic State Parks. Snowshoe rentals available.

Snowmobiling

One of the most popular ways to travel through forests, farm fields, and along frozen lakes in winter is by snowmobile. In Minnesota, find snowmobile rules and registration, youth safety classes, and

Snowmobiling in the St. Croix County trail system

other information at www.dnr.state.mn.us/snowmobiling. In Wisconsin, find the same information at https://dnr.wisconsin.gov/topic/Snowmobile.

In the upper portion of the St. Croix River Watershed, four long-distance snowmobile trails pass through state forests and natural areas:

Matthew Lourey State Trail: eighty miles in Minnesota, linking St. Croix State Park with Chengwatana, St. Croix, and Nemadji State Forests: www.dnr.state.mn.us/state_trails/matthew_lourey.

Gandy Dancer State Trail—northern segment: thirty-one miles in Minnesota and fifteen miles in Wisconsin from Danbury to Superior: https://dnr.wisconsin.gov/topic/parks/gandydancernorth.

Cattail State Trail: eighteen miles on a former rail corridor between Amery and Almena, Wisconsin: https://dnr.wisconsin.gov/topic/parks/cattail.

Wild Rivers State Trail: 104 miles through Douglas, Washburn, and Barron counties in Wisconsin: https://dnr.wisconsin.gov/topic/parks/wildrivers.

Other Winter Diversions

Sandstone Ice Festival

Ice climbing is the focus of this festival in Sandstone, Minnesota, in early January each year: https://sandstoneicefest.com/.

World Snow Sculpting Championship

During the winter, Stillwater, Minnesota, hosts fun outdoor celebrations. The World Snow Sculpting Championship takes place in January and includes several events and activities. https://greater stillwaterchamber.com/WSSC

Hudson Hot Air Affair

Each February, thousands of visitors descend on Hudson, Wisconsin, to watch colorful hot air balloons rise into the sky above the frozen St. Croix River. Founded in 1990, the Hudson Hot Air Affair is a unique way to chase away the winter doldrums: https://hudson hotairaffair.com.

Dozens of balloons take flight during the Hudson Hot Air Affair in February.

In January, Stillwater hosts the World Snow Sculpting Championship at Lowell Park on the St. Croix River.

TIPS ON EXPLORING

Children in Nature

WHEN THEY'RE THIRTY, WILL THEY REMEMBER LAUGHING AS DAVID leaned over with a mischievous grin and crushed Charlie against the side of the trailer? "It's called jelly!" I called back to them. "We used to play it in the backseat of the car when I was a kid." Will they recall the sound of our hollers echoing off the hills as we yee-hawed down the gorge? Surely they'll remember the baby snapping turtle, no bigger than a silver dollar, which we passed from hand to hand. Then again, they might forget the entire day—lost like so many others into a jumble of ice cream, skinned knees, and endless childhood adventures.

I spent my grade school years in a mid-sized city in central California where the edge of town moved out about a mile each year. Like most children of the 1980s, I roamed the neighborhood from dusk until dawn, usually by bike and always with at least one friend. When we got hungry, we'd pluck pomegranates from a tree in the neighborhood or scrounge up nickels to buy candy from the ice cream truck. We dug holes in the ground in vacant lots, searching for buried treasure, and when the vacant lots gave way to houses, we pedaled farther to find the wild beyond our fences.

Out in the country, we sometimes patrolled the irrigation canals or snuck into nearby apricot orchards. More often, we turned down an unmarked dirt road where grapes grew wild near a curve at the bottom of a hill, and no one ever seemed to be around. Once, when I took the hill too fast, my bike flew off an embankment and

Molly, my ever-present companion for outdoor adventures, navigates a bluffside trail along the St. Croix River at Somerset Landing, Wisconsin.

Lily, Eloise, Ingrid, and Zachary explore the prairie.

into a pond. I jumped off just in time but had to go home and get help to pull my bike out of the water. Thinking about this now, I'm sure someone owned that land.

Sometimes I wonder if our children can still find the wild familiar to many of us adults as we grew up. There are parks, playgrounds, and railroad tracks turned into beautiful trails. But can they still ride their bikes to woods or a field where the world is theirs to explore?

Exploring the outdoors with children can be wonderfully rewarding, and in our modern society it is also increasingly important. A study in 2018 by UK-based National Trust showed that English children on average play outside only four hours each week. Studies in the United States reveal similar statistics. The average American spends just 5 percent of each day outside, and that is usually little more than the time spent walking to and from our cars before and after work and while running errands. Meanwhile, American children spend an average of five to eight hours each day in front of digital screens.

In his 2005 book *The Last Child in the Woods*, Richard Louv coined the term "nature-deficit disorder" to describe the problems facing many modern children whose lives have become too busy for unstructured playtime outdoors, sit-down family meals, and physical activity. Louv noted that a number of childhood problems seem to be on the rise as a result, including obesity, attention disorders, anxiety, and depression.

Tips for Enjoying Nature with Kids

Teaching children how to spend time outside and enjoy nature can improve their (and your) physical and mental health, but it can also be stressful if you don't plan ahead and start the experience in a proper frame of mind.

The first thing you need to know is that at least one child will become ravenously hungry the instant you're out of sight of the parking lot. Be prepared to fuel a four-hour adventure in the wilderness, even if you are taking only a thirty-minute walk in the park. Also, don't imagine that anyone but you will eat that Luna bar flavored with lemon zest. The second thing to remember is that however far you think you'll be able to walk, you won't. In fact, you should count yourself lucky if you even make it beyond sight of the parking lot. Many families don't.

Here are a few additional tips for enjoying the outdoors with children.

> Let go of the idea that you need to travel a certain distance to enjoy your time in nature. In my experience, children will usually walk a short distance down a trail until they find a fun place to play and then park themselves there and play for hours until you beg them to leave. Instead of fighting against their natural desire to stay and play, relax and enjoy a moment of peace for yourself. Bring a book to read or help them build that fairy hut out of sticks and dandelions.

> Don't be afraid to step off the trail. Some outdoor destinations request that visitors stay on the trail, but in most places it's fine to wander into the prairie or woods. Stepping off the trail allows little feet more time to wander without being trampled by horses and hikers, and you might have a much more immersive experience.

> Go to the bathroom ahead of time. Seriously—I can't stress this enough. Go to the bathroom before you leave the house. Go to the bathroom at the trailhead before you begin hiking, biking, or canoeing, and bring toilet paper with you in case they need to go to the bathroom again while you're in the woods (and they will).

Charlie creates a shield of skunk cabbage leaves and scrambles up a steep hill in the woods.

Almost any weather is good weather to explore outdoors if you're properly dressed. Like most people, I most love the outdoors when it is 70 degrees, sunny, and bug-free. I have also had memorable (though not always enjoyable) experiences in nature when it was raining, snowing, or sweltering hot. The key is to dress appropriately—whether that means rain boots and an umbrella; a winter hat, scarf, and snow pants; or a tank top and sun hat. Think strategically about which outdoor destinations to visit at different times of the year. For example, head to the woods on a blustery winter day, as the trees will help to shield you from the wind. On a hot summer day, pick a trail near a stream or lake so that

Dandelions and sticks create an inviting fairy hut.

you can play in the water to cool off. You don't need to go outside *every* day, but you'll be amazed by how much better you feel after spending even a little time outdoors during a long winter or rainy spring.

Plan an activity . . . or not. There are numerous kid-friendly outdoor activities you can plan if you feel uncomfortable stepping outside without a little structure. My favorite simple activities include bringing along a butterfly net to catch and release bugs; collecting fall leaves to take home and press; or looking for animal tracks in snow and mud. Nature tends to inspire creativity, so don't be afraid to walk out the door empty-handed and let the prairie, woods, and water be your inspiration.

If you're interested in trying out a new outdoor activity but don't know how to get started, check out the Minnesota DNR's "I Can!" program, which is designed to give families hands-on experience with camping, paddling, fishing, mountain biking, and archery. The programs are low-cost or free and include all necessary gear. Learn more at www.dnr.state.mn.us/state_parks/ican.

The St. Croix National Scenic Riverway also has a Riverway Junior Ranger Program. Pick up a booklet at the visitor center in St. Croix Falls or download it online to begin the adventure: www.nps.gov/sacn/learn/kidsyouth/riverwayjuniorranger.htm. After completing the activities, kids earn a badge and a certificate.

Charlie (right) and a group of kids pledge to earn their Junior Ranger badge after a National Park Service Program.

Getting Older Shouldn't
Mean Staying Indoors

We know that spending time in nature helps reduce depression and anxiety, lowers blood pressure, and keeps us fit and active. For older adults, there are additional benefits. According to the Elder Care Alliance, getting outside regularly can help seniors recover more quickly from surgery or illness and retain better memory. Vitamin D from sunlight helps our bones to absorb calcium, which protects against osteoporosis in older age and can also lower blood pressure and reduce the risk of diabetes and rheumatoid arthritis.

Unfortunately, mobility issues, lack of transportation, fear of falling, and other concerns keep many older adults indoors, away from Minnesota's woods and water. In late 2020, I spoke with Randy Thoresen, who was then a recent retiree of the National Park Service. He shared a conversation that he had had several years earlier with the division chief for conservation and outdoor recreation, while he was still working at the St. Croix National Scenic Riverway. "I enjoy doing all of this work with youth," said Thoreson to his colleague, "but I think we're missing a major sector of the population. The outdoors aren't just for kids, you know."

Soon, Thoreson was traveling around the country, giving presentations at AARP conferences, Rotary Clubs, Lions and Kiwanis Clubs, and National Park Service meetings, where he advocated for new programs to help seniors get outdoors in nature. He pointed to Wilderness Inquiry as an example of an organization that plans inclusive outdoor adventures for people of all ages, abilities, and backgrounds. Thoreson suggested that the National Park Service and other conservation organizations begin planning similar programs that cater specifically to seniors.

In addition to bringing seniors to parks and natural areas, Thoreson said that it is equally important to bring nature into the places where we live. "Ask your community leaders what they are providing in town for residents," he advised. Outdoor recreation boomed during Covid, and people of all ages began looking for local parks and trails that they could easily access without having to drive. Likewise, Thoreson noted that developers building new senior living complexes should consider site design and think about how to create outdoor experiences for residents with trails, gardens, and sitting areas.

Randy Thoreson was passionate about helping seniors remain active and connected with nature.

Research from the University of Minnesota backs Thoreson's advice. In particular, researchers find that "green and blue" spaces (environments with running or still water) are especially beneficial for healthy aging in seniors. "While our research may seem intuitive, it creates conversations on how to build communities that serve people across their entire lifetime," says Jessica Finlay, a researcher involved in the project. "We don't just need playgrounds for children, we also need sheltered benches for grandparents to watch them."

In terms of health benefits, it is most important to get outside regularly, even if you don't travel very far. AgingCare, an organization that connects families with home care, assisted living, and caregiver support, offers advice to help seniors with mobility concerns to get fresh air and sunshine more regularly. Suggestions include spending time every day sitting outside on a patio or porch (if possible) or near an open window (if not).

Try mounting a bird feeder near the window or back door where it is easy to see and access; plant a garden with native plants alongside a patio or deck to attract birds and butterflies; or grow native plants in containers or window boxes if a garden isn't possible. For container gardens, Minnesota Extension recommends columbine, aster, black-eyed Susans, Jacob's ladder, wild geranium, purple coneflower, and coreopsis as native options that will bloom throughout the season and do well in a pot or window box.

Looking at long-term trends for Minnesota, demographers expect seniors to comprise a larger percentage of the population in coming years. Currently, 15 percent of Minnesotans are older than sixty-five years, but that number will grow to more than 20 percent by 2030. At the end of our conversation, Thoreson noted that he had recently retired and become a senior. "Now that I'm retired, I guess I have skin in the game," he laughed, "but I've cared about this topic since before it affected me. I don't do this to get rich, you know. I just really want to see more people of all ages get outside to experience the benefits of nature. It's body, mind, and soul."

An adapted version of this story was published in the Stillwater Gazette *in 2020. Randy Thoreson passed away on October 28, 2022.*

Outdoor Safety

There are so many fun ways to explore nature in the St. Croix River Watershed, but there are also inherent risks. Because the St. Croix is a designated Wild and Scenic River, there are very few roads and accesses within the riverway, and cell phone reception is poor to nonexistent, even close to the Twin Cities. Weather conditions change dramatically from one season to the next and are especially unpredictable during the spring and fall, when it might be sweltering one day and snowing the next.

Building your outdoor skills and planning ahead will keep you safe and happy when exploring the St. Croix. This is particularly important if you'll be traveling or adventuring alone.

Build Your Outdoor Skills

Learn and practice outdoor skills such as map-reading, plant and animal identification, how to change a flat tire on your bike, and

The key to safety is being prepared. Typical supplies I'll bring on a day hike include a backpack with built-in water pouch, snacks, sunscreen and bug spray, a foldable cloth dish to fill with water for my dog, headlamp, first aid kit, compass and map, pepper spray, pocketknife, lip balm, and a journal and colored pencils. If you'll be out for more than two hours, it's a good idea to bring a light jacket in case the weather changes.

how to build a campfire. As you spend more time outdoors and develop your skills, your confidence will increase and it will begin to feel "normal" to go for a hike, regardless of whether you're with other people or alone.

Here are a few suggestions for programs to build your outdoor skills.

REI Co-op offers classes and guided trips to help you build outdoor skills: www.rei.com/events.

The Sierra Club, a national environmental organization, offers guided trips through its Outings program. National and international multiday trips have an associated cost, but there are also local outings in the Twin Cities that are free and open to anyone: www.sierraclub.org/minnesota/ outings. You can also volunteer with the Sierra Club's Inspiring Connections Outdoors program, which takes kids and adults with limited access outdoors on half-day, full-day, and overnight outings to local and regional parks.

Minnesota DNR offers a variety of programs, including "Becoming an Outdoors Woman" (www.dnr.state.mn.us/ education/bow) and the "I Can" program series (www.dnr. state.mn.us/state_parks/ican).

North Woods and Waters of the St. Croix Heritage Area offers a online community calendar (www.northwoods andwaterslynx.org) where you can find nature and recreation events in the watershed.

I highly recommend seeking first aid and CPR certification and attending training every two years to maintain your certification. The American Red Cross offers numerous training opportunities (www.redcross.org/take-a-class), as do other organizations. I took a two-day Wilderness First Aid course several years ago through National Outdoor Leadership School and REI that focused specifically on first aid scenarios in the outdoors—how to manage heat and cold, injuries that happen far from the road, and deal with snake bites, poison ivy, and other natural ailments. Information about similar classes can be found online at REI (www.rei.com/ events) or NOLS (www.nols.edu/en).

Plan Ahead. Plan Ahead. Plan Ahead.

I can't stress enough how important it is to plan ahead for outdoor adventures. If you'll be exploring a new destination, study a map ahead of time to familiarize yourself with the river, park, or trail. Is there a visitor center with bathrooms and water, or will you need to fill your bottles ahead of time? If you're planning a long bike ride, are there gas stations along the route where you can stop to get extra food and water? How far do you plan to travel?

Know your body, your physical fitness, and your own limitations. For example, I know from experience that I drink about one bottle of water per hour if I'm running or biking during the warm season, and I need to eat a small snack after about seventy-five minutes to avoid getting light-headed. I also know that a ten-mile run can feel like a breeze when I'm training for a marathon—or an arduous trek if I'm not.

It is helpful to have a standard collection of gear that you pack for different activities. For example, when heading out for a hike with my son, I carry a small backpack with a one-liter water pouch plus an extra bottle of water for him, a first aid kit, compass, pocketknife, snacks such as jerky or granola bars, lip balm, emergency money, a camera, and a journal and colored pencils in case we decide to stop and dawdle. When going on a bike ride, I carry a fix-it kit, spare inner tube, water, snack, phone, credit card, and emergency cash. The longer the distance you'll be traveling, the more gear you'll need to bring.

Check the weather ahead of time and dress in layers so that you can adjust to changing temperatures during the day. If you'll be going out on the river, always bring a long-sleeved shirt or lightweight jacket along, even if it feels warm when you first depart.

Solo Adventures

What if you love hiking, biking, skiing, and kayaking, but you're short on friends who enjoy those activities? Or perhaps you prefer to spend your time outdoors alone?

Though I am a top-notch extrovert, the realities of daily life (busy schedules, far-flung friends, and a husband who is not especially outdoorsy) have led me to many solo adventures over the years. *Usually* things have gone okay, but not always. What steps can you take to ensure that solo nature adventures are as safe and enjoyable as possible?

As is the case for any outdoor adventure, it is important to build your outdoor skills and plan ahead for any trip you take. If you'll be traveling solo, it is particularly important to let someone know where you are going and the approximate time when you'll be back.

I enjoy bringing my dog along on outdoor adventures. She helps me feel safer when I meet men along the trail, and she is also a conversationalist, or at least a very good listener! Many people I know bring along bear spray for personal protection when they are solo.

The biggest challenge I've encountered when exploring the outdoors alone is not having another person along to intervene if I start making poor decisions due to heat, cold, or fatigue. This is why it's so important to practice outdoor skills and wilderness first aid skills so that they come more easily when you need them most.

After offering these words of caution, it's important to note that I've been exploring the prairies, woods, and waters of the St. Croix River Watershed for nearly twenty years and have rarely had a problem that couldn't be solved by either calling a friend to pick me up early or turning around and struggle-bussing myself back to the car.

Nature as Medicine

Many humans intuitively recognize a healing power in nature, whether or not we can spin the leaves and soil into poetry like Henry David Thoreau, Mary Oliver, or Wendell Berry. Some find solace in quiet fishing trips; others head north to cabins in the woods. I have a collection of favorite local trails where I return time and again to work out the worries of the day.

If you've ever noticed that you feel happier and more relaxed after spending time outdoors, you won't be surprised to hear that research shows a strong connection between time spent in nature

Sun over prairie at Lake Elmo Park Reserve

and reduced stress, anxiety, and depression. In fact, according to Harvard Health Publishing, "calming nature sounds and even outdoor silence can lower blood pressure and levels of the stress hormone cortisol, which calms the body's fight-or-flight response" (2018).

In the growing scientific field of ecotherapy, nature is prescribed as a therapeutic treatment to improve both physical and mental health. The University of Minnesota's Earl E. Bakken Center for Spirituality and Healing brings together professors and researchers from the School of Nursing, Medical School, College of Veterinary Medicine, College of Pharmacy, School of Public

A fern in the woods

St. Croix River in Scandia, Minnesota

Health, and School of Dentistry to conduct research and develop innovative engagement programs and models of care.

They have found that being in nature, or even viewing scenes of nature, softens feelings of anger, fear, and stress, in addition to reducing the physical manifestations of these feelings—blood pressure, heart rate, muscle tension, and the production of stress hormones. Other research has shown that children with ADHD are better able to focus their minds when outdoors in nature and retain an increased attention span later when they return inside.

Unlike prescription drugs, nature doesn't require a precise formula to work its magic. You can spend twenty to thirty minutes in nature three times a week, take a deeper dive into the wild during a multiday camping trip, or craft a quiet corner in a garden to visit every day. It doesn't matter whether you immerse yourself in nature alone or with friends and family. The researchers at Harvard University noted that people suffering from a serious illness, unemployment, or the death of a loved one experienced the greatest mental boost from spending time outdoors in nature with other people. For a busy parent, taxed by the daily grind of work and home and school, a moment of leafy solitude could be just what the doctor ordered.

Whether or not I understand the exact ways in which nature alters the neurons in my brain and the beating of my heart, I can appreciate how I feel when fresh air hits my face and the busy noise of modern life fades away. I am happier in nature, and for me that is enough.

ACKNOWLEDGMENTS

IN FEBRUARY 2022, I TOOK A WEEK OFF WORK, LOADED UP MY DOG, my computer, and an ample supply of coffee, wine, and chocolate, and headed north to a cabin in the woods. One week later, I returned home with a nasty case of Covid and a pretty good outline for this book. Over the next year, I stayed up into the wee hours of the night writing, compiling photographs, and watching the book take form.

I thank my husband, Gary, for providing emotional support during this journey—both the journey of writing the book and life in general—and for keeping Charlie, Molly, and me outfitted with an abundance of snacks and gear to carry us through our outdoor adventures.

I thank Charlie (the son) and Molly (the dog) for joining me on countless adventures and explorations on and off the water. I'll never forget the first time I decided to try fitting all three of us on my stand-up paddleboard and thought, "This will be either one of the best or one of the worst decisions in my life." I know a lot of people who love the outdoors but not that many like these two who are ready to head out into the woods whether it's sunny and warm, -10°F, windy, rainy, or thick with fog. I won't pretend they never complain, but they almost never say no!

My mom also gave me great support as I was writing this book. She stepped in many times to watch Charlie for the day or take Molly for a walk when Gary was traveling and I was buried in work, and she was always willing to listen to me prattle about the latest developments in the project.

Thank you to Erik Anderson, my editor at the University of Minnesota Press, for walking me through the process of writing my first book ever and for transforming a collection of words and photographs into a guidebook with style and substance. I'm also grateful to Emma Saks for painstakingly placing and labeling hundreds of photographs.

Several people offered invaluable advice before and during the writing of this book. Spike Carlson and Natalie Warren both shared their experiences as writers and gave suggestions for how to get started. Greg Seitz, Jim Almendinger, and Diane Hilscher were early readers who were delightfully detail-oriented and provided excellent edits to the scientific details and information. I consider Greg's StCroix360.com website my go-to source for information about the St. Croix River and the surrounding watershed.

I thank the many people who were willing to share their St. Croix stories with me to include in this book: Sharon Day, Keeli Siyaka, Josh Leonard, Sinthang Has, Nor Olson, Susan Haugh, Katie Bloome, Gordon Dietzman, Dave Medvecky, Kathy Bartilson, and Randy Thoreson. I extend a special thanks to Giiwedin for inviting me to come wild ricing with the Water Protectors and to all the Anishinaabe people I met that day who were so gracious in sharing their culture and expertise.

I am grateful to everyone who provided photographs for this book, including Sinthang Has, the Northwest Passage Gallery (including photographers Derek, De'Vante, Chris, Clayton, and Anthony), Brett Stolpestad, Gordon Dietzman, Connie Taillon, Tom Furey, Aaron DeRusha, Ryan Schlagel, Carrie Rolstad, Kathy Bartilson, Kelly Randall, Matt Downing, Jessie Thiel, and Randy Thoreson.

Finally, I thank the St. Croix River for being my constant refuge and source of renewal, as well as the thousands of people who work tirelessly year after year to protect the prairies, woods, and waters of this beautiful place.

RESOURCES FOR VISITORS TO THE ST. CROIX WATERSHED

Where to Stay

FOR INFORMATION ON HOTELS, CABIN RENTAL, AND CAMPING IN different regions of the St. Croix River Watershed, visit these tourism bureau websites.

St. Croix Valley Regional Tourism Alliance (Lower St. Croix Valley): https://saintcroixriver.com

Explore Minnesota: www.exploreminnesota.com

Afton Area Business Association: http://exploreafton.com

Discover Stillwater: www.discoverstillwater.com

Chisago Lakes Water Trail: www.chisagolakeswatertrail.com

Hinckley Convention and Visitors Bureau: http://hinckleymn.com

Taylors Falls, Minnesota, and St. Croix Falls, Wisconsin: https://thestcroixvalley.com

Travel Wisconsin: www.travelwisconsin.com

Prescott Area Chamber of Commerce: https://prescottwi.com

Hudson Area Chamber of Commerce: www.hudsonwi.org

Hayward Lakes: https://haywardlakes.com

Cable Area Chamber of Commerce: www.cable4fun.com

Planning and Online Information

National Park Service—The St. Croix National Scenic Riverway encompasses two hundred miles of the St. Croix and Namekagon Rivers. The National Park Service offers trip planning advice, including maps, river conditions, and outfitters. The visitor center is located in St. Croix Falls, Wisconsin, at 401 North Hamilton Street: www.nps.gov/sacn.

North Woods and Waters of the St. Croix Heritage Area—Event and Cultural Guide. Check out this handy online resource to find activities related to history, art, nature, kids and family, food, and community throughout the watershed: www.northwoodsandwaterslynx.org.

ArtReach St. Croix is a nonprofit organization that connects community and arts in the Lower St. Croix watershed. The annual Take Me to the River event in September encourages people to explore art along the riverway, and the Navigate collaboration brings together artists and environmental professionals in the region: artreachstcroix.org. ArtReach St. Croix also offers a free events calendar with music, art, and nature activities in the lower watershed: www.stcroixsplash.org.

St. Croix 360 is an independent blog-style news source with stories about the St. Croix River to inspire stewardship. Subscribe to a weekly email digest with events, nature stories, and environmental updates from across the St. Croix River Watershed: www.stcroix360.com.

St. Croix Scenic Byway is a 124-mile driving route that follows the St. Croix National Scenic Riverway through Washington, Chisago, and Pine Counties in Minnesota. The nonprofit organization promotes "sustainable tourism through education and experience." A Historical Travel Guide with maps and locations of designated historic sites is available online: http://stcroixscenicbyway.org.

Wild Rivers Conservancy of the St. Croix and Namekagon
is the official nonprofit partner of the St. Croix National
Scenic Riverway and promotes land conservation,
water quality protection, river corridor and watershed
stewardship, and celebration of the river and its watershed.
Wild Rivers offers events and guided outdoor activities
and operates the My St. Croix Woods and Rivers Are
Alive K-12 Environmental Education programs. Wild
Rivers also offers guidance for local governments,
landowners, and realtors on Riverway regulations:
https://wildriversconservancy.org/.

INDEX

Angie Hong has been an environmental educator for more than twenty years. She is coordinator of the East Metro Water Resource Education Program (EMWREP), where she works with thirty local government partners and implements educational programs that teach and inspire local residents and community leaders to protect water resources in the region. Her weekly column in the *Stillwater Gazette—Valley Life* newspaper that shares tips and tales about keeping water clean is available at www.eastmetrowater.org. Follow her outdoor adventures on social media @mnnature_awesomeness.